AF539972

1. 'Diwali' Greetings - lighting the way.

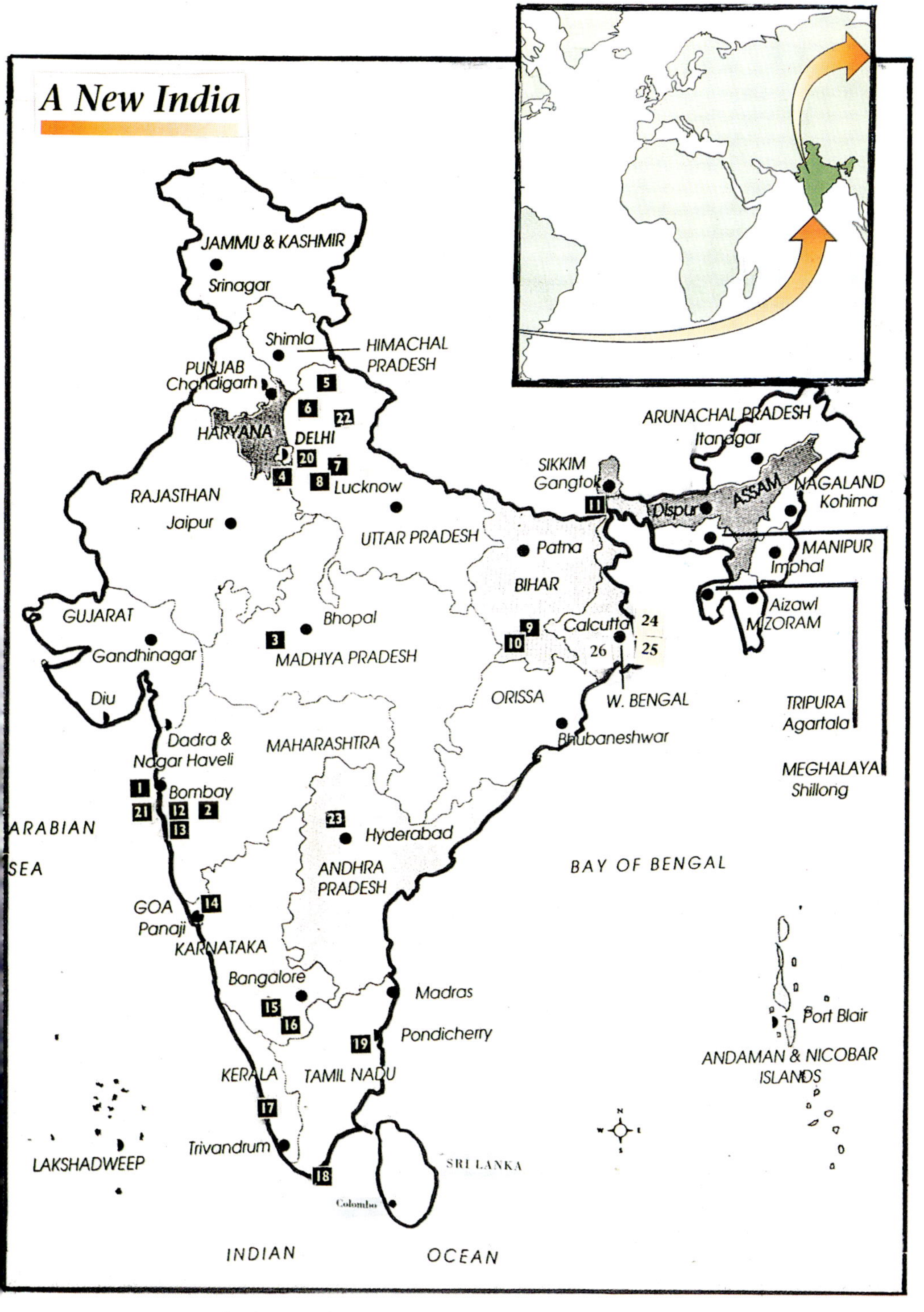

2. Map of India - highlighting each location.

"INDIA

a tryst with destiny"

- discourses on a burgeoning democracy

(told like never before)

David William Martin
(Author of ***The Changing Face of Calcutta***, 1997)

Originals
(an imprint of Low Price Publications)
Delhi-110052

Distributed By
D.K. Publishers Distributors (P) Ltd.
4834/24, Ansari Road, Darya Ganj,
New Delhi-110002
Phones: 3278584, 3278368, 3261465,
e-mail: dkpd@del3.vsnl.net.in
visit us at: www.dkpd.com

© David William Martin
First Published 2001
ISBN 81-7536-242-1

Published By
Originals
(an imprint of Low Price Publications)
A-6, Nimri Commercial Centre,
Near Ashok Vihar Phase-IV,
Delhi-110052
Phones: 7401672, 7452453
e-mail: lpp@nde.vsnl.net.in
visit us at: www.lppindia.com

Printed At:
D K Fine Art Press P Ltd.
Delhi-110052

No part of this book may be reproduced, stored in or introduced into a retrieval system, or transmitted in any form or by any means (electronic, mechanical, photocopying, recording or otherwise), without the prior written permission of both the copyright owner and the above mentioned publisher of this book.

The views expressed here are those of the author and do not reflect the views of the Publisher.

PRINTED IN INDIA

Acknowledgements

Frontspiece	From "INDIAN AND FOREIGN AFFAIRS" Journal, (New Delhi)
Frontspiece	Taken from INDIA MEANS BUSINESS (Six Parts)- Compiled by ECONOMIC CO-OR. UNIT of EX. AFFAIRS given by C.I.I. New Delhi
Facing page	
34.	London Sunday Telegraph (17.1.88)
38.	Travel Brochure
48.	"Illustrated Weekly of India"
58.	"Indian and Foreign Review" (15.8.87)
66.	"Indian and Foreign Review" (15.8.87)
72.	Dustcover of *The Scope of Happiness* (1979)
74.	Letter to author (from VLP)
84.	Reproduced in "Soma" (Oberoi, House Magazine)
90.	Copied from Brochure bought at Dayalbagh
100.	Picture supplied by TISCO Public Relations Dept.
106.	Possibly from 1987 copy "Indian and Foreign Review"
116.	Insert, Tourist brochure
118.	Transparency (author)
126.	Unknown-Possibly from Airline Magazine
130.	Picture supplied by Tata & Sons (of JRD)
134.	Pictures from TISCO in-house publication
144.	Various travel brochures
160.	"Soma" (OBEROI) House Magazine
168.	Transparencies (author)
170.	Bits supplied by THURSTONS, Liverpool
176.	Unknown (some Indian magazine)
176.	Brochure given by St. Francis Church, Cochin
182.	Transparencies (author)
190.	From Tourist Brochure
	Back ("Business Today" 22/8-6/9/1994
194.	Transparencies (author)
200.	(OBEROI) management
214.	Travel brochures
226.	Travel brochures
238.	Travel brochures
248.	Transparencies (author)
270.	(author)
276.	(author)
290.	Book cover "TCFOC" (author's transparency)
296.	Unknown from travel brochures
300.	Colour prints (author)
324.	Picture from "Centenary Volume" R. Tagore

List of Maps, Illustrations and Photos

Unless Mentioned are Colour Photos

Contents

India lies wholly in the Northern Hemisphere and is a Sovereign Socialist Democratic Republic with a parliamentary system of government. Covering an area of 3,287,263 sq. km., with a population of more than 1 billion people (2001), the principal indigenous languages spoken* throughout its 25 states and 7 union territories provide an insight into its great diversity.

States	**Languages Spoken**
Andhra Pradesh	Telegu, Urdu
Assam	Assamese
Arunachal Pradesh	Monpa, Miji, Aka, Sherdukpen, Nishing, Apatani, Tagin, Hillmiri, Adi, Digaru-Mishmi, Idu-Mishmi, Khamti, Miju-Mishmi, Nocte, Tangsa and Wanche
Bihar	Hindi
Goa	Konkani and Marathi
Gujarat	Gujarati
Haryana	Hindi
Himachal Pradesh	Hindi and Pahari
Jammu and Kashmir	Urdu, Kashmiri, Dogri, Pahari, Balti, Ladakhi, Punjabi, Gujri and Dadri
Karnataka	Kannada
Kerala	Malayalam
Madhya Pradesh	Hindi
Maharashtra	Marathi
Manipur	Manipuri
Meghalaya	Khasi, Garo (and English)
Mizoram	Mizo (and English)
Nagaland	Angami, Ao, Chang, Konyak, Lotha, Sangtam, Sema and Chakhesang
Orissa	Oriya
Punjab	Punjabi
Rajasthan	Hindi and Rajasthani
Sikkim	Lepcha, Bhutia, Nepali and Limbu
Tamil Nadu	Tamil
Tripura	Bengali and Kokbarak
Uttar Pradesh	Hindi and Urdu
West Bengal	Bengali

Union Territories	
Andaman and Nicobar Islands	Hindi, Nicobarese, Malayalam, Bengali, Tamil and Telugu
Chandigarh	Hindi, Punjabi (and English)
Dadra and Nagar Haveli	Gujarati and Hindi
Daman and Diu	Gujarati
Delhi	Hindi, Punjabi and Urdu
Lakshadweep	Malayalam
Pondicherry	Tamil, Telegu, Malayalam (English and French)

***Hindi is the most widely spoken language - approx. 40% of all people.**

Introduction

- a 2001 overview

In many respects India is a timeless land, for good or for ill, obstinately-consciously or otherwise, refusing to discard, or allow to drift, any part of her neverendingly fascinating, rich heritage. Events happening hundreds of years ago, or just yesterday, meld into the whole which is today. There are few or no subtractions, only additions.

While her cities become more and more crowded, for the greater numbers of people who live in rural India on the agricultural estate, apart from advances in modern irrigation and plant technology augmenting the old, not a lot in the methodology used or in how attendant village life is lived has changed, from what the situation was hundreds, or even thousands, of years ago. Peace and tranquillity and the contentment that accompanies it, qualities so frequently undervalued and dismissively ignored by India's critics, have been enhanced with the threat of starvation no longer a constant.

In India's incomparable way, life moves on. The 'living' time capsule simply takes on more appendages, as more years, more experiences, and more people are added. No other country offers more. Few others in this, the industrial age, possess more potential.

Half of the essays/discourses included in this volume were compiled (and taped) for the enjoyment and edification of visually handicapped people, from material the author collected on numerous visits made to India, over the past decade. Except for the most adventurous and courageous of their number able to partake individually, fascinating India, through these glimpses and 'word pictures', could have been denied to many less self-equipped.

But as well, except for the serious scholar and the genuinely curious, most visitors to India rarely leave the well-trodden trails, being hostage to the stereotyped narrowly formal 'diet' meted out by travel agencies, themselves only sketchily familiar with the enormous reservoir of interesting people and interesting facets that abound everywhere in India. These essays could provide added stimulation for those people seeking next time to delve deeper and to learn and enjoy more.

There are few adjectives that would not fit India, or which have not been used by writers and historians over the past couple of hundred years, to describe the myriad aspects of India, and her colourful history. India provides prodigious helpings of every conceivable kind - diverse cultures; multiple languages and dialects; religions and religious architecture; of great tracts of history witnessing the triumphs and the tragedies of powerful, and sometimes philanthropic empires, reaching back to Asóka and ending with the creation of the modern State of India, from 1947, when a new dawning for Indians began.

The complete disappearance from India of British 'imperialism' has not happened (argument for and against retention, so far as any freed nation is concerned, will never abate. Practical vision is often left very much in the rear of the field, by the erupting euphoria). Unlike some other parts of Britain's erstwhile Empire, no transmigration from Britain occurred, and no nucleus of 'permanent' white population was assimilated into Independent India beyond a small number of expatriates who chose to stay.

Ordinarily, it is not part of normal Indian culture to believe (or behave) in any way that suggests that one is better than another, whether through birthright, inheritance, superior education or position of office. Arrogance and pompousness is considered ungracious.

Humility is a virtue and attracts greater acceptance and recognition, from all (there will always be some whose vanity is beyond containment).

For the most part, Indian expatriates and those Indians who have migrated to other countries have steadfastly maintained these same commendable virtues. Most prefer to keep a low-profile, while continuing to keep close ties with their native land.

For real exemplars of Indian behaviour one could not go past several of her most eminent (bearers of really great scholarship, true feeling and marvellous normality on a universal scale) world respected personages, Professor, Dr. Sarvepalli Radhakrishnan (1888-1975) and his modern contemporary, Professor, Dr. Amartya Sen, recently the recipient of the Nobel Prize for Economics. Both of them wonderful examples amongst a host of 'feet planted firmly on the ground' and 'good sense always the victor', of their compatriots - hundreds, in fact almost a billion of them.

If more reasons, (for non-assimilation of British ways on a wide scale) are needed, millenniums' old religious fundamentals were (and are still) too solidly entrenched and especially so with the greater part of India's population, those who reside in the rural regions. There are very few parts of India's three million square kilometres that are not lived in. Very very few, are the persons who can claim intimate knowledge, with all parts of India.

This was no less the case in British times, when not many of their ilk got far into British India, and hardly, or not at all, into the other areas not within their 'direct' control, *ie: the Princely States.* Getting conglomerate vast India into true/proper/sensible - perspective, will always set a poser, for everyone, and more so, for every foreigner. Indubitably it was ever thus (and will remain).

Bearing all these circumstances in mind, it was entirely predictable that British ways could not, or would not have been implanted in any all embracing way (even had this been the objective of the British which with any serious intent - was improbable), in what became Independent India, in 1947.

But notwithstandingly, India has seen great value in retaining much of the structures and procedures put in place by the British up to 1947 *viz.* jurisprudence and the governmental structures, political and bureaucratic, and not least military, (army, navy and airforce) style and formation. The latter very jealously taken aboard, and very creditably so.

Various international spokespeople from time to time have been critical of India for predominantly (giving equal priority and value to vintage cultural mores and progressive twentieth century economics) favouring and preserving its age-old cultural principles at the threshold of her modern existence (unlike other liberated Asian [and some African] countries, which too eagerly embraced western-world economic and capitalist procedures, and the blandishments of greedy hard-headed unsympathetic loan sharks, whilst believing there'd be no inroads made into their primary cultures).

In the light of the difficulties and economic turmoil being experienced by many world countries, including many of India's regional neighbours, near and far, uncomplimentarily few bouquets have been passed India's way for its pursuing the more patient, cautious, conservative path – to supposed 'quick' prosperity. Raising living standards for all the people to partake of, and to more permanently enjoy, seems to be the goal and the objective India preferably seeks. Their avoidance of aggravated problems by sticking with carefully measured fiscal controls was more than fortunate fortuitousness. India has never gone about anything rashly. It seems unlikely she is about to change.

Beyond everything else the most radical change in India since Independence would be the dramatic increase in indigenous population growth. Whilst in the twentieth century, nearly all western nations have experienced declining natural populations (propped up by transmigratory quotas and refugee intakes), India's population has trebled to over 900 millions, soon to join China in the one billion population league. Advances in world medical discoveries and distribution of services to everyone across the whole of India, previously mostly left to *ayurvedic* remedies, has dramatically raised life expectancy, in some cases by as much as one hundred per cent.

Other very significant advances have been made in agriculture and in industry. One source, often quoted, recorded that prior to 1947, just a few cities and towns in India were touched by industrial development, with ninety per cent or more, of the people, consigned still 'to the dark ages'. Hyperbole is no stranger to India, but there could be much truth in this assertion, if only using today's population displacement as some sort of measuring stick.

Coming off relatively low bases (agricultural and industrial), and grappling with the concurrent explosion in population, the advances that India has made reflect great resourcefulness on the part of all those Indians who have 'stayed at home' to build up the country and its improved conveniences - for everyone. Great unselfish effort is everywhere to be found.

The following statistical information taken from the 28th July 1997 issue of *The Hindu* confirms the great strides that have been made by India in seeing to its own vital needs in the area of food grains and other basic commodities.

Foodgrains - Rice, wheat, oilseeds, sugarcane, pulses, coarse cereals

- Production (in million tonnes)	1950/51	(50)	1996/97	(198)
- Per Capita availability - grams per day	1951	(375)	1966	(498)
- Yields - all foodgrains per hectare/kg	1950	(500)	1995/96	(1499)
Irrigated area (millions of hectares)	1950	(20)	1995/96	(80)
Fertilizer Consumption (million tonnes)	1950	(Zero)	1995/96	(14)
Production of milk and fish				
- Milk (millions of tonnes)	1950	(17)	1995/96	(66)
- Fish (thousands of tonnes)	1950	(7)	1995/96	(4949)

Yields have climbed dramatically - rice, three times; wheat, four times.

The foregoing also serves to remind us that rushing into rash dogmatic assertions about India, is to be avoided. Never short of critics, the path leading up to India's door, is metaphorically strewn with relics of mistaken unhelpful pessimists. But it has not been very much different down through history, wherein India has always proved capable of confounding its critics and just as it has done by finally shrugging off a succession of invaders and dealing with other natural pestilences, it has survived and gone forward, as it will continue to do. Not ordinarily apparent or readily perceived, and when it is, often not firmly enough acknowledged, there is embodied in the Indian people an underlying and invisible binding force of great strength and tenacity, which holds the strands together.

It was several moments of inattention (figuratively, in India's long history), that allowed Partition to happen, a schism of the peoples and of the sub-continent, most informed commentators contend should not have come about. Their views could appear to have support from subsequent analysis and events, not least the creation of the separate nation of Bangladesh and the marginalizing of those Muslims who moved across to the west, to help form the new nation of Pakistan ('the land of the pure'). The theories keep pouring in, all of them wreathed in speculation, for no one could accurately predict what the ultimate outcome will be.

Resolving the big points, (and the sub-continent has always thrown up plenty of these - and doubtless there will be more and bigger ones to come), requires infinite scrutiny and discerning analysis, and the removal of conflicting and misleading emotions. Reaching to clear unbiased opinion - about anything, will always be complicated and never be simple.

A foreigner either loves India and her warm-hearted people, warts and all (and if one takes the time to look below the surface, there is an explanation for everything), and very passionately, or is upset by so much of what he or she sees. The latter- failure to measure up to expectations (yet most go to India either wholly unprepared beforehand, or considerably under-prepared. So why go there?) - produces an antagonistic belittling attitude, one that is often quite unrealistic and based on fragmentary association with wide-scale India and additionally biased, by their own rigidly held concepts of what life should be, as lived by them in their quite unrelated countries. Indians just might like - *living as Indians*! and why not?

I am unashamedly one of the first group. Wonderfully, some are immediately smitten from the very start. However, for most people a long apprenticeship must be served before pre-conceptions are overcome and things are valued for what they are, and not for what one believes they should be. Wonderful rewards are there for those who reach out to others and who bring proper understanding into the equation.

Curing or altering the prevailing 'long-distance' foreigner's view of India may never happen. The 'no-change' foreign media approach was given another opportunity recently to be more generous, more expanding and more discerning, when the world's focus fell on the Memorial service for Mother Teresa. It turned out a classic repeat of unshakeable (unrepentant) stereotyped archaic attitudes.

A heaven-sent opportunity was there for a better more sincere and accurate depiction of the 'real' Calcutta, of the true expansiveness of contemporary India (*sans* the usual anachronistic stereotyped portrayal), but it was skipped over, by the predominantly unversed, under-informed, visiting contingent. Indian/Calcuttan input was barely sought or proclaimed, although the gracious host factor must bear some of the blame for this - the homesters bowed to the more assertive, instead of marshalling their forces, and 'getting in some overdue practice', at presenting things, their way. Had this happened, more compassionate and lasting signals may have been flashed abroad.

The humble nature of Indians precludes most of their number offering spirited challenge. Attending to one's own (and family's) daily needs gets priority over expenditure of energy on extraneous matters. Whilst there's a whole lot of good sense in this, it also perpetuates an attitude of 'leave civic matters, for reform / for improvement', to others. Collaboration on a wide, consistent and sensible scale, could bring more of the things that the masses can benefit from, ensuring that development occurs on broader terms of equality.

Indians are not a literal people. What you see on the surface tells only a small part of the story. That they move away from public display of naked patriotism (a highly significant feature amongst other aspects of the Indian psyche) is a trait more due to the much more personal and stronger pull, of regionalism, than of no love for their country, India.

It is ordinarily enough for most Indians in the *mofussil* (seventy per cent of India) to concentrate upon what directly affects them. Other wider issues that are highlighted by the indigenous, and sensationalised by, the foreign-media, are too remote to claim anything more than scant attention, if any at all, from the masses, more reliant by far upon very localised sources for their economic and social information.

What goes on in the Lok Sabha or in the State Assemblies, connects very little, with the average rural (or urban too) dweller's daily life. To compare everything that happens everywhere around the world in like terms, to how events are seen and treated, in one's own 'neck of the woods', is bound to leave one none-the-wiser, if one is regarding India.

For all today's marvellous electronic communications, the real position remains that beyond a few factors, one half of the world has precious little comprehension of how the other half lives. Until broader education occurs, tolerance (a by-product of strong education) on any wide-ranging scale, can not happen. The world media living on sensations (how quickly news dulls), needs to indulge in a lot more patient preparatory study before it does proper justice to India.

But as well, the ball is in India's court for it to tell its own story, to market itself. Meanwhile, city-bound foreign reporters might find that venturing into India's *mofussil* (rural areas), could bring deeper understanding and a wider truer perspective (told as it is) of the whole country, and of all of its people.

An in-depth analysis of India's population mix brings many surprises. In essence, it is many countries. At over 900 millions, and equal to ten Germanys in population make-up, the number of skilled professionals its seats of learning (and know that these skills have been in evidence for a long time - algebra, zero-maths.artifact, chess, the decimal system - all bear 'made in India' tags) turn out, borders on the astronomical.

To illustrate the dimension of educated Indian scholars, your author once asked an Indian friend - a PhD. graduate of Harvard University and now O.C. Computer Research at another large U.S. University ...... *"how come you Indians excel at science, mathematics, medicine, engineering, computer technology (particularly software), and in fact in some, lead the world?"* His answer ..... *"we don't"* .... pause ..... *"it's just that there are so many of us"*. A truism so little known or acknowledged, around the world, in some respects due to contemporary India's own extreme reluctance (or mistaken omission) to broadcast its quality wares.

Many Indian graduates go on to the United States, Britain and Germany *et al* for post-graduate training, a situation that has resulted in large numbers of Indians becoming an integral part of foreign academia, industry and science. India's prodigious body of talent for higher mathematics and its contribution to advances in computer technology (acknowledged by Bill Gates, himself) receives world-wide acclaim everywhere.

When this awesome 'pool of cerebral resources' is diverted to progressing India's own cause in the twenty first century, tremendous advances seem assured.

Turning from these lofty heights meanwhile, and giving attention and cognizance to current matters, helps reveal an India, where people get on with their daily business. We observe the teeming activity that unceasingly goes on very organizedly, everywhere throughout the country, night and day. The interlocking systems, that engage a vast corpus of manual labour, have been handed down through the centuries.

Many of these manual workers would be illiterate, whatever that term in present day parlance may be construed to mean, but it would be a mistake to consider them as robotic and devoid of nous and great dollops of intuition. Most have a very clear understanding of what is going on, but in 'labour intensive' India (beware the threatened advent of economic rationalism, to India!) people don't question - particularly when it could be to their likely personal detriment! There is always another to take one's place. Logic prevails, in every layer of Indian society.

The 'work ethic' is deeply ingrained in Indians, particularly amongst manual workers, the many millions by whose labour the wheels are kept turning day-in-day-out, all across the country. *Sust admion* (lazy people) there may be, but non-participation in some form of paid work, would not get one very far. Idleness (among the active) would more likely be tantamount to handing to one's self a passport to starvation. Where in developed countries, welfare leaning is frequently related to an unwillingness to do (any) work, such has no place in India, where most manual workers continue to perform some kind of paid work throughout the whole of their (active) lifetimes.

The hardest workers, and worked of all, are those men (and women) who - till the fields, plant the rice paddies; mind the cattle; do all the heavy porterage at railway and bus stations; pull the heavily laden hand carts; who carry on their heads, in boxes, in baskets, the huge quantities of fresh produce and merchandise that is moved around the whole land every day. For most of these workers, there is no (regular) 'knock-off' time, but they toil on until the task is done.

This concentrated, repetitive and devilishly hard physical work goes on (much of it through the night), for most of the three hundred and sixty five days of the year. Sunday sees a slowing down - but not for everybody. Annual leave, *chutthi,* when some itinerant city workers return briefly to their native villages, is still uncommon outside union-controlled occupations. For many, a temporary substitute 'a *badli*' has to be supplied to toil in one's absence, virtually meaning that the more permanent worker goes unpaid, for time off.

It is a hard unforgiving system, but few complain. Paid work is paid work, whatever or however meagre the remuneration, for it constitutes the only means by which great numbers of Indians can survive. Wrongly condemned by many observers not looking to the core of everything (that exists in the huge conglomerate that is India), beyond everything else, and most significant of all, is the grit and fortitude of all these splendid people, mostly uncomplainingly - 'getting on with it'. Until their labours can be relieved in some measurable way, I personally hugely respect them, and doffs my lid to them.

One aspect of India that is considerably misapprehended outside India, concerns language and particularly that used -

1. in the general administration of the country by Central Government in New Delhi, and by the State Administrations in the 25 States, and as well, in the 7 Union Territories (administered by New Delhi);
2. in newspapers and in business and scientific journals;
3. in matters of formal education.

Central Government Publications are printed in both Hindi and English. The official language for conducting business in both Houses of Parliament in New Delhi (the Rajya Sabha, - Upper House 'The Council of States', and the Lok Sabha - 'The House of the People') is English. Steps to introduce Hindi - the widest spoken indigenous language - as the official national language, have been withheld, notably due to significant opposition from the southern States, Karnataka, Kerala and Tamil Nadu, where the local languages Kannada, Malayalam, Telegu and Tamil, predominate amongst nearly two hundred million people.

Less subject to 'foreign' influences for much of the last several thousand years (few invaders from northern climes reached down to the Deccan region of India, beyond the Vindya mountains, leaving religion to be the dominant factor in an otherwise substantially agricultural society) and much less industrialized than North India, in the southern half of India, widespread use of regional languages has been maintained for nearly every purpose, and significantly so for education in the public sector, right through to tertiary level.

Outside the main business centres of the larger cities (of India) not a lot of English is either in evidence or spoken, for not unnaturally, people are most comfortable using their most familiar local language or dialect. This is particularly and noticeably so, in South India.

While most newspapers are printed in the (local) regional vernacular, every major city has its English language daily, or more usually, dailies. Next to the old Soviet Union, India publishes more daily newspapers, over 4000 of them, than any other country in the world. One news-vendor on Chowringhee, carries over fifty daily newspapers in many different scripts, for his varied customers.

As is the position now everywhere in the world (now that television fills the questionable role of 'people informer' arising from its distinctly less-demanding personal contribution), all newspapers attract a particular readership and compilation necessarily pays cognizance to such. There are very many discerning Indian readers avid for knowledge of every sort.

Among the top ranking Indian English-language newspapers is *The Hindu* printed in Madras and circulated throughout India (as are also the other top national newspapers, *The Times of India, The Statesman, The Indian Express, The Pioneer* and *The Asian Age*). *The Hindu* is a standout amongst a number of very good newspapers. Its regular content and erudition and journalistic excellence, would rank it for quality of content, alongside the classic London dailies, *The Daily Telegraph* and *The Times*. India has avoided tabloids and the notoriety they (can) bring.

India recognizes the great and increasing value of good education. For the majority of young people receiving their tuition in the public schools' system, the medium of instruction is the particular regional language, with some Hindi and/or English. There are many Church schools and private institutions throughout India, where instruction right through from primary grades, to secondary and tertiary levels, is in English. In nearly all of India's 222 Universities, English is common and in most of them, it is the principal medium of instruction. Hindi rates next.

You should not be surprised if an Indian addresses you in splendid (though sometimes pedantic) English. It is perfectly normal, for he or she has learnt their English at school, in the traditional and thoroughly strict way. It may not always be 'formed correctly', the result of too little practice in everyday terms, but what counts most of all, is *understanding* what another says (is driving at). Most foreign language speakers, as a second language, everywhere in the world, suffer similarly from pronunciation boo boos and other shortcomings. But it points up a warning, to delay/avoid using body language. It can be discourteous, even insulting - especially to an Asian.

Many will know that Indians have a remarkable capacity for knowing and speaking many languages - foreign as well as local. They have grown up in a multi-lingual country, where a score or more major indigenous languages and hundreds of local dialects, are used, intermingledly too, everywhere. A Babel of tongues, there are few Indians amongst its millions, who do not possess an innate understanding of the differences.

Intuitively, and also from a person's name, speech and attire, picking a person's home habitat *etcetera,* comes readily to most Indians, formally educated or not. Many millions, even tens of millions, speak two, three, four or more languages/dialects, including English. Jumping to abrupt conclusions is neither the smart nor the appropriate way to go - in India, for intelligence and comprehension abound there in considerable measure.

Reporting (accurately) on India, requires much patience, deliberation and a whole lot of proper discernment. Contrary to the scribblings of (short-term) foreign journalists, intended anyway not for Indian readers, but for their own home country readers, fed a diet often quite removed from the factual position, and accordingly retaining different /differing perceptions (of India and the Indian people, of the twentyfirst century), India is moving ahead very significantly, and in very many areas. It is a 'big' country in everything. Generalizing on the basis of a 'small sample', can be wholly inaccurate - and ungenerous.

Covering the enormous breadth of all of this activity change, can not be readily observed from just 'standing on the corner of Park and Chowringhee', or of 'Janpath and Connaught Circus', or worse still, from afar off, 'from on the Strand', or 'from Madison Avenue'. Its dimension is far too complex, too big - for that. Objective reporting of today's India calls for much more profound discernment.

How refreshingly enjoyable therefore, that there is one segment of India that needs no apology, no explanation for its being, except that it is there. Any explanation would be quite superfluous. For those privileged to 'explore' some of India's incomparable array of architectural and art treasures, there is none finer, more breathtakingly magnificent, or more captivating and compelling, to be found - anywhere.

But most surprising of all, Indians very rarely, or never, boast about it. On the contrary, they underplay it. In so doing, they innocently separate their present-day accomplishments from the magnificent work accomplished by their antecedents, who down through the millennia, created this great bank of artwork.

Unlike the situation in Western countries (and cultures) where the genius of a Michelangelo, a Titian, a Donatello, or a Cezanne is hugely acclaimed and revered, most of the great art everywhere in India, is anonymous. The designer (or designers) of the greatest architectural monument of all, the magnificent Taj Mahal mausoleum at Agra, is not positively known or is ever likely to be conclusively known. Much the same position relates to the vast majority of India's prodigious art treasures.

Instead of lamenting (or being told) that the great eras of Indian art are past and over, contemporary Indians might justifiably believe that their ancestors' great skills have been descended upon them. While funding factors, combined with the extent and awesomeness of many of the tremendous structures, ensures that much of the older art treasures can not be replicated, art of many kinds and themes lives on, gaining more ground and admirers, every day.

An inhibiting factor is an Indian's normal retiring nature, and preference for privacy. Boastfulness is not a normal trait of Indians. It is rare that they make exorbitant haste to declare their personal genius. Western style marketing technique on any scale has yet to inflict itself on Indians, sports and film stars, aside.

It was these unique (and endearing) factors present in India, and in the Indian people, that claimed my attention and my huge interest and admiration. Attitudes are critical. It is not so much help that India needs but recognition. Their social graces and manners exceed those of their western cousins. However and sadly, the missing factor (with the majority) is pride, something their inherent humility and self-effacing nature, denies them. Pride and boastful aggression are two opposing things. They sometimes get blurred and merged, with disastrous consequences. Quiet character uplifting pride - pride in being an Indian; pride in its great history; pride in the great contributions India has made to science and to humanitarian causes - will serve India best.

I readily perceived that relating my impressions to others (gained from long and varied personal experience) and from many 'research' visits, would help me, and could assist others, to a better understanding and appreciation of Indians and of their country *as it is today*. There was an urgent need to get away from lions and tigers and caparisoned elephants and camels (the usual depiction of India). Kodak might satisfy the needs of most casual visitors to India, but to fulfill my mission, only 'three dimensional word pictures', those which could provide considerably more impact and meaning, would fill the bill.

My original plan was to begin my 'mission' in India, and to move on from there to other familiar stamping grounds, Sri Lanka, Burma (Myanmar), Thailand, Indonesia, the Philippines and points north. However, the realization soon crystallized, that stories with an Indian backdrop would be so numerous that inter-territorial travel would become unnecessary. Indeed, this is what happened. My enquiries and peregrinations for this volume of essays (discourses) became solely confined to India.

Bombay (now re-named Mumbai) was the ideal place from which to start, and virtually from the historic 'Gateway' on the seafront, India's western citadel. While the attached map delineates the trail I covered, every story can stand on its own and no particular sequence is essentially required. Such a situation fits in with what India is - a great admixture of people brought together over thousands of years speaking many tongues (the Indian Constitution officially lays down English and Hindi; in practice, as many as fifteen major languages are widely recognized, and hundreds of dialects spoken amongst its population) and following many religions, but principally Hinduism and Islam.

While some persons may regard this diversity as India's weakness, others perhaps more rightly, look to the fundamentals, and see it, as providing the colour, and the enormous extra 'variations on every theme' that are embodied in Indians. Over the many centuries much hybridity has also entered the situation, ensuring that from this time onwards, any repeats of the horrendous internecine problems which accompanied the winning of Independence, are remote.

Train travel in India is always fascinating and the short run up to Pune confirmed this, as the second story relates. Nowadays a bustling, fast developing Maharastrian city, the frenetic activity came as a surprise to me, wrongly expecting a lovely calm well ordered cantonment (military) town, as of old. It has now left all that far behind.

Correctly, I had anticipated that New Delhi would present some colourful pageantry. As well, the train journey up to Delhi covered new territory for me and also represented my initiation to AC2 (air-conditioning second class) transportation, in India. The 'open-plan' sleeping accommodation introduced me to a whole host of 'Indian' experiences - family activity at close quarters including cooking pots and rich smelling food. It was a much enjoyed experience and a *different* one!

Delhi, with its Lutyens' created new parts (1912 - 1931) and the older Mughal dynasty - enhanced city, provided many novel experiences. I had been there years earlier, on a few occasions, and have spent longer periods there in more recent years but do not yet know it as intimately overall as I should like. In recent years, the expansion outwards, has been enormous. In the dry season the Jumna, around Delhi, is non-distinct, which is possibly the reason why it plays virtually no part in the normal life of the city beyond its crucial function of supplying water for its hugely expanding population. Strangely, Delhi faces *away* from the river, unlike most cities blessed with a decent river artery.

Also, artificially separated as it is from the hustle and bustle of its commercial hub, the administrative and diplomatic areas of 'New Delhi' are totally different from what could be termed 'normal India'. In normal Indian terms, 'unusually privileged', the Central Government of India in New Delhi artificially divorces itself from the searing reality that affects (and afflicts) the rest of the country.

What suited the aloof British administration may not necessarily produce the best results for independent India. Fitting into the 'same' shoes always risked perpetuating the British way and delaying the implementation of the more natural and better suited 'Indian' way so essential to instilling and developing the required Indianness that is vitally needed.

As Mohandas Karamchand Gandhi, the prime mover and spiritual 'father of the modern Indian Nation', once very succinctly defined (syn. with the rationale of the Indian Nationalist Movement) .... *"I am not against the British, I am only against their civilization"*. It could seem that many since have misunderstood the nub of what Bapuji was stressing, and have strayed from strenuously pursuing an 'Indian' India.

The opportunity to go north to the mountains and to Mussoorie was very welcome. I'd been there before, savouring the crisp mountain air, after several weeks inspecting industrial sites in Uttar Pradesh and in neighbouring Punjab, as far as Amritsar.

On the particular occasion in 1987, I had broken my journey just north of Dehra Dun to pay a call on Mrs Vijaya Lakshmi Pandit, one of India's noblest ladies and sister of the great statesman and first Prime Minister, Jawaharlal Nehru. A wonderful gracious woman, it was a great pleasure to meet with her and to interview her. I remember being so thrilled and afterwards I took her wonderful expressive interview to London. Going to see the Daily Telegraph's Peregrine Worsthorne down at the newspaper's new Dockside premises, I felt extremely confident his paper would grab Vijaya Lakshmi's testimony with alacrity. But the reality was disappointingly different. Strangely too, as Americans are fond of Indians and their country, knocking on the door at Times Square received the same (negative) reception. The great Indian lady had been off the front page for several years and was seemingly - no longer news. A great disappointment - and too, the lost chance of putting India's genuine and sincere feelings, to the world.

The next two stories at Agra and at Dayalbagh (Soamibagh) will live with me for ever. The sheer breathtaking magnificence of one and the inspiring enterprise of the other. Another cheering aspect of the latter 'temple building at Soamibagh' is the confirmation of the statements I made earlier that the artistic abilities of Indians are still very much alive and being productively employed.

The ancient skills being used at Dayalbagh (now for over ninety consecutive years) are being similarly duplicated in many other places in India. India is a big country and despite the fact there are thousands of newspapers published daily, it is an impossibility to report every constructive incident happening throughout the country. But, be sure there are many busy hands, many millions of them, active everywhere across the land, too numerous to specifically notice.

One of India's indigenous pioneering industrial groups - Tata and Sons, enjoys a 'second to none' reputation throughout India; one that extends to the rest of the world. In 1987, displaying an efficiency and promptitude on par with anywhere, the Tata organization invited me to their major location, Jamshedpur. A crisp, rat-a-tat-tat organization, their ultra efficient management, over a fortnight, had me visiting every one of their multiple enterprises within a hundred mile radius of their core business - TISCO.

I might please be forgiven for including three stories which have a Tata flavour. I ask that the commercial aspects be put to one side and the magnificent excellence and humanitarian qualities, a distinctive and important part of the Tata Group's whole history from its very beginnings, be given proper and just, priority. Whether it be consideration for its workforce; or for its total community, or for the enhancement of Indian management skills and practices, the Tata Group provides a wonderful example for all Indian enterprises to emulate, and there is no reason for such to stop at India.

The re-settlement of the tribals has been carried out with commendable tact, patience, and skill. The great man, J.R.D. Tata, must rank as one of India's (and the world's) finest gentlemen of any era and one of the most gracious international ambassadors ever for India. His exemplary selfless life would serve as a supreme example of unselfish successful service, not just to other Indians, but to everyone. J.R.D. was assuredly that kind of person.

One of the wonderful benefits of working from Calcutta was the opportunity it provided for going to the mountains. At the beginning of every cricket season, at Puja time conveniently (October), we journeyed to Darjeeling (and as well during the season - to other places in the tea growing areas of north-east India) to play the Planters XI, then all expatriates, many of them very talented cricketers.

It was convenient to go on to Sikkim, and to the lower ramparts of the Himalayas, for hard trekking and some stiff climbing. I did this on a number of occasions enjoying quite marvellous times, absorbing the superbly breathtaking scenery, and much of it adjacent to Kangchenjunga, arguably the most beautiful section of the Himalayas.

The story gives a picture of life in Darjeeling today, although ongoing political problems still disrupt any distinctively new progress and new investment in the region. Notwithstandingly, Darjeeling still ranks as the finest and best located hill-station in the whole of India and easily accessible from Calcutta just hours away by plane and road. In any world assessment Darjeeling and its magnificent backdrop Kangchenjunga, would figure in the top ten. Unquestionably.

It may be coincidence that J.R.D. Tata was a Parsee. It is no coincidence that Parsees, by their great endeavour, have served Bombay (and India) to a remarkable degree. Not familiarly known to many others in the world, one could not sojourn for any time in Bombay without telling their story. Their good works, good citizenship and business success, represents a very distinctive part of Bombay's modern history.

I first went to India in 1952. Though not entirely an innocent abroad, nevertheless I would have fitted my own description of young British scions sent as young men to India, namely 'young bloods there to get their knees brown' (i.e., acquire good experience), or alternatively, 'to remove the down from their cheeks' (grow up into resourceful young men).

I departed India for Indonesia in 1961, serving periods for specialist duties in Sri Lanka, Burma, Singapore and Malaysia between 1952 and that time, besides travelling to many countries and around the world several times. Returning to India briefly in 1963 I did not renew my acquaintance again until 1987, when I returned with a vengeance, repeating the exercise in 1988, 1990, 1992, 1994, 1995, twice in 1996, and in 1997 - three times!, and into 1998.

The intensity of my visitation (from 1988 onwards) was due to a great urge to research India forty years and more on from Independence, to note the changed situation of the country and to write a lengthier book whose message might reach extensively within India and as well, serve to faithfully depict contemporary India, outside India.

While a book encompassing the whole position of India was a possible choice, my greater allegiance was to my erstwhile 'temporary home' Calcutta. The welfare of Calcuttans themselves deservedly claimed first priority.

The result of these endeavours is *The Changing Face of Calcutta.* My sincere hope is that its message will hit home, where the need is greatest - to Calcuttans, and more tangibly, achieve more, much more, lasting results, than other sensation-seeking books have done, less concerned about improving the lot of millions of very deserving Calcuttans.

After the intensity of nine years researching, visiting, compiling, writing, seeking publishers, editing and promoting my book, written for India (in India and equally importantly around the world) to combat the 'fiction' which has been circulated about the people who actually populate and make India what it is today, and marketing too - pointless going to these lengths, if people don't read the stuff! - it seemed reasonable, even for my own remembrance, to record how the idea for "*The Changing Face of Calcutta*" came about and was executed.

In relaxed conversations with my learned friend, Mushtaque Murshed, I.A.S., longtime involved bureaucrat in West Bengal and Central Government affairs, he put it to me to 'put something down' in writing, of the Calcutta (the India) 'of my *chokra* days', at a time when significant British commercial business interest in India was drawing to its end, in the second decade after Independence. Most of my experiences remain pretty vivid and compiling story number twenty-five proved quite fun.

With minor variations, British commercial 'occupation' of Calcutta, of West Bengal, of India, carried on after Independence for another twenty years, very much as before 1947. The social prejudices were little changed and the disciplinary self-control observed by the expatriate community still occupying the grand mansions at Alipore, Tollygunge, Ballygunge and within the rectangle, Chowringhee, Park Street, Rawdon Street and Lower Circular Road, still strongly persisted.

Allowed such extraordinary licence, courtesy and extreme tolerance, by a gracious still re-grouping India, few expats thought too much about our 'right' to be there. A remarkable liaison, for most part, and astonishingly devoid of any rancour, particularly from Indians (an amazing commentary too of an Indian's forgiving nature), it worked wonderfully well, for everyone.

The Indian saga, which has occupied half of my adult life, is still not ended. Other subjects, of much contemporary interest, rapidly project on the screen. I have added more stories arising from other wonderfully interesting (and eventful) visits to Goa, with some of the residual 'magic' that still persists from its long Portuguese period; to Mysore (famous for Tipu Sultan and its colourful Maharajahs); Ootacamund (now called Udagamandalam) and its glittering Club where the game of Snooker first won its 'world' legs; Kerala and lovely Kovalam Beach; India's colourful southern extremity - Kanniyakumari (Cape Comorin); Trichinopoly (Tiruchchirappalli) or simply 'Trichy', as it is fondly termed; Pondicherry (highly interesting former French enclave with palm fringed beach setting); Mamallapuram (major seaport of the Pallava Kings and a marvellous open-air 'museum', south of Madras. The 'rathas' carved out of the monolithic rocks. The Shore Temple in its fabulous setting), and other absorbing places, everywhere in India. Finally to Hyderabad - a jewel in the making.

I wish you well to read these stories, mainly of India. May they evoke a mounting desire within you to learn more about today's India, best satisfied by sincere preparation and personal visitation.

1. India Re-discovered

- the allure never diminishes - but burns ever more brightly

If there is one certain thing in this world it is that India is the supreme cultural experience. It is an historic land of enormous contrasts - of sounds, of colour, and of aromas! Distinguishing trade marks, all of them, yet so often trivialised, and disappointingly for the brief visitor, either barely noticed or not allowed the full play so essential to better understanding of India, leading to greater enjoyment of that country.

The world's fascination with India and her teeming diverse millions, very naturally and properly, puts it in a category of its own. Whereas in former times it was the vogue to quote Frenchmen as the arbiters of opinion, it seems incontestable that the fortunes of 900 million Indians are destined to play a significant role in the shaping of tomorrow's world.

People from other lands either have an intensely passionate love and regard for India, and for her friendly smiling people, or else they feel uncomfortable. Getting their thoughts to rise above the unfamiliar environment and often grimy conditions that are encountered, can so easily cloud compassionate feelings. It takes time to assimilate. Ordinarily, it is a transition that can not be managed with a flick of the switch. It has to be worked at.

Many (and film directors possibly purposely - in order to create tension) rarely 'cross the divide', yet fundamentally, India presents few real problems for visitors. It is a safe country where everyone is accorded respect - not just visitors. Fear and personal danger is normally absent. Disregard David Lean's screen version of Forster's "Passage to India" which in a purposely misrepresented way played up 'fear', for 'awe'. The latter condition would more realistically be a truer representation of much that one exults about, in India.

In reality, India is many lands rolled into one. Its great diversity, complexity and even paradoxical simplicity (it is a land of immense ethnic diversity nurturing numerous cultures, languages and religions) allows no convenient, glib explanation, and deep down, everyone must search out their own answers.

It is also very possible that more people everywhere in the world, find India and Indian history more fascinating and a greater study, than just about any other people or anywhere else! For many, India's colour and complexity acts as a magnet.

In previous times (and possibly still today), many children the world over, enjoyed a brief 'growing up association with the awe-inspiring tales of the Great Mughals. Rudyard Kipling also helped with his many fascinatingly 'different' portrayals of life in colonial India, set down in his "Jungle Stories", and in his universally heralded novel, "Kim".

Youthful fascination and wonder (regrettably, a quality which invariably evaporates when people reach adulthood) thrills readily to exotic pictures of life, and in some respects, at any rate, so far as children are concerned, tingeing fact with fantasy, is no bad thing.

Who hasn't heard of the fabulous Taj Mahal at Agra. It is quite probable that this quite superlative architectural creation is better known than any other single edifice in the world. Every facet of it - its origins, location, design and construction, and not least, its magnetic drawing power - for everyone, is possibly unequalled.

Few persons could dispute that the Taj Mahal represents the greatest material tribute man anywhere has paid to his wife, in its time (c. 1650), before or since. In our times millions of Indians and visitors view this wonder every year. How astonishing then that a British scholar visiting there in 1790 could report that the shrine was deserted! Indeed, a remarkable commentary of fluctuating fortunes.

And so it was that beautiful memories such as these might have remained undisturbed. However, as time advances, the urge to again explore old haunts and to add new delights, is persistent in its call to just about every one of us.

Hence it happened that your scribe decided to lay fantasy aside and to pay a long visit to India of the eighties. Clearly such an adventure would be enhanced by travelling with Air India International, that was it!

The afternoon setting, at Sydney's Kingsford Smith International airport unwittingly provided a dress rehearsal for events to come. The queues of joining passengers were seemingly endless. Thoughts intruded themselves "Would the flight get away on time?". But more importantly - "Would the Jumbo be jumbo enough for so many people?"

Nowadays, no one complains about sensible security arrangements (seemingly the culprit for our delay), but nonetheless, there was a surprising absence of strained tempers and frayed nerves amongst the 400 and more passengers due to board our 747. Doubtless, nearly all were too occupied, mulling over anticipated good times ahead.

The preliminaries over and welcomed graciously aboard, the good Captain Das soon lifted his mighty charge "CHANDRAGUPTA", up and away into the skies. A long curving turn portside soon had us headed north-west and towards every sort of perceived thrilling expectation.

Strolling soon after dawn next morning, in the Senapati Maharaj Shivaji Gardens along the ramparts of Apollo Bunder in Bombay, (excitement had pushed into the background any thoughts of catching up on lost sleep, for there was too much to re-explore and rejoice about), it seemed appropriate that a singularly pleasant and loquacious early morning air-taker should be named Mr. Placid. The 'o' had been dropped from the normal Portuguese spelling.

Indeed, the atmosphere I felt, described to a 'T' the distinguishing quality, which from the start had set the tenor of Air India's service - always (graciously) there, but unobtrusive.

Fortuitously too, the strongest cue yet for foreigners moving around India had been signalled, naturally and spontaneously, at the outset. Put simply, it was this - "keep smiling, observe self control and most things will be satisfactorily and happily resolved". This same recipe operates universally, but never more so than in modern India, where many millions besides yourself require to be considered.

It is salutary to keep these virtues solidly in mind. If you do you will banish most concerns and uncertainty. This advice is especially pertinent when one is struggling to catch a train or a bus, in apparently, impossibly crowded conditions.

To arrive at Bombay's International Airport at Sahar at 2.15 a.m. on a humid summer's morning (it was 29° Celsius) is an experience. Immediately, you are engulfed in a sea of people all jostling for attention. Language difficulties affect more than just foreigners, as a man from Calcutta or Madras or Cochin, could find just as much difficulty in being understood (and assisted), in Bombay. But in spite of everything everyone survives and the day goes on its inexorable course, looking to do the same things to its next batch of victims.

The airport is thirty kilometres from the city centre and provides a hectic taxi ride for arriving travellers, even startling - if you are visiting Bombay (or India) for the first time.

In due course we reach the famous Taj Mahal Hotel. It is the mecca for people from all around the world. It would not be exaggerating to reckon, that in the spacious gleaming marble lobby of the 'Taj' Hotel, the world of east and west meets. In essence, the gateway 'in' and 'out' of the Arab world and to the Persian Gulf, is via Bombay.

The scene is always captivating with people gathered from all points of the globe hurrying about their business. The 'Taj' (along with Oberoi's magnificent modern hotels at Nariman Point) has a wonderful history of excellent hospitality. This famous hotel was conceived and built by one of the noblest and most dynamic of Indians (a Parsee), Jamsetji Nuserwanji Tata, at the turn of the (twentieth) century - 'to supply a need!'. Yes, astonishing as it now may seem, in those far-off days rights of admission to many top hotels in India did not extend to everyone - regardless of how much money you might have in your pocket!

Jamsetji, a man of enormous vision and achievement (he also pioneered the indigenous Indian Steel Industry in 1911) acting in his usual forthright and positive manner, soon put the 'problem for his countrymen' to rights!

At its rear the 'Taj' Hotel stands cheek by jowl with innumerable small shops selling merchandise of every description. *Caveat emptor* is acknowledged on both sides of every transaction. The passing traffic from daybreak until far into the night, is thick, swift and hectic.

3. The Gateway to India, Mumbai: one place to begin an "awe-inspiring" experience.

Bombay's taxi cabs dominate the congested thoroughfares and bear down in waves on the hordes of pedestrians, forced to use the roads because of the miscellany of commercial activities conducted everywhere on the pavements.

But, Bombay is, when you look at the splendidly architectured buildings, a 'fine old lady' underneath it all. Before it was overtaken by too large a population, it was surely very gracious and even beautiful.

The motor car gives much food for reflection in India, and it is not simply that seat belts are not compulsory, or, that good and capacious roads everywhere in India are a rarity. India is possibly unique in the (western) world in its attitudes to the motor car industry, for in most respects the shape and appearance of cars has remained visually almost unaltered, since the 1950's. (See Epilogue).

The Hindustan "Ambassador" (an Indian version of the 1954 Morris Oxford produced by the Birla organization - production is now up to the Mark IV model) and small Indian made Fiats completely dominate the scene. A returnee might pinch himself in disbelief at a road-scene which seems hardly altered in thirty years!

Not so long ago, in Melbourne when I was showing some slides of Assam taken years before, some smarties in my family had quipped that 'the cars' were a dead giveaway (of Dad's age). Incredible in a way to think how wrong they could be!

There would be few countries as India, where out of sheer economic necessity a measure of this sort for rationalizing attitudes to motor cars has been adopted. In reality, it is an object lesson to other countries, and to besieged car manufacturers the world over. But one thing I think all of us could be reasonably sure of - 'wherever he is, Henry Ford would undoubtedly be applauding loudly and long' and feeling vindicated that his theory and sales pitch, has lived on in India of all places!

To start one's Indian adventures at the sumptuous Taj Mahal Hotel with its stupendous past and obvious great future is a bonus. It will be something for me to look back upon and to savour (sigh for, might be more apt?) as I plunge into old haunts and into totally new areas, in all four corners of India.

Tomorrow, I take the "Deccan Queen" to Pune, going on from there to many magical sounding places on the plains, and right up into the highest and most majestic mountains of all, the Himalayas. There will be many interesting encounters and chastening experiences. Nothing will be the same again and I am sure my admiration for India and Indians will be increased.

How can it be otherwise? Any country with a civilization going back 4500 years clearly provides an illimitable study. Many very great men testify to this. How India tackles her future must surely play a significant role in this world's affairs in the twenty-first century.

Just about everyone will be watching and noting -and that includes me! A great reckoning is needed everywhere to ensure that the world in the twenty-first century, about to dawn, will be a fit place for everyone and where everyone and his or her needs, claims rightful consideration.

EPILOGUE: While eminently sensibly, India made do with just a handful of makes and models of passenger cars for forty years and more, with the advent of the economic liberalization programme from 1991, as many as ten or more new makes of small passenger cars have now been introduced (through local and multinational manufacture). This, despite the fact that India is pitifully short of decent roads and highways, and the roads of its principal cities and towns already heavily congested. It is difficult to understand India's departure from good sense. One without the other makes little sense.

2. "A Piece Of The Road"

- a place for everyone

It was 5.30 a.m. The sun was not yet up. Scores of homeless using the entrance hall for shelter were beginning to stir. Yadu, licensed Bombay railway porter No. 488 hoists my baggage up on to his head as if it were a featherweight, and then signals me to follow him!

We are at V.T. (short for Victoria Terminus. Indians have a penchant for abbreviations, especially reserving reverential tones for nostalgic former English connections). I wished to catch the early morning 'DECCAN QUEEN' out of Bombay but my problem was that I had no reservation and I had been told that none would be available for days.

In the world's second most populous country the extensive railway system, a legacy of the British, provides the means of moving vast numbers of people around the country. Railways crisscross India in all directions and whether they pay for themselves or not - fares are geared to the paying ability of users, and the poorest classes are the principal travellers - you can depend on it that there is rarely, if ever, a vacant seat, whichever line you are travelling on.

Encountering Yadu was a stroke of good luck, for where it came to finding a seat on 'full' trains, he was the master tactician. Illiterate he might be, but endowed with omniscient native instinct, skill and experience, he readily demonstrated his unmatched knowledge of the system. Whisking me into a vacant seat, he stood by, proud of his enterprising capabilities, waiting for his reward. I had to admire him - and his bargaining sense.

If time had permitted and a reliable interpreter been available (my long distance remembrance of Hindi allowed for too much misunderstanding), a thumbnail biography of Yadu would surely have made amazing reading. It is the Yadus who provide the links in the system, and thankfully India has many tens of thousands of Yadus.

While the scene around the vast concourse scarcely portrayed the bustling activity usual with Indian railway stations, bang on 6.45 a.m. the loco's shrill whistle sounded (more like a fanfare really, as though rejoicing to be away) and our journey had begun. There is something pleasant about a train moving off. For me there was a tinge of relief as well.

Ambling along at a leisurely pace, clearing the environs of Bombay occupied a long time, for the city stretches endlessly out into the country, while in reality there are few parts in the whole of India where there is no habitation. A saga of life beside the tracks was unfolded the likes of which most of us could never conceive of. Foreigners have been credited with labelling it, 'picturesque poverty'! Very easy said quickly, but one would have to ask what really does go on in the minds of Indians? What do they observe around about them and what are their feelings. What emotions trigger off their responses to life going on around them? Are they too involved in surviving themselves, to think about it, or even care? To outward appearances the average Indian displays an insouciance which masks his true feelings, but which allows him to endure conditions beyond anything we could comprehend (or cope as well with?).

The Monsoon (synonymous with life-giving seasonal rain in India) had been tardy this year and this was in evidence as we reached out into the rural areas. It is six weeks into the wet season and large tracts of country in the Western and Northern regions have so far been ignored, while in the East, floods are devastating life and property.

Much more than pan splattered pavements cry out for refreshment. Meagre rains, in a country striving to create reliable water storage facilities, often means harsh agricultural results and widespread suffering for the rural population, until the next uncertain rainy season comes around. It is not just a minor hiccough along the way, but a dramatic lessening of even the barest sustenance for countless millions.

It is no wonder that many Indians flock to the big cities (and by doing so put more strain on already greatly strained resources and facilities) in the hope that even paltry earnings made there, will sustain them and their families, back home in their native villages, until better times come around again. All this has a see-sawing effect; for although it temporarily redresses the problem, India's relentlessly accelerating population, substantially happening in the lower, poorer sections

4. Resplendent architecture - VICTORIA TERMINUS, Mumbai.

everywhere in the country, virtually ensures that the problem may never be overcome. It is a sad fact of Indian life that it does little more than postpone the eventual evil day.

After a tortuous journey up the Ghats we reach the plateau. As though exulting in its achievement the loco now bowls along whistle joyously blowing loudly and often. Soon we will reach Poona (Pune), a name many of us readily associate with wax mustachioed British Military pomp and ceremony. I too, was expecting to see traces of these past glories, but strangely, even disappointingly, it now is none of those things.

Realistically, I suppose, the fairy tale past had to be superseded by modern India. Regrettably then, nostalgia must take a back seat, and although one tries vainly to conjure up the sounds of bugle calls (how Kiplingesque bugle calls always appear. Without him, the bulk of Britain's military presence in India, particularly kept out of the towns in cantonments, might have passed unnoticed) and the clash of hockey sticks on a Saturday afternoon, any pictures that come are blurred.

But far-away thoughts were sharply banished as stark reality returned! We had arrived at Poona and hordes of porters and purveyors descended on all of us disembarking passengers. In an twinkling your scribe found himself propelled into a Bemo, India's motorized answer to the betjak (those familiar with Indonesia and the Philippines will know that ubiquitous conveyance) - a contraption with three wheels, sounding like a not-so-well-maintained rotary lawnmower and need I add - a highly vulnerable road transporter to boot, with their operators' death defying penchant for weaving imperiously and cheekily in and out and around heavily laden trucks and buses.

I had imagined beforehand that I would find Poona of the eighties a quiet gracious country town but this was not to be. What I found was a contrary situation and a strong burgeoning industrial centre, in which all of its one and a half million citizens seemed to be on the move, at one and the same time, and using every conceivable kind of conveyance. Although normal sense evoked a teeth gritting, 'hold on tight' attitude, to my surprise and delight it was a novel (first) experience, and most exhilarating! Especially as well to arrive against seemingly all the odds, in one piece, after negotiating the dense-est and easily most diverse road conditions imaginable. By any comparison, the mayhem around the Etoile is a tame experience.

I was graphically struck by the urgency of every users demands, by their wordless entitlement to 'a piece of the road'. It all seemed so typical of life in India where great tolerance must be (and is) practised and whatever there is has to be shared. Whatever the time day or night, wherever you are, there always seems to be someone 'sharing the road'.

The conglomerate mass sharing the road in Poona does so in the most deregulated way. It seemed for all the world like a giant computerized meccano board, where incredulously, just enough space for everyone was provided. Possibly providence helps preserve life and limb (or some otherwise gracious Hindu deity). You may regard it how you will - either awe-inspiring, or sheer fatalism in action! A bit of both I'd reckon. When I am told that India ranks eleventh in the world in car numbers, but has the highest road accident rate, I cannot be surprised.

One could not pass Poona by without recording that it is the home of the world's second largest motor scooter manufacturer and most probably, the town itself holds the world's record for most motor scooters. The BAJAJ people must be highly gratified to have such a huge user population on its doorstep. The scene in Poona may be likened to that in Bombay where we have just left, where ten diminutive Fiat motor cars seem to occupy every square metre, appearing to the people like an unparalleled Italian 'advance' of frightening proportions as hordes of Fiats hurtle towards them in waves! While literally swamped with Bemos, likewise no similar concerns appear to bother loyal Poona dwellers.

My arrival in Poona coincided with a significant day in the commemorative life of independent India, a day when the leaders of the 'Free India' movement made their intentions absolutely plain by running up the Congress Flag (the future flag of free India) publicly, for the first time. It was on 9 August 1942 that Aruna Asaf Ali, then a frail young girl, unfurled the tricolour at Gowalia Tank, Mumbai defying the might of the British Empire, while Mahatma Gandhi's call to "Quit India" ignited the hearts and minds of every Indian.

The vision of one man (Bapuji) became the vision of the entire nation. The country became one in its fight against colonialism and imperialism. The final phase of the freedom struggle had begun, guided by the principles of truth and non-violence.

Ninth August continues to be counted as a red letter day in the life of modern India. While many illustrious patriots including Mahatma Gandhi and Jawaharlal Nehru were thrown into gaol for their efforts, it marked an important step along the road, which ultimately saw independence won in 1947.

Looking back on those events it does seem extraordinary (or even, wholly monstrous), that people with so profound a heritage allowed themselves to be subjugated by foreign masters until 1947. Also, that in such a richly endowed country, Indians were still living on the margins of hunger after suffering horrific famines! Thankfully today, famines are a thing of the past, for ordinarily, good seasons permitting, India now grows enough food to provide at least minimum nourishment for the whole of its population. But, the balance still remains ever so fine combating the demands of an exploding population which rolls on inexorably, in spite of significant birth control programmes.

It is a measure of the greatness of India that down through the ages it has always generously found a place for the many differing cultures which have made their way to its shores. Everyone has been welcomed (take or leave a skirmish here and there, although none of these conflicts ever wholly involved the entire nation) and calm reason has resulted in a synthesizing of all the various strands, providing a classic object lesson for other nations around the world. If internal political ambitions could be stifled as well, and unwanted rarely properly understood mis-directed intrusions of foreign media kept at bay, the generous and friendly disposition of all her people would ensure tolerance for everybody.

There can be no doubting the fact, that it is only truly great men who can show the way and nowhere moreso than in a country as diverse as India post-1947, in which year it came together as it is now, for the first time. This situation is not always realized, a fact which also legitimately negates all attempts to compare present performance with the past.

India has produced great leaders with exceptional moral fibre, many of them being also imbued with exceptional humility. How many leaders of other countries could say with Pandit Nehru - "they call me the Prime Minister (of India) but it would be more appropriate if I were called the first servant (of India)" - and mean it? Not very many, as most of us can testify.

This was the man who with all his mind and heart, loved India and the Indian people. Many other great Indians also stood alongside Nehru.

There was much deserved rejoicing on August 15, 1987 when 40 years of independence was celebrated throughout India. Transition to united nationhood had been slow, which may seem incongruous, in a land whose history stretched back 4,500 years. There are still some gigantic problems to be overcome but considering all that has been achieved since 1947, if it is the will of the people, the raising of living standards for everyone will surely happen. It may just take a little more time.

Contrary to generally held views outside India, India's post independence record shows that few nations have done so much in humanitarian terms, as modern India has done, to alleviate the plight of the distressed, and to bring about the eventual prosperity of all her peoples.

The magnitude of this achievement requires to be seen in the context of a hugely diverse ethnic population, speaking a score of major languages, and which has trebled in just over forty years, to 900 million. An enormous feat to manage, economically and socially. Sharing and consideration for everyone is a lesson all nations around the world are still learning. Only when everyone's entitlement to 'a piece of the road' is properly comprehended and met, will men and women everywhere live in true harmony with each other. Fair play and justice have still a long way to go.

The law of the jungle and of the survival of the fittest and strongest, should be seen for what it does to human beings, for it condemns the underprivileged to permanent inescapable impoverishment. By democratic means, the balance must be redressed, and with it our consciences, so that life becomes for everyone, more meaningful and endurable.

3. All Aboard For Jammu Tawi

- a train journey through middle India raises intriguing issues

Pune (Poona) had been warm, dusty, pungent and cluttered. The Monsoonal rains which constitute the most significant feature in the lives of nearly all Indians had put off their visit - a very serious thing! These rains satisfy every conceivable component of life and besides, the seasonal drenching scarifies and cleanses. It is the Nation's "Hoover", provided by nature. But in spite of everything, the general lively demeanour of the townsfolk seemed to be little affected. Life must go on - and indeed, it does!

It is a proud city, with great traditions and the home and principal manufacturing seat of some of modern India's great pioneering industrialists - Kirloskar made its small beginnings here eighty years ago (with no encouragement at all from the Raj) and is now a household name throughout India and neighbouring countries. In more recent times Bajaj has provided motorized transportation for the masses - the company is presently gearing up to manufacture one million units of motor scooters a year! Affording convenient and relatively cheap own transport, motor scooters figure very high amongst first 'non-essential' purchases by Indian households, hence their great popularity and ever increasing numbers.

Also, the presence in Poona of several arms of the great Tata organization, lends enormous prestige. The Group's major truck (and now passenger vehicle) subsidiary TELCO, has added to the region's considerable prosperity, while its Management Services and Computer Technology sectors gain much from collaborating with other National Technical Institutes, also located in the area.

Of more recent vintage, though of less noble renown, is the presence in Poona of the Bhagwan Maharajrishi, the self styled Messiah, who flourished in the United States for a while, with a stable of 91 Rolls Royces! Since Oregon dealt with him, he sits again in Pune, licking his wounds, or perhaps planning more depredations? The amazing ever forgiving Indian society finds room for everybody!

My initial introduction to the motorized rickshaw, and in Pune, was like nothing I had ever previously experienced. It sent the senses reeling and the physical assault from all sides was utterly fantastic. To come out of the hurly burly of the indescribable traffic unscathed, is to go back again and again into the fray, each time to marvel at it all, and to be exhilarated. Riding by taxi thereafterwards (another occupation in India not without its own drama and hazards) pales as a 'non-event', and is even stately by comparison! When you reflect, it is a truly remarkable thing how we attune to the startling and even dangerous, and the way we make our preferences.

But all this frenetic activity is no more than another 'picket' in the myriad fence that is India. When, and if, one can get one's values into proper context and begin to evaluate everything from this base, only then can the temperament of the Indian and his ability to co-exist be seen in proper perspective. Without this great trait (habit, penchant? call it what you will) he could not possibly endure the myriad situations, otherwise seen and irrevocably regarded by outsiders as quite horrific, impossible, and beyond toleration by the normal human. In reality, most Indians, and in particular the lowly Indian, have wonderful qualities and they should be marvelled at, and certainly not (and thoughtlessly) reviled! Left to his own devices and adaptability, I believe that the average Indian citizen is able to aspire to a satisfactory level of happiness. He or she is blessed with a lot of humility and are grateful for any kindnesses shown to them. While in real terms there is a high degree of acceptance of one's lot in life, expectancy is geared to the reality around them, which inevitably dismisses most chance of disappointment occurring.

Where it comes to durability and ability to endure all manner of hardships and deprivation, almost without demur, the Indian has much to teach the foreigner. In so many things in fact it is *not* as the west is all too ready to believe, but quite the contrary, it is the other way round! How mindless and awfully sad it is then that western civilization unthinkingly and erroneously feels a compulsion to impose its ideas on others, without scarcely any consideration or thought being given to drawing something *from* those countries, whose life experiences stretch back millenniums and way beyond our own relatively recent origins.

But the Stationmaster reports all is ready and the Jammu Tawi mail is on its way. North India beckons. The journey up as far as New

Delhi was to produce its rash of new experiences, of fresh shocks and, of new delights.

My diverse companions for the next twenty-seven hours would do much to improve my understanding of what it is that makes the Indian tick. Forget the conventional, the humdrum, you won't find any of that here! Nothing stands still in India, everything is in a state of constant flux, which of course presents the daily challenge and paradoxically is the catalyst which keeps the driving wheels turning round. I have no doubt that a great stupor would descend if this ever stopped and catastrophe would quickly follow. Mercifully, it seems unlikely.

Before reaching New Delhi we would cover 1740 kilometres and traverse five States - Maharashtra, Madhya Pradesh (literally Middle Province), Rajasthan, Uttar Pradesh (Northern Province) and Haryana. We would marvel at the fact that nowhere would we see boundary fences dividing one agricultural property from another (except for a small pocket south of Madras, the writer has never encountered boundary fences in rural areas anywhere in India. The prohibitive cost and scarcity of fencing materials ensures that 'western' methods of separating properties cannot happen). The essentiality of a substitute effective 'moral' code is immediately raised. You may ask, "how can anyone be totally certain which is their land?" Factually, the problem of identification is not so awesome, for many small landowners never move during their lifetimes, from their birthplaces. The same plot of land is passed down from generation to generation. The bigger question is perhaps, "how does one prevent others stealing one's crops?"

It makes one smile to think of the trouble the western world goes to, to keep unwanted trespassers out. Sometimes in India, there must be times when ripening crops are pillaged, but by and large, 'title' is respected, although how land ownership in a country covering over three million square kilometres, one third of the size of the U.S.A. and with more than three times America's population, could ever be meticulously registered, and of course every bit of it is, defies logical thinking! It provides another instance where our format for living has no place in the scheme of things here, where, if problems do arise, they are accepted as not abnormal but all in the normal scheme of things. It seems that one of the visual methods used for demarcating different ownership is the growing of trees at the corners of the plot, or many trees along the perimeter. "But", you may again say, "your own particular type?" It is another local feature to boggle and wonder at! - in this fantastic land of India, where there are literally tens of millions of agricultural landowners. Owning even the very smallest plot of land has enormous importance, and is often the difference between subsistence level living, and starvation.

Leafing through a copy of the Indian Railways' Year Book revealed to me that there are over sixty-two thousand kilometres of rail track reaching into every nook and cranny of the country. Instead of closing down lines, as is happening in many developed countries, more new areas are being serviced every year, for the railway system is the lifeblood of the country. Rail communications are seen as vital, and contrary to what uninformed sceptics may trot out, the very latest international technology is being used to carry out these extensions including too, the considerable upgrading of existing track. Along with India's other millions of train travellers, I am heartened to read that mobile electronic detectors regularly scan all the rails on major routes for metal fatigue and other problems!

The number of people using India's vast railway network every day is mind boggling. Daily users run to tens of millions. When the Colonial Governor Sir Leslie Orme Wilson opened Pune Station in July 1925 he could never have imagined the numbers travelling the line sixty years later! It is sobering to reflect upon the insignificant increases in the populations of western countries in the same period. Here in India where the population has trebled in the last forty or so years, 'big' is synonymous with 'gigantic', and 'small' rarely comes into the vocabulary!

My attention turned to my immediate travelling companions. "Who were they?" "What did they do for a living?" "Why were they travelling north?" Taciturnity not being a normal trait of the average Indian I had not long to wait before I knew these answers. From the great admixture of their speech - Maharasthan, mixed with English and Hindi or Urdu (the extensive multi-lingual capabilities of large numbers of Indians is not generally known and accordingly, acknowledged and respected) - I was soon to make some deductions.

Shasti held a doctorate degree in engineering (he had secured his Ph.D at age 50 - from Texas University!) and Laxmi was barely less qualified. Their specialty was (is) harnessing power from the ocean tides and as officers of the Central Water and Power Research Station in Pune, they were journeying to New Delhi for a day's conference. Money is the one commodity India hasn't enough of - but unlike some other (western) debtor nations, it has long since stopped squandering precious capital on non-essential imports (where else are they using predominantly the same dies as thirty years ago to manufacture just a handful of makes of cars, and also of heavy road vehicles?), and strives to 'live within its own self created means'. But not all foreign credit raisings can be avoided, as essential infrastructure needs for rising population can not be indefinitely put off, nor indispensable food imports in crisis situations.

I marvelled that my new-found Indian engineer friends thought it was no great hardship to put in 54 hours laborious train travel out of a total period away from their homes of little more than 72 hours, simply to put in a few hours at a conference! It is even more astonishing but creditable that they undertake the same journey frequently, yet nearly always cheerfully, and uncomplainingly. Plane travel is considerably dearer and ordinarily restricted to very senior officials and emergency situations.

Shasti and Laxmi are highly enthusiastic about their work which particularly affects the region around the Gulf of Kachch (Gujarat) where 7 metre tides occur. Exhaustive feasibility studies take years without any guarantee that the scientists' labours and achievements will be rewarded, for when the time to employ their findings does eventually arrive, no money may be available to put their plans into operation! It seems a tragic imbalance of values as projects of this sort (and right now many countries, with Canada which has 20 metre tides, in the vanguard - are intensively researching the same objectives) might ordinarily come within the category labelled "TOP PRIORITY FOR MANKIND" being pollution free, unlike fossil fuelled methods still substantially employed around the world for power generation.

In mid-morning next day we cross the Narmada River. Many religions co-exist harmoniously in India. It is a daily ritual with Hindus to pay great respect and reverence to their gods. More than all the man-made laws Hinduism teaches people how to discipline their lives, that theirs and the lives of others may be enriched. Rivers and mountains (even hills) everywhere, have their devotees. Pilgrimages of long or short duration, or of greater or lesser hardship, engage just about every Hindu during his lifetime. Paying *dharma,* or duty to society, is seen as an obligation and it is rarely ignored or avoided.

Homage to the Narmada (one of India's many huge river systems - all of them sources of life and worshipped as such) is a case in point. It is one of India's most sacred rivers, almost as holy as the Ganges. In its vast basin live tens of millions of people, many of them tribals or scheduled castes. In the forests along the river banks is a huge wildlife population. Flowing majestically westwards to the Arabian Sea the Narmada has sustained the people living adjacent to it, both materially and spiritually, for centuries.

Pilgrims regularly gather at the mouth of the Narmada at Bharuch in the Gulf of Khambat (Cambay), and then proceed 1,000 kilometres *on foot* up to the source of the great river at Armarkantak situated high up in the Maikala Range in Madya Pradesh, where prayers are offered to the deities. Then they about-turn and cover the same distance back to the Arabian Sea. Such a journey (pilgrimage) may take a whole year! Non-Hindus may scoff at all this determined devotion and question its efficacy while at the same time just probably quietly marvelling at such tenacity.

To pilgrims, devotion and sacrifice has very great merit, and doubtless every pilgrim experiences great inward satisfaction and elation from having accomplished what he or she has set out to achieve. Many possibly never manage to complete their mission, but fall down on the way. However, this is not seen as any reason for not setting out. There is something singularly fantastic in these personal (communal) efforts and I for one readily accept that ""half a billion or more Hindus surely cannot be wrong", in their strong unwavering religious convictions.

But it is time now to eat! The *khansamah* (railway steward) delivers the food previously ordered. Our man is quite a character, scruffy and wonderfully simple, and so solemn, with an ability to readily forget, for he had taken the same orders at least six times! But he means well and no one takes the slightest offence. Most enlightening of all to me is that no one gets mad and abusive.

Indians usually partake of their food with relish, treating meal-taking seriously, although I am not aware of any religious ritual requiring this observance (here I exclude Muslims who have very strict

5. India's fabled tiger - "Lord of the Jungle".

meal routines). Conversation invariably ceases (in this regard, and with respect, it might be said that it is possibly the only time many are silent during their waking hours for Indians are ordinarily exceedingly gregarious and love to converse). A great variety of cooking styles exists but in most respects it is true to say, that Indians do not ordinarily depart very much from their own basic (regional) tastes, throughout the whole of their lifetimes.

Bhopal was now behind us. A long-held grievance I and many others have with the fourth estate is that many events and the Bhopal 'leak' was one of them, are all too often obliquely reported. For instance, I doubt many foreign 'observers' of the tragic Union Carbide disaster at Bhopal drew very much, and in perspective, from newspaper reports. This situation is all very sad and extraordinary as well, when so many persons died and thousands of others suffered brutal and ghastly injuries. Rightly or wrongly, it could seem overdue that western nations stop shrugging off multiple deaths in India as 'all in a days course'- it certainly is not that! Even the poorest of the poor have feelings, no different to anybody else.

It is an unseemly attitude and shows an ignorance of India and of Indian life, for contrary to the impressions sometimes left with (western) readers, every life is precious regardless of whether it is lived in a populous country or not. Suffering and bereavement know no borders. A more sympathetic sharing of tragedy and sorrow would have benefits for everyone.

In reality, Bhopal is not a very imposing place and lies in the midst of fairly harsh countryside. The peoples' trials this year were not helped by the late onset of the monsoon and the countryside for as far as the eye could take in, was dry and parched.

We pass through Jhansi, popularised by John Masters in his racy narrative *Night Runners of Bengal*. One hundred years or more on, the tumult has indeed died down and it would require a lot of concentrating to conjure up very much of the heroic and glorious episodes played out here, during the time of the Mutiny. Ears and eyes would be strained to catch even an echo from the ruins of the past. Such is history, so much of it now gone and buried, the way left clear for more to be made.

It would be remiss to pass Jhansi without noting that it was the birthplace of the greatest hockey wizard of them all, the immortal Dyand Chand, a great exponent of the game and athlete, more revered and celebrated perhaps than another local heroic figure from Indian history, the 'Ranee of Jhansi', renowned for her valiant resistance to the British during the Mutiny, a role still hugely popular in present times, with Indian filmgoers.

Gwalior is a name familiar to many people through its excellent potteryware (in former times they also had a quite celebrated Maharajah). Back in my halcyon days in Calcutta as a young *chokra* (new chum), I owned a lovely Gwalior vase. It had not cost me much, but it was quite large, a lovely yellow colour (like ripe corn) and beautifully glazed. At any dinner party it always occupied a prominent, eye-catching place, filled with fine blooms.

It was always so convenient to collect a large flower arrangement from Calcutta's New Market, get home, unwrap it, and pop it straight into my yellow Gwalior. One evening I was rushing and left the formalities to (new) servants. Emerging soon afterwards, I was quite shattered to find the arrangement had been disembowelled and six inches were being hacked off most stems, preparatory to the stuffing of smaller bunches of blooms into numerous glass (jam) bottles - I was aghast! So much for my lovely Gwalior vase!

John Masters knew his India very well (to many Indophiles he is compulsory 'light' reading) and might well have been inspired to write his *The Deceivers* from glimpsing the extraordinary land formations which cover a large area adjacent to Morena and the Chambal river. It is 'dacoit' country and I fancy some Hollywood directors might see much potential in the topography for making 'goodies and baddies'.

Soil erosion happening over centuries and stretching to the horizon and beyond it, has created a quite unique landscape - literally thousands upon thousands of miniature 'mountains' (and steep valleys) none more than forty metres high *and all below ground level*! Imagine if you can an embossed relief map of the vast Himalayas, set *into the ground*! It is like opening the lid of a large cardboard box and seeing inside a simulated Chinese burial ground, or an excavated Nubian Kingdom there before your eyes. Here man never came into it, but it is nature's work alone!

Shades of Lilliput, but indeed, India's modern *dacoits* (bandits) were quite real and gave great trouble until recent years, when after the waging of an intensive para-military - police campaign, most were either captured, or induced to lay down their arms. It couldn't have been very funny being held up and robbed (the old time caravan trains) in such a spooky 'Dartmoor-ish' region. The *dacoits* had found a marvellously invulnerable place in which to hide out, for with a sameness about every square metre of it and no visible signposts about, the wonder is that even they themselves were able to find their way, 'in and out', of what is, a gigantic Hampden Court Maze! But these strange events did actually happen and the amazing ground formation is there for everyone to see.

For some time there had been a terrible din from down the carriage? Everybody tolerates it, nobody sees any reason to do anything about it! Regarding it as strange, I enquire of my friends. It seems that we have a *prabatikar* (*pujari*) amongst us. A professional storyteller, he is regaling a dozen or so wide-eyed listeners with an exciting tale from Hindu mythology, doubtless suitably embellished (so I am given to understand), with a few of his own original adaptations. All boredom is banished as the audience is held in thrall. Traditionally in India much of their vast folklore is still passed down, or on to others, by word of mouth. With high illiteracy still prevailing, particularly amongst the older people, the professional story-teller still has a special and very important role to fill.

I take notice, not only because I am impressed with the *prabatikar's* superb enactment, (if the test of such, is the total attention of one's hearers), but also with his lung power and his stamina, which are exceptional. The gripping high pitched tones rattle out with the speed of a machine gun and the oration occupies perhaps forty minutes in all - maybe longer. Hardly one eyelid dared a blink. Marvellous theatre, and the irony of it all was, that perhaps the raconteur got no more than a few rupees (fifty cents) for his enthralling effort. India provides some fascinating moments - millions of fascinating moments in fact, every day, everywhere up and down the length and breadth of the land.

We have passed through Agra (that is a major topic in itself for other times) and we are entering the final stages of our journey. It is evening and we will reach New Delhi at 9 o'clock, a little sadly I profess, for what could have been a long drawn out train journey largely endured by the reading of a western novel, had developed into a wonderful voyage of discovery and in the process, my esteem for Indians, had been considerably enhanced.

I bid Laxmi and Shasti *au revoir*, perchance to meet them again at Pune, where they have promised to show me their engineering models and to explain the mysteries of power generation from the tides. Another day, another chapter.

EPILOGUE: Three important events which have since occurred could have some interest for readers.

The river Narmada, the 'pleasure-giving' Goddess, has become the focus of the world's largest river project, stirring up great controversy in India. Permanent (stored) rain water is vital to life everywhere, often being given priority over all other considerations.

The Narmada Valley Project envisages the construction of thousands of dams, large and small, with the two biggest - the Narmada Sagar in Madhya Pradesh and the Sardar Sarovar in Gujarat - larger than all others anywhere in India. Large tracts of country will be submerged, including extensive areas of agricultural land and irreplaceable forests. Millions of people will have to be evacuated and re-settled.

Environmentalists as well, stridently resist the Government's objectives, arguing that much wildlife will be destroyed and that the river basin's ecology will be permanently destabilized.

The grandiose Narmada Project has been embroiled in controversy ever since it was first mooted. Crucial to huge minimizing of submerged land will be the height of the Sardar Sarovar dam wall (and resettlement of displaced people). The converse is, that whether the height of the wall is 436 feet or 455 feet, completion of the Scheme - and soon - is vital to life for millions in Kutchch, Saurashtra and North Gujarat.

The second, relates to the extraordinary land formation surrounding the Chambal River (dacoit country) and the celebrity status being enjoyed by Poolan Devi, one of India's most notorious dacoits. Uniquely a woman dacoit and describing her crimes as revenge for

indecent treatment by men (she alleges that she was repeatedly assaulted and raped as a young woman) after capture and a term in prison, Poolan Devi is now getting 'icon' treatment from sections of the women's movement and from the media. In the 1996 elections she went one further and won a seat in the Indian Parliament (*Lok Sabha*).

A recent film "The Bandit Queen" allegedly portraying Poolan Devi's exploits in the Chambal region, created much controversy, leading to its being withdrawn by India's film censors. Associated publicity has boosted the once loathed Poolan Devi to national prominence.

The third point relates to upgraded concerns for the world's environment, a situation which highlights what Shasti and Laxmi are doing to reduce India's dependence upon fossil fuels for power generation. The importance and urgency of finding and improving alternative methods, viz. hydro-electric, wind, solar and the huge potential contained in harnessing the tides, has been heavily underlined at the Rio, Berlin and Kyoto environmental conferences. In wishing Shasti and Laxmi and their colleagues speedy success, we pay due homage to the great importance of their work, they and others are doing, around the world.

4. Forty Years On

- the day I rose early to hear Rajiv Gandhi

In New Delhi on January twentysixth every year, (Republic Day), a gala parade takes place down the Rajpath, which stretches in a straight line for many kilometres, from the ramparts of Rashtrapathi Bhawan (the President's Palace) to India Gate. Few processions held anywhere in the world, surpass India's Independence Day parade, for sheer size, martial order, variety and colour (there's plenty of this), and for its superb setting. The Rajpath and modern magnificent New Delhi, Edward Lutyens' creation this century, is the new world's answer to London's Mall and to France's Champs Elysees, both of which are also wonderful thoroughfares for ceremonial parades.

I had gone to India in the month of August expecting to correct a previous omission. However, in my ignorance (though not for the want of enquiry for I had written ahead asking about the form the festivities were to take but had received no response), I had presumed that the celebration of free India's fortieth year of independence on 15th August, 1987 would include a monster parade along the Rajpath - Bengal Lancers on magnificent steeds, Rajputs on superb chargers, bedecked elephants, camels, etc., in fact - the complete works!

But although I was indeed five months too early, I was still privileged in another sense, for Proclamation Day 15th August also has great significance for the modern nation of India. The India of 1987 that I found, was sorely afflicted by much internal strife and other acute problems, leaving the nation in little mood for celebrating. No amount of glitter and razzmatazz would be enough to banish the serious strains which the nation was enduring at this time. Indians love processions whether for religious purposes or whatever, and her people being very naturally gregarious, will always turn out in substantial numbers, if only for the break in the everyday harshness of normal life, that such occasions provide. Native curiosity also ensures that attention will nearly always be given to exciting, out of the ordinary, events.

But after forty years, the euphoria which had accompanied initial independence, (in 1947), had noticeably eased. Maintaining national fervour for such a length of time amidst difficult circumstances, would call for extraordinary zeal, enthusiasm and energy. Reflecting a moment, it seems to be a fact that in not many places in the world now, are big parades still regularly held - for one, they cost a lot and two, there seems to be less public appetite for them, or for formality. Precision, discipline and orderly marching, smack perhaps of 'military might' and no longer produce pride and thrills. Mores the pity.

But returning to my story, I accepted my ill luck and resolved to redress the balance on some other 26th January. Better I felt, to concentrate upon the moment and obtain for myself a ringside seat at the next best Indian celebration - the Leader's national August 15 address given from the ramparts of the Red Fort in Old Delhi. It is interesting to note that the newest new world settlement Australia, and one of the world's oldest civilizations, India, share the same celebratory date. But this is where all similarity ends, for life lived in each country is really very different.

I sought and obtained a Yellow Pass at the Government Tourist Office on Connaught Circus which would entitle me to a place in the official enclosure to witness, as an admirer of India, an epic event in their calendar.

Up to this point it had seemed all too easy to manage, for I had personal remembrances of Bulganin and Krushchev (and other huge gatherings too, when Pandit Nehru addressed the people), on Calcutta's Maidan in the fifties, when upwards of half a million people attended a huge welcoming rally.

"How many people were expected at the Red Fort?", I had asked. The answers kept coming back to me "Oh, a great many, maybe up to a million!" Aghast, I had second thoughts about attending, especially as it meant getting up very early and being 'seated' by 6.30 a.m. I was told that the Prime Minister, Mr. Rajiv Gandhi would commence his speech an hour later.

But loyalty to my original intentions guaranteed that I would take the thick with the thin, and also tolerate the additional but not so comforting thought, that there would be huge jostling crowds all clamouring to hear and possibly catch a close glimpse of their leader.

It was going to be a hot sticky day and already even so early in the morning, the temperature was already burning, as it does at this time of year everywhere on the plains, in India.

Waking was no problem, for I was agog with excitement at the forthcoming prospects. (What an anti-climax it all ultimately turned out to be!).

In plenty of time, I emerged from my hotel (Oberoi Maidens in Old Delhi), ready to do battle. But like me many others had also anticipated that a great throng of people would be present, and very wisely, taxis and motorized rickshaws, conscious of being trapped in a horrible traffic jam, were having no part of it. The roads adjacent to the Fort would be soon closed, locking in those foolish enough to have already entered, with their cars.

A ride part of the way on a truly 'low flying' bus (I counted myself fortunate to be able to alight from it - there was such a crush!) left me only a few kilometres to tramp, up by the old Kashmiri Gate to the Red Fort (Lal Qila). To my dismay and disappointment too, activity all around was not very hectic, for I had geared myself to expect a tumultuous gathering. Very surprisingly, far less interest was being shown than I had expected, remembering pictures I had seen in the press when I lived in India years before, of those occasions when Pandit Nehru annually addressed the throng. Nehru had an enormous following particularly amongst the poorer classes, who saw him as their champion.

I couldn't help wondering why things had changed? Where was all the enthusiasm I had expected? Why wasn't I being jostled by great crowds all eager to hear their national leader speak from the rostrum from which the great Jawaharlal Nehru had proclaimed India's Independence on that momentous night in 1947, forty years before?

Only the day before, I had looked over the Jawaharlal Nehru Memorial Exhibition at the Trade Fair Grounds, and had read that great man's stirring words, uttered at the birth of the Nation. These thoughts which came from a great person, from a great humanitarian who was also a great statesman, were delivered in an atmosphere of great euphoria. It would be hard to adequately describe the joy, the relief of the millions, all over India, as these words poured forth from their great freedom fighter, and first Prime Minister.

"Long years ago we made a tryst with destiny and now the time comes when we shall redeem our pledge, not wholly or in full measure, but very substantially. At the stroke of the midnight hour, when the world sleeps, India will awake to life and freedom.

A moment comes, which comes but rarely in history, when we step out from the old to the new, when the age ends, and when the soul of a nation long suppressed, finds utterance.

It is fitting that at this solemn moment, we take the pledge of dedication to the service of India and her people, and to the still larger course of humanity.

As long as there are tears and suffering, so long our work will not be over."

Such an epic speech, and one full of great hopes and of great expectations. There was an enormous job ahead in building the nation, for indeed when independence ultimately came, many critics would claim that Britain had let the new nation down, by withdrawing with unseemly haste. In Britain's defence, every decision along the road to Independence seemed to create its own multiple problems. Discussions could have gone on interminably. Better, the British decided, to wield the axe, withdraw, and let the people themselves sort out their differences, which is what happened. To the eternal disappointment of Mahatma Gandhi the 'father of the nation', Independence contained one other very bitter pill - Partition and the religious division of the country. It was a dreadful irony after a long and often intense struggle to keep the country and its people together, irrespective of class or creed, to remain living together, and harmoniously, as they had done for thousands of years, prior to British intervention.

The scene surrounding the magnificent seventeenth century Mughal palace, the Red Fort in Old Delhi is itself captivating. At the Chandni Chowk side, it boasts ramparts very high up, which overlook an open space large enough to accept very large crowds. But it could never be regarded as the ideal speechifying place as it is located in a very crowded heavily populated area, which invites traffic chaos whenever large numbers gather. I'm sure that on the night of 14th/ 15th August, 1947, the crush must have been terrifying. However, retention of the original location doubtless embodies much symbolism and accordingly, it would be no easy thing for Indians to remove to a

6. India's first Prime Minister, and great statesman, Jawaharlal Nehru, addressing the nation, from the ramparts of the Red Fort, Old Delhi, on Independence Day, 1947.

different and more suitable location, for getting consensus from the people could be fraught with problems.

Security features high on the list in India these days. Assassination of political figures poses a constant threat. It is not so long ago that the Prime Minister, Mrs. Indira Gandhi was shot and killed by Sikh extremists agitating for a separate state. It is ironical that her assassins belonged to her own trusted bodyguard!

I had intentionally left my camera at the hotel, for ordinarily they are taboo in the highly charged atmosphere of public gatherings. As well, they may not be carried into any of the central government buildings in New Delhi but must be left at the reception. But I did not count on an embargo on *all* bags! Mine held the essential water bottle (a necessary precaution against a long speech on what was a humid morning), and a few nondescript and harmless miscellaneous items. But all my polite protestations fell on deaf ears and it was no go. Being loathe to entrust my belongings to uncertain trustees, and at a gathering of unpredictable parameters, I chose not to enter any seating enclosure.

One Sepoy (military type) after another, primarily not wanting to waste the opportunity to show off their authority, shooed off all loiterers i.e. anyone who couldn't show the right card or had a bag or a camera - to somewhere, to anywhere, so long as it meant removal from their beat!

My instincts warned me against any show of antagonism. Much wiser to tread warily for there was no point in being silly, particularly remembering that after all, it was their day - not mine! When in Rome .....

While all this kerfuffle was going on, two army helicopters hove into sight, flying in tandem, the P.M.'s in front emblazoned with the Indian tricolour. A buzz immediately went up from the crowd. While the hoped-for large gathering of party faithful and Indian zealots had not materialized, among those who were gathered, there was no doubting their patriotic fervour.

Nevertheless, I got the distinct feeling that if Rajiv Gandhi's popularity was measurable by the numbers that were present, he might well have tendered his resignation letter there and then. For inexplicable reasons the gathering was not only unexceptional, but it was also very sobersides, and surprisingly (to me), not the emotionally-charged occasion I had led myself to expect it would be. Maybe it was the heat? Maybe it was the 'failed' monsoon? On the other hand, one had only to read the current newspaper editorials to deduce some of the reasons for the poor turnout. Indian newspapers especially hammer home any whispers of corruption involving their politicians, and the Bofors gun affair would haunt Rajiv Gandhi for the rest of his life, allegations of personal corruption, proven or not.

Yet whatever the reasons for the disappointing turnout, it did seem sad that after only forty years, the spark has apparently gone out of things, and that much of the nation's burning patriotic fire had been extinguished.

The organization on the ground was good, and ever faithful to the indigenous motor industry, the P.M.'s cavalcade of five gleaming white Hindustan Ambassadors soon arrived at the ramparts and disgorged Mr. Gandhi and his entourage. The great moment had arrived. But had it? I expected tumultuous support for Mr Gandhi and the crowd to erupt. But the greeting was quite tame.

Rajiv Gandhi is a very deliberate and clear speaker. More interested in other things and not having been raised to be a politician in the footsteps of his mother Indira Gandhi and of his grandfather Pandit Nehru, he appears to lack the usual politician's enthusiasm and fervour, whether contrived or not. On the other hand, his grandfather and mother grew up in a different age, when fever for freedom ran high. Even after Independence was gained, politicking called for great eloquence, to set the population alight, so that the further great objectives might be achieved for the benefit of all, rich and poor alike.

It is true that nothing stands still for long, but it sometimes would be helpful if certain fundamentals managed to endure. It is increasingly evident that we live in greatly changed times. Political fervour nowadays is all too often perceived as having a false ring about it. With the untimely death of his brother Sanjay and the shock assassination of his mother, Rajiv Gandhi was thrust into the Prime Minister's job and made leader of the ruling Congress Party while not wholly willing or ready. Nonetheless, he carries out a huge programme tirelessly, while it seems clear that much of the real 'country first' service has gone out of Indian politics. The old zeal, sincerity and patriotic fervour is nowadays rarely evidenced.

There are many difficult issues. On all sides, India is assailed by unstable political regimes - Pakistan! The Afghanistan war! (The Russians may call it something else), Sri Lanka! Bangladesh! Burma! Much of South-East Asia and the Persian Gulf area is in ferment. India is the largest country in the region numerically and in land area. Few people would be game (or foolish) enough to try their hands at predicting the future, even ten or twenty years from now!

Such is the present jitteryness of Central Government that even the poor homeless boy temporarily sheltering right near where I was standing in the fork of a 'centre of the road' tree was not left in peace. For today at least, he was a security risk and must remove himself, his tattered bedding, meagre worldly possessions and all!

So what does Independence really mean forty years on? Clearly many things, to many men, but not always those goals Jawaharlal Nehru held firmly in his sights on that historic night in 1947.

India, and the world, has some serious thinking to do. Has resolve and political honesty deserted the scene? Until decency and incorruptibility and fearlessness (of integrity and of purpose) is once again commonplace, not very much that is enduring will be achieved.

How very much then might all mankind like to see embraced and lived everywhere in the world, the commitment, the high ideals and noble aspirations, so magnificently embodied in the epitaph for Jawaharlal Nehru -

> WHILE HIS LIFE'S LABOUR WAS FOR HIS PEOPLE AND THEIR FREEDOM HIS VISION WAS ONE OF A WORLD WITHOUT POVERTY OR FEAR AND BLESSED WITH PEACE

What a wonderful world that could be, one which everybody might enjoy and appreciate. Regretfully, until man's proclivity for obtuseness is overcome and common sense allowed its rightful place, such a pleasant and satisfying world, for India and for all the other nations, will be beyond reach.

EPILOGUE: Rajiv Gandhi, in a duplication of his mother's fate, was assassinated on 21st May, 1991 at Sriperumbudur near Madras in South India, after addressing a public electioneering rally.

The assassin, believed to be an adherent of the Sri Lankan Tamil separatist movement, blew herself up in the same attack.

5. Faded Glory - In The Tehri

- a glimpse into the past - of another 'Savoy'

The name "Savoy" has a ring of richness about it and it is hard to stop oneself from slipping off into a world of fantasy. "The Ritz" is another salubrious name that similarly conjures up visions of extreme opulence. It is easy to picture in one's mind's eye magnificent drapes, burgundy-red thick pile floor coverings, gilt furnishings, beautiful women elegantly gowned and scrubbed clean handsome immaculately attired men.

Imagine then, how our thoughts raced, when we discovered that we would be putting up at the "SAVOY". It was not that famous Victorian hostelry on London's bustling Strand the personification of all that is best, but another "SAVOY" in a remote corner of a once proud empire!

It had been exceedingly hot down on the plains, the monsoonal rains had not yet arrived this year, affording the usual annual relief. Some pending business matters in Delhi could wait, for here was an opportunity to go to the nearby mountains. The "SAVOY" beckoned.

How very pleasant it can be to let memories run unbridled, back to grander days. The prospect before us of open fires at night induced a warm glowing feeling, for oh, how lovely it was going to be, putting the different energy sapping heat of the plains behind us, for even a short while.

But we reminded ourselves it was not 1942 but 1987! Much could have changed, for in the interim the British regiments which had graced the scene at Roorkee and Dehra Dun since Queen Victoria's day had lowered their flags for the last time, long since.

Feeling in an adventurous mood, we decided to take the Inter-City bus, for train travel is usually uninvolved and misses the spontaneity and hurly-burly of bustling everyday life encountered on the country's highways. Negotiating the crowded roads and the hundred and one different situations that overland travel inevitably produces in India, promised far more excitement. The 'de luxe' special was going to whisk us over the 280 kilometres to Mussoorie for the princely sum of just five dollars! How amazingly cheap for a dress circle seat which would provide all the fun of the fair on the way as we passed north from Delhi through extremely congested villages and towns which bisected hectare after hectare of rich agricultural farmlands.

The mighty Ganga fed from the melting snows of the Himalayas spreads its blessing over these lands through the agency of immense man-made canals. The irrigated fields bountiful with corn and tapioca and sugar, rejoice in their good fortune, while not so far south in the U.P. (Uttar Pradesh, India's most populous state), there will be no harvest this season, for that region has experienced no significant rains for over a year.

The farmland scene (not everywhere in India do you see broadacres farming as occurs in the Punjab and in the northern parts of Uttar Pradesh) here and there changes. Grove after grove of mango trees now peppers the landscape for as far as we can see.

Occasionally, paw paw plantations add to the rich scene. Noticing so many cooking fires in the villages as we hurry past, sets us to wondering how fuel needs in this vast and heavily populated country can possibly be satisfied. Visions of the plight of Ethiopians and of people of other African countries haunt one, and you think "well, India could easily be the next country to be cruelly affected" as essential vegetation is marauded and irrevocably consumed. Keeping one step ahead of inexorable population increases requires very involved planning. The huge scale of everything in India makes minor problems in other countries gigantic ones to be overcome in India. The situation can be likened to the inevitability of the encroaching deserts, the advance of which, everywhere around the world, defies most human efforts to arrest.

But the experiences of other populous countries have not gone unheeded by India and there is some reassurance in the sight of thousands of spindly Australian eucalypt trees lining both sides of the roads for kilometre after kilometre, on the way to Dehra Dun. The F.R.I. (Forestry Research Institute), an institution headquartered in

Dehra Dun which has achieved world-wide acclaim, plays a major role on India's own doorstep. All over India, major reafforestation programmes are in full swing, evidencing the seriousness with which the Government treats the problem of fuel supply and environment control. It is stupefying to think of the huge quantities of fuel (of one sort or another), needed every day, to cook just one hot meal for all of India's accelerating population, now approaching 900 million.

Never dull as we traverse the action-packed highway, after several hours we leave the plains and begin to climb. Soon we shall reach Dehra Dun once a lovely town in the Terai at the foothills of the Garhwal Himalayas but sadly now over-populated and faded. Going on and after we pass through Rajpur the steep bit of the road takes over for the final thirty kilometres up to Mussoorie - and the "SAVOY"! We again project our thoughts - will it be as grand as we suppose it must once have been to warrant this appellation?

As the gradient steepens, the hair-pin bends get tighter, until it is a fact that the bus is actually into the next bend while it is still proceeding out of the preceding one!! The blaring of horns forewarns passing down-traffic of danger. Miraculously no vehicles touch, yet sometimes it seems that a collision cannot be avoided. The visibly dilapidated condition of most of the vehicles hardly exudes confidence, but in spite of everything we reach our ultimate destination, the 'Library Bus Stand'- we have arrived at Mussoorie.

The engine of our bus has hardly cut before we are besieged by hordes of rickshaw pullers, all clamouring to secure a fare to add to their extremely meagre seasonal earning opportunities. We are amazed to find that the old two-man-shafted hill country rickshas are still being used, no different to how people and their luggage were transported in the mountains one hundred years before! We prefer to give the Ricksha puller a small tip and walk, for it is only a short distance through the interesting and colourful shopping mall to the top of the rise from where the "SAVOY" commands a view of the town and a three hundred and sixty degree vista.

The hard foot-slog up the hotel drive is an instant reminder to us that we have just come from the plains and we are now standing at an altitude of 6,500 feet. Our lungs have yet to adjust to the rarefied atmosphere.

By now we are standing at the office, a small quaint low building set a little apart from the main complex. Sadly we note that the brass plate has not been cleaned for years. Panic starts to mount but we cannot turn back now and we are resolved to see it through! A warm greeting, from a world that our world has passed by, soon soothes our concerns, and we quickly decide that we are going to enjoy ourselves, no matter what.

Giant deodar trees in the compound said to be nearly three hundred years old, lend dignity to an otherwise faded glory. We console ourselves that many famous men have graced these paths, including a forester whose name has been forever immortalized, Sir George Everest. His once proud villa lies rotted and unrecognizable in the vicinity of the local Municipal Gardens.

We are shown to our 'suite'. We are aghast, but consider it would be uncharitable to complain and so we keep our feelings to ourselves. It is not every day that one finds oneself in a situation like this. The compensations for us are really manifold for despite the decadence all around us, we are provided with an unscheduled opportunity to look into yesterday's world. Unlike lost 'Shangrilas' (this is the romantic Tibetan name often given to uniquely strange and remote idyllic places) and Bavarian villages to this day still preserved in appearance in their sixteenth and seventeenth century form, our "SAVOY" has had to withstand the ravages of time and the cruelly destructive climatic extremes of North India, where nothing is spared.

Opened to the public in 1902 as the SAVOY Hotel, the complex (and it is a substantial collection of buildings which started out life as the 'Mussoorie' School) was put together in the days when every bit of material had to be hauled up the mountain cart track from where the motor road ended at Rajpur. The first motor car did not reach Mussoorie until 1920. We can only marvel at the ingenuity and perseverance of Mussoorie's town builders.

While Mussoorie in the years preceding its emergence as a 'hill-station' had hosted many visitors from the scorching plains below, with the arrival of the Savoy, it meant that it could now provide amenities similar to the other hill stations, Simla and Naini Tal. To Mussoorie now flocked Maharajahs and their glittering entourages, also landowners and civil servants, and British military officers on leave. The "SAVOY" catered in all its finery to a melange of guests.

7. The Savoy Hotel, Mussoorie.

Thinking back upon this, we paused, and allowed ourselves to listen in our fancy to imagined music, wafting as an echo through the whole complex. Unlike the cacophony that accompanies life down on the heavily populated plains, up here in the mountains there is no noise, and only the twittering of birds and the croaking of frogs disturbs the stillness.

We go into the dining room - once grand, but now resembling a mausoleum. A peep into the kitchen puts beyond all doubt our suspicions that here we now have the crumbling remains of a once resplendent establishment. Time has indeed stood still! How very sad it all seems. Why does glory have to fade.

Tradition and form die very hard in all of the British inspired 'hill-stations' in India and so it was no surprise that the 'Markers' eyes lit up when a game of snooker was suggested. The British were certainly ones for organization - and nowhere more so than in their Clubs. The 'Marker' besides being the attendant and the one who 'marked up' the progressive score, also filled in as a playing partner - whether one was playing billiards/snooker *or* if on the tennis court, the opposition on the other side of the net.

It was probable that the drapes had not been removed from the tables for years, but true to form at the end of two frames, *the* 'book' was produced and forty rupees (AUD4.00 at the current rate of exchange) requested from the sahibs. It seemed so unreal, but this was (is), the stuff of old India, along with the rest of the relics. Change is slow where people have been used to rigid order for centuries. A bottle of Grand Marnier stands on the shelf in the bar alongside a bottle of Port. Vintage brews indeed, for all else bears the label of indigenous concoctions - available in some variety since Independence, for the adventurous!

Long gone were the heady days pre-war, when the Mussoorie Savoy's orchestra, playing every night in the hotel's festooned ballroom, duplicated the musicology of their famous namesakes in London. The years rolled back in an instant, to memories of my father's old seventy-eights and the haunting strains of *Get Out and Get Under the Moon,* performed by Carroll Gibbons and his renowned band, the Savoy Hotel Orpheans. Our imaginations were delightedly allowed full play.

Two vastly divorced situations - the regal Savoy on London's Strand, and this once equally luxurious one, tucked away in the remote mountains of north India. Separated by thousands of miles but simultaneously both capable of exhorting their lovestruck couples to - *Look, Look, Look at the Stars Above.* Now fifty years on, the fantasy slowly and sadly faded, and was gone.

But now we have a new problem - without any warning the lights go out. Enormous increases in population and of associated industry, has put a great load on available electricity supply throughout India and electricity rationing must also be accepted by the hill-ites. Even more so now are we with the ghosts haunting the whole place in an eerie, though it must be said - unfrighteningly way, for we must believe that only friendly ghosts could reside in this marvellous old mansion-like establishment.

By the time the lights come on again our appetites have gone. We return to our musty suites, there to once more let our imaginations flit back to the glittering times of the past, until exhaustion overcomes us and we float off to sleep wearing curious half smiles on our faces.

Next morning, we decide we will take another bus and explore further east along the Tehri road. We are not disappointed and after it has all ended and once again we have descended from the mountains, and are speeding back to Delhi, we are left, shaking our heads in admiration, at the great industry and fortitude of the splendid hills people, who go about their daily business so diligently and uncomplainingly. Although the next day for them may seem hardly different from the one before, adherence to tribal ways and religious scruples avoids major troubles and brings equanimity and peace of the kind we all seek.

Our visit to marvellous Mussoorie and to its erstwhile showpiece, "the SAVOY", had been a journey of a difference and an enjoyable thought-provoking experience. Whilst indubitably staid old Savoy on London's Strand has its own colourful past, we still pause for a moment, and give thanks that we have been privileged, albeit fleetingly, to mingle with the 'other' Savoy. To have had our imaginations titillated by going back into times which are now but a memory, has been a bonus along life's way and one to be treasured and sweetly savoured for the rest of our lives.

6. "Your Most Gracious President"

- a birthday tribute to a wonderful lady

The setting sun on the mountains just across the verdant valley and the accompanying big wispy clouds drifting ever so weightlessly across the sky, matched the situation perfectly.

So it seemed to me, as I stood looking out from the lovely terrace while I awaited a lady whose quiet dignity and unfailing graciousness was so sincerely admired for very many years by so many people of every nation and political persuasion. Like me, you too must have wondered what had become of her after gracing the world's stage so illustriously for so long.

As a highly interested observer of Indian affairs over many years (I had lived for ten years in India), I was making a long revisit to India. In the course of my journeying I had come to Dehra Dun in North India to pay my respects to someone whom I had always considered to be one of the twentieth century's greatest world ambassadors for good, Mrs Vijaya Lakshmi Pandit.

By their devoted unselfish and unremitting service, few families anywhere can have rendered so much, particularly to their country, and by their example, to people everywhere, as the Motilal Nehru's of Allahabad. Motilal, the great Indian advocate, turned freedom fighter at the height of his fortune and success. His son Jawaharlal Nehru, India's first Prime Minister and one of the greatest leaders this world has seen. Motilal's daughter and Jawaharlal's sister, Vijaya Lakshmi (aunt of Mrs Indira Gandhi; herself mother of Rajiv), through her lifetime of service to India and magnificent diplomacy around the world, for India, and in the United Nations. All of them had been inspired by that most exceptional mentor of all, Mahatma Gandhi (no relation).

Although I had not previously met Mrs Pandit, her completely natural manner and genuine warmth immediately created a lovely atmosphere. How indeed, all of us might wish we could be of similar disposition as we were about to celebrate our 87th birthday! I believe that each of us appears as we have lived and that our inner qualities are reflected in our faces and by our demeanour.

Everything I had felt as I read her quite delightfully sublime autobiography *The Scope Of Happiness* was confirmed. In truth, I never doubted for a moment it would be otherwise, for there is a genuinely delightful ring about her writing. True sincerity can never be stage-managed and only a great and essentially good person can leave such a lasting impression on a reader. As a great Indian patriot she also writes as a champion for good in all of the world.

I felt very honoured and privileged to be sitting with this exceptional lady in her own lovely garden discussing her illustrious life's work, peppered as it has been with great names and associated with significant events.

Like the incomparable "Father of the Nation" Mahatma Gandhi, and her own brother Jawaharlal, Mrs Pandit also wears comfortably and modestly the Churchillian accolade 'of having overcome Man's greatest enemies - 'fear and hate'. There is no higher plane to aspire to, or higher praise than this.

First woman in the world to hold Cabinet rank (1937); unflinching disciple of Mahatma Gandhi in the ultimate winning of Independence for India (and for her allegiance suffering the ignominy of jail); first woman President of the United Nations General Assembly (1953). Her contributions to so much for the common good of men and women everywhere, would fill many volumes.

Persons with her human touch, moral fibre, intellect, and unfailing tolerance and graciousness, rarely pass this way. For one possessing such impeccable credentials, it seemed very natural and completely right to invite her views on numerous aspects of her wonderfully fulfilling life and where she saw all the present conflict and divisiveness was leading to - for India, and for the world?

Question: Mrs Pandit, thank you for receiving me today.

Throughout your lifetime you have shown great concern for your people's welfare and happiness. When did you commence your public service and how did it come about?

Mrs Pandit: I was nineteen in 1919 when Gandhi came to my father's house and turned my life upside down. I wanted to help at the grass roots and for many years I worked in the villages amongst the people helping them organize better, and caring for their health. As well, it was enormously important to rally vast numbers of people to the 'Free India' movement and to get them to join the Congress Party.

I went about explaining what this meant, to the illiterate masses, in the towns and rural areas, for the movement could only succeed if all sections of Indian people were behind it. To illustrate the point, Gandhi once graphically stated that "if every Indian spat at once, every Britisher in India would be drowned". After eleven provinces were given local government autonomy (by the Act of 1935), I was able to do more as a Cabinet Minister in my state, the U.P., particularly in health matters.

Question: With the winning of Independence in 1947, great hopes were held that now the day would be hastened when sweeping changes would come to India, greatly enhancing the welfare and prospects of the people. What do you believe are the most enduring benefits that have been introduced?

Mrs Pandit: The really great change that came about with Independence was the raising of the people's self esteem. It was amazing and wonderful and had to be seen to be realized. Whereas previously, Indians followed a 'two-ness' policy i.e. they submitted to the Raj from sheer necessity while their feelings really lay in the other direction, now all pretence was cast off. There was a remarkable transition and everyone's spirits soared for the first time. A great sense of national pride replaced former lip service. Retention of the bureaucracy was one of India's wisest moves and these systems endure with suitable modifications, to the present day.

Question: Looking back on the last forty years' events you will probably agree it is much too simplistic for commentators to continue to dogmatically opine that right from the start Partition killed all reasonable chance of Independence being a success. You were a prominent member of the Congress Party and must have laboured long over that issue. While Partition was for very many a tragedy, and the road to Independence almost indecently accelerated, despite Wavell's entreaties to the British Government to allow more time, was Congress nevertheless reasonably confident that with the effluxion of time, differences would be settled and problems created by Partition diminished or was there great apprehension that Partition would be forever a running sore - for both India and Pakistan?

Mrs Pandit: It is easy to be wise after the event, but the facts were that the momentum towards Independence could not be halted and the chance to be free could not be missed. It is true there were grave misgivings of the arbitrary and hastily contrived demarcation processes, but nothing could be done about it, Pakistan had to be accommodated.

It is perhaps a touch ironic that North Indians, and this includes that part which is now Pakistan, share very much in the way of language, eating habits, and clothes that are worn, and much else, while being quite removed from South India, where so much orthodoxy exists, and where nearly everything is different (from Northern India), with the only significant common bond being that we are all Indian Nationals.

Question: In 1965, during the first armed conflict with Pakistan I happened to be in Karachi and Bombay in the same week. The situation was tense in Karachi with troops and mass hysteria everywhere, while in Bombay there were few signs that anything untoward was happening. How would you explain this juxtaposition, in the light of overall attitudes of the Indian Public generally to 'differences' with Pakistan, and I expect one would have to include Bangladesh as well?

Mrs Pandit: You are quite correct. To the average Indian nowadays the presence of Pakistan has no great significance. Where we are concerned though, is with the rebel activity in our border districts and the increasing insurgency within India generated in part, at least we believe, from Pakistan. India has existed for a very long time (thousands of years) and the people have a singular capacity to accept and absorb invaders and just about every happening. No, I don't think Pakistan is an everyday concern to most Indians, certainly to nothing like the same extent as Pakistanis view India.

Question: It seems a reasonable premise that for a very long time to come, population numbers will decide a great many things for India internally. Natural catastrophes, whether drought or flood, often happening together, place a tremendous strain on already stretched fiscal resources. What hope do you see on the horizon for mitigating these problems by perhaps restricting the growth of the population? Do you have any solutions to offer, how this may be achieved without seriously affecting other strong religious and traditional factors?

Mrs Pandit: Education is the key, but unfortunately relentless population increase and restricted funds for infrastructure needs, make providing education for the masses, a major task. While the Constitution says that every

David Martin Esqr.
Madhuban Hotel
Rajpur Road.

202

URGENT

VIJAY LAKSHMI PANDIT

181-B RAJPUR ROAD
DEHRADUN 248 009
21. 8. 87

Dear Mr Martin,

When you called I made a stupid mistake. I am not free tomorrow morning. I wonder if you could come at 5 pm? Please call me & confirm.

Sincerely
V.L. Pandit

8. Author's memorable meeting with a great lady.

child to the age of fifteen may receive education, the headway we should all like has not been made in the public sector. As well, private education gets more expensive and out of reach to the majority of the population. It is a matter for regret that we were the fifth member of the Nuclear Club, when we had so much else to spend our money on.

Question: Do you consider that the Indian political scene has markedly altered since the first flush of independence? In your opinion, are India's politicians today motivated by the same high ideals, zeal and selfless service, that were the hallmark of her earlier Parliaments?

Mrs Pandit: The old days of higher values and unselfish public service are gone. Instead of 'what can I give?' it is now 'what is there in it for me!'. The great Gandhian concept of unremitting selfless service no longer moves the politicians. At Independence there were many great men (and women) who gave tirelessly of themselves for their country - Sardar Vallabhbhai Patel, C.R. Rajagopalachari, Rajendra Prasad, Maulana Azad, Rajkumari Amritkaur and so many others. Unfortunately they passed on, and have not been replaced. These men and women knew what democracy meant.

Question: By her great and long heritage, religious leadership, land size, population and industrial strengths (and nuclear capabilities), India occupies a very strong position in South-East Asia. Does it worry you that India may become expansionist?

Mrs Pandit: No! We are too big already! We must give leadership. That is something we can pass on to other countries in our region not as fortunate in their heritage as us. In spite of intermittent internal problems we have stayed united, because I believe this is what we fought so hard and long for, and we will not give it up readily. Anyway, we have enough problems of our own without adding more!

Question: Changing the mood, and looking back on your very full life, what pleasurable and momentous events spring readily to your mind?

Mrs Pandit: More than anywhere else I enjoyed my time in Britain. My upbringing, language and early life had been associated with 'British ways'. I felt at home there amongst so much I could understand and I had many friends. America brought 'new' experiences, but I preferred the atmosphere of Britain best of all.

Question: When you first met Mahatma Gandhi how did he impress you? Did you get the instant feeling you were in the company of a towering personality?

Mrs Pandit: No, I did not feel anything of this! I was only sixteen and saw Gandhi only over the heads of a large gathering. At that time Gandhi still wore his turban and Gujarati clothes. But when he came to my father's house in 1919 he was wearing only a loin cloth to identify himself with the poorest Indian. It was totally different and everyone was very excited and greatly affected.

Question: Where do you think his magnetism and drawing power lay? What was the intangible/tangible 'thing' which convinced you to 'follow' him?

Mrs Pandit: His presence was like a great rush of wind! His great sincerity touched everybody. He never asked anyone to do anything he was not prepared to do himself. Through his example he utterly convinced everybody with his message, not just me, but everybody in my father's house, and there must have been forty of us and as many servants. At that time we were a joint Hindu family all living under the one roof. I can remember tearing at my bracelets and other jewellery (an unheard of thing up to that time when a woman's jewellery was her most precious possession) to donate them for party funds. There was a great urgency that no time must be lost.

Question: Where were you on the 15th August, 1947, when Independence was proclaimed? Would you like to describe your feelings at that historic moment?

Mrs Pandit: In Moscow, as India's first Ambassador! My brother had insisted that I go there about 10 days before (Independence). He said it was important that the Russian people should be made aware of the historical happening in India. I never forgave him for doing such a thing to me!

Question: You were leader of the Indian delegation to the United Nations for a number of years. How did you come to be elected the Assembly's first woman President and did you attach any particular significance to your election?

Mrs Pandit: I was never permanent Indian head of mission at the U.N. but I would go there from my particular diplomatic post. It was the turn of the Western bloc to fill the post of President and the honour was really to India, and not to me.

9. A wonderful ambassador for universal good-will, Vijaya Lakshmi Pandit.

Question: The U.N. has had some extremely fine and capable Secretaries General and world-shaking decisions and happenings regularly affected its sittings in its formative years. Where do you see the big differences between today's seemingly ineffectual U.N. and its former great presence when almost daily it consistently captured the world's attention?

Mrs Pandit: Dag Hammarskjold was easily the best Secretary General. He was a scholar and a diplomat greatly admired and respected for his capabilities. In the early days of the U.N. it attracted only the very best people of the highest calibre, from every country. Its decisions were vital to mankind. Regrettably the same qualifications and honour of representing your country rarely applies now. Political 'competitors' are often shunted off out of harm's way to the U.N. The best men are required at home. This is some of the reason why it is no longer respected and their decisions mostly defied or ignored. A sad turn of events.

Question: While you attended the U.N. and also in your years of representing India in the diplomatic service, what particular occasions gave you the greatest pleasure?

Mrs Pandit: I always come back to my time in Britain. There I liked best. I was very interested in the arts and enjoyed meeting the great performers. In London and later in America it was my very great pleasure to form a very warm relationship with Paul Robeson and his family. He was a lovely person and it was an education for me as an Indian to note the wonderful racial tolerance observed in his home and amongst his friends.

Question: Of all the famous and interesting people you have met in your lifetime (apart from members of your own family), which of them stand out above the rest?

Mrs Pandit: I greatly admired Charles de Gaulle as a person. His countrymen needed a moral and spiritual boost and he did much to provide it.

Then there was Andrei Vishinsky, whose oratory in the U.N. captivated all of us, irrespective of which political camp we were in.

Margot Fonteyn and her wonderful dancing remain a great memory and as well the supreme acting of Laurence Olivier.

Ingrid Bergman was my great friend, so natural, so very sweet. Yehudi Menuhin too was marvellous.

Sir Richard and Lady Casey were special friends. We had met when he was Governor of Bengal. I later was their guest in Canberra when he was Governor General.

Then there was my protege, Zubin Mehta, so charming, so talented.

I was also most impressed with Jan Smuts, then quite an old man. I had proposed a motion in the U.N. protesting against discrimination against people of Indian origin living in South Africa and won a two-thirds majority when the vote was taken. As Smuts was a good personal friend of Gandhi, I went over to him afterwards and said that I had done nothing more than uphold Gandhi's high standards. He clasped my hand in both his hands and said quietly, "My child, this has been a hollow victory". How correct Smuts' observation was to become.

Question: Coming back to the Indian scene, how deeply concerned and disturbed were you when your niece Mrs Indira Gandhi as Prime Minister saw fit to rule India using emergency powers? And how were you personally affected by it all?

Mrs Pandit: I was very concerned indeed! Although I was not inconvenienced much personally, it was most upsetting and it did untold damage. Emergency powers have no place in a truly democratic society, it lowers standards and seriously affects morale.

I campaigned strongly against Mrs Indira Gandhi when the next free elections were held. I endeavoured to point out to the people the great wrong done them and you may know that Mrs Gandhi was roundly defeated at the polls.

Question: Do you consider that it has left a bad precedent or have most people now put it out of their minds?

Mrs Pandit: I think it has now passed. It would take a very courageous person to repeat it.

It is highly dangerous and the people have shown that they want no part of such political exercises, which strike right at the heart of our Constitution.

Question: I seem to recollect it was your brother, Pandit Nehru, who quizzed the ridiculousness of so many unofficially declared wars being conducted in a world supposedly at peace, and rightly wondered how it could be and where it would lead. If today you were asked to propose a workable policy for an end to all wars (even those conducted in peacetime), what would you suggest?

Mrs Pandit: Well, that is a difficult question. I think the U.N. should be retained, but its status should be restored if it is to be effective.

Pandit Nehru actually appealed for a 'YEAR OF PEACE'. His appeals were heard, but after three months' observance man's weak spirit capitulated and the shooting started all over again. Medals and honours are given for fighting. There are few monuments erected to men of peace.

Conclusion: Thank you for being so patient and for your readiness to discuss any points.

In wishing you continued good health and happiness, is there some message or advice you would like to pass on to people everywhere?

Mrs Pandit: I think it would be presumptuous of me to tell people how to live their lives. Whatever I've done, I've done with sincerity and conviction and with a belief in what I was doing. If other people can learn from that, then this will be satisfaction enough for me.

Epilogue: Srimati Vijaya Lakshmi Pandit celebrated her 87th birthday on 18th August, 1987. She died on 1st December, 1990. A wonderful woman.
Her splendid beautifully written autobiography *The Scope of Happiness - a personal memoir* was published by Weidenfeld and Nicolson Ltd., London - 1979. All those genuinely interested and who love India, will enjoy reading it.

7. Reviving Memories Of Gulbadan - "Princess Rosebody"

- the glories of the great Mughal Dynasty relived

Gulbadan Begam or "Princess Rosebody" as her name beautifully translates, was the youngest child of the first great Mughal Emperor, Babur. She was born in 1523 at Kabul and travelled to India as a small girl as part of her father's royal entourage. Princess Rosebody was also a contemporary of Henry VIII, but living their lives at different ends of the world, it is quite probable that neither would have known of the other's existence, nor had any real knowledge of how each lived their lives, in their particular worlds. It is interesting to pause for a moment and reflect upon the blessing, or the curse, of modern day communications?

To visit the twin cities of Agra and Delhi (the old town), is to enter the realm of the Great Mughal Dynasty. This is the period which describes the rule of India by the first six Mughal Emperors, beginning with Babur (1526) and ending with Aurangzeb (1707), who reaching to 90 years of age lived longest of the six Great Mughal Emperors. The Mughal dynasty fell away after Aurangzeb's reign reaching its nadir at the Mutiny in 1857.

Both Agra and Delhi abound with noble and beautiful buildings from the Mughal era which embody a combination of Indian ideals and Persian inspiration and - one would have to add, tremendous ingenuity, craftmanship *and* the sweat of many many thousands labouring mightily over lengthy periods - the Indian counterpart of the great Egyptian periods, millenniums before.

The advent of the brilliant Mughal Court brought a stream of scholars and architects from Persia, all seeking fame and fortune. Many of them stayed to make considerable contributions to Indian culture, and to play significant roles memorialized in great works done at the behest of the Great Mughals, whom they were pleased to serve.

I had come again to Agra to refresh previous experiences and I was not to be disappointed, for so much of the Mughal architecture is so magnificent. Not even the searing summer heat, or the high humidity which affects this part of the world during the monsoon period, could in any way detract from the marvels I was again to feast upon, with my eyes and my senses.

Beyond all doubt, the pull of the irresistible Mughal creations near at hand was unquestionably far greater than any small concerns, about being uncomfortably hot!

Babur, a Turk, was the first of the Great Mughals (the word 'Mughal' is a corruption of Mongol - a description accorded people in those times who were thought of as barbarians). He had come as a conqueror from Kabul in Afghanistan to India in 1526, to form an empire. Babur founded a line of Kings who performed great deeds in their adopted country, India.

Regrettably, early death cut short Babur's reign in India. Succeeded in 1530 by his son Humayun, very few notable changes occurred until the advent of his grandson, the mighty Akbar, the greatest Mughal ruler of all. Succeeding his father Humayun, in 1556, Akbar was a man of action and a proven leader of men. He aroused the passionate loyalty of his subjects, irrespective of their caste, religion or race. During his reign there was a unity in India, not experienced since the days of the great Asoka, two thousand years before, and even possibly, never since.

Gulbadan, our lovely loving and much loved Princess Rosebody lived through the reign of three emperors, her father Babur, her brother Humayun, and her nephew Akbar, and during her long life witnessed the creation and building of many superlative structures, including the fabulous Agra Fort and the unique palace at Fatehpur Sikri, a short distance from Agra.

The earlier Mughal Emperors had lived in the palace at Badalgarh overlooking the Yamuna River. When Akbar succeeded to the throne he had the old buildings torn down and in their place rose up the stupendous Agra Fort, a huge moated palace compound semi-circular in shape, and nearly two miles around the perimeter walls.

Allowing full vent to one's imagination, it is spellbinding to walk through Agra Fort. In the halcyon days of the Mughal dynasty it contained as many as 500 different stone buildings - all put to different uses - within its compound walls. It is impossible not to let your mind and senses fantasise on its past intrigues and glories.

Conjecturing upon what it all must have been like in its heyday, provides wonderfully exciting mental gymnastics. How all of us might wish that we could be taken back in time and be able to behold its fabled and colourful activity. Tens of thousands of people lived or traversed within the Fort compound every day.

We must therefore be exceedingly grateful to Gulbadan for her memoirs which she set down in her writings, entitled "the HUMAYUN-NAMA". They preserve for us descriptions of the magic that prevailed, although regretfully, her splendidly woven tales can only provide a fragment of the overall picture of the colourful pageantry of the times, some of which thankfully, has also been preserved, to a degree at least, in paintings from the Mughal period.

Standing amongst it all and regarding the marvellous opportunity that seems to cry out to be perceived and responded to, one cannot help wishing the past could all again come to life. Instead of today's empty buildings and courtyards, how much more the Agra Fort could entertain and enthral if it was reanimated, allowing one to thrill to what it was actually like at the height of its Mughal fame. Sometime perhaps (?) the Indian Government might be inspired to create a Museum within the Agra Fort, providing tableaux consisting of scale models, paintings and drawings accurately depicting those times and something of the various daily activities and the way life was then lived. Such would prove a boon to better comprehension and greater enjoyment now, of things as they were then, over four hundred years ago.

Consider how marvellous it would be to gaze at a (living) tableau of the Khas Mahal and its adjacent Angoori Bagh, complete with its daily occupants all going about their pleasures or their chores? Gulbadan would have frequently moved about within the Angoori Bagh (garden) when it was resplendent with grape-vines and meticulously arranged flower beds, as well as fruit trees and playing fountains.

But great men pass on. Jehangir succeeded Akbar, to be followed by Shahjehan. Unusually perhaps (for those days!) and before his death, Akbar had planned his own memorial. After he died in 1605, Jehangir completed his father's superb Tomb at Sikandra, which is only a short distance from Agra up the Grand Trunk road, along the road north which leads to Delhi.

In the mortuary chamber of Akbar's Tomb at Sikandrabad, in a hallowed recess in the marble pedestal, the famous "Kohinoor" diamond (since 1849, part of the British crown jewels), once reposed. The Chamber is famous for its inscription - on the northern side "Alla-ho-Akbar" (God is Great) and on the south side "Hille-Hilalhu" (magnificent to his glory). Around these inscriptions are carved the ninety nine "most beautiful names" (al-asma al-husna) that are the glory of God.

As reigning Emperors, neither Jehangir nor his son Shahjehan saw any significant reasons for changing the social structure that had been so skilfully created by Akbar. Accordingly, their reigns were comparatively peaceful.

How eternally grateful we must therefore be to Akbar for this state of affairs, which left his grandson Shahjehan largely free of problems on domestic issues, and able to indulge his great passion for creating architectural masterpieces. The pinnacle of his remarkable achievements will forever be the Taj Mahal, arguably the finest Memorial ever conceived and brought to fruition.

From whatever direction this incomparable edifice is viewed, every sighting one catches of the Taj Mahal (literally 'CROWN OF PALACES') has a magical quality about it. Approaching the complex from above or below the town, and seeing snatches of the dome of the Mausoleum and of its minaret sentinels, raises ecstatic and urgent responses, as you get closer. You feel like a child going off to a seaside resort for a holiday - searching, searching eagerly, for that first sight of the sea. When at last what you are seeking is bared before your eyes, you experience a feeling of exultation and even of relief. Similarly, the exhilaration upon first sighting the incomparable Mausoleum of the Taj Mahal, for most people is overwhelming. The 'Taj' magic surges and grows inducing great awe, for it is endlessly superb in whatever direction it is viewed, or whatever circumstances absorbed.

It is worth stopping and reflecting for a moment about the composition of the world when all this history was being made. Shahjehan was a contemporary of Louis XIV of France, le Grand Monarque, and the Thirty Year's War was raging in Europe. So, while Versailles was taking shape, the Taj Mahal and the Pearl Mosque were also taking shape in Agra. Those other magnificent monuments to Shahjehan, the Red Fort and the Jama Masjid in Delhi, were also built at this time.

These four Indian architectural 'wonders' represent the height of Mughal splendour and architectural achievement, and all have survived for us to marvel at, today.

Mumtaz Mahal, or Arjumand Bano Begum as she was then, became the second of Shahjehan's wives when in 1612, as Prince Khurram, he married her. Her father was Prime Minister in Jehangir's Court as well as being the brother of Jehangir's wife, the powerful Nur Jehan. Upon her marriage to his son, Emperor Jehangir gave to his daughter-in-law the title 'Mumtaz Mahal', which means "Exalted of the Palaces".

Prince Khurram did not succeed to the throne (as Shahjehan) for another sixteen years. Meanwhile, his devoted and loving wife Mumtaz Mahal bore Prince Khurram many children, scarcely ever being without child at any time during their marriage.

In 1631 and following the birth of her fourteenth child, Mumtaz Mahal succumbed to post-natal problems leaving Shahjehan, now Emperor, broken-hearted, shocked and distraught. They had been inseparable companions.

To commemorate that deep love and to keep a solemn promise made to his beloved wife, Shahjehan set about planning a unique tomb, different and more wonderful than anything that had been built anywhere before. But first, the Court entered upon a long mourning period of two years, for the deceased Empress.

Controversy has raged now for a hundred years or more regarding who designed the Taj Mahal. Speculation continues about the identity of the true architect (or architects) of the quite majestic and incomparable complex at Agra. Situated on the bank of the Yamuna (or Jumna) River, the shrine contains the white marble mausoleum, the "Taj Mahal", the burial place of Mumtaz Mahal (joined in 1666 by her husband, Shahjehan).

Whoever it was who designed and supervised the construction of this memorial to surpass all memorials (M. Grousset, the French savant, said that it is "the soul of Persia incarnate in the body of India" - which suggests the possibility of Persian participation to a significant degree) it is indisputable that they created something, which before or since, has not been surpassed.

This mystique seems to be in rightful keeping with the complete uniqueness of the Taj Mahal.

The uniqueness and quite extraordinary exactitude of construction, and the sheer exquisiteness of the Taj Mahal has drawn many exultant responses but none more explicit and expressive than that of one observer who saw the mausoleum 'as a temple of white ivory, wrapped in exquisite white Brussels lace'. A fair, and wonderful description indeed! It really is fabulous and a sight not repeated anywhere else in the world. Truly, Shahjehan succeeded handsomely, in immortalizing his beloved wife. In a similar way that Michelangelo's exquisite statue of 'David' in Florence has those who gaze upon it searching for superlatives, the Taj Mahal inspires enormous awe, from the feeling one derives from looking, upon something wholly removed from the ordinary; at an object of singular and rare greatness.

We are fortunate that some records pertaining to the construction of the magnificent complex have survived. The little of the whole that these reveal tell us that craftsmen from Turkey, Persia, Afghanistan, Uzbekistan, (Samarkand and Bukhara) and also Arabia, as well as from India itself, combined in a work-force of tens of thousands for between ten and twenty years to complete the work.

Whilst the 'centrepiece' of the whole complex is undoubtedly the mausoleum, properly regarded, it (the superlative Mausoleum) forms only a part of the whole architectural extravaganza, for the rest of the overall complex is as well, outstanding. Costs of building the whole complex were defrayed from many sources. Precious stones, gold and silver were donated in abundance. Many of the different materials used in the construction were either given or imported from far off places. It was clearly a tremendous joint effort culminating in a finished product, the likes of which may never happen again.

10. The Taj Mahal, Tomb of the Emperor Shah Jahan and his Queen.

The spectacle on the day when it was all finished and the mortal remains of Mumtaz Mahal were consecrated and laid to final rest in the crypt in the Mausoleum, must have been quite fantastic. The colour and pageantry which surely attended the sacred Muslim solemnity might well have rivalled the celebrations of the Pharaohs thousands of years before. But nowhere is there any record of any great celebration taking place? Why is this so?

Many will know of the custom in our times when ships are ready for launching or great buildings and majestic new bridges reach completion when the builders of these constructions gather with official guests to celebrate their inauguration.

It would then be easy to imagine a vast religious cavalcade and great fanfare attending the ritualistic blessing of the 'Taj' complex (mosques were incorporated in the vast walled perimeter and function still today). It would be equally conceivable that many dignitaries from within India and from far-off lands as well, came to bear witness on the great occasion. Hundreds of thousands of people might have been present. What a great Italian painter would have made of the scene can only be conjectured?

The surprising and even paradoxical thing is, that no author in English, or any scribe, either in Mughal times or since, has referred to any official opening taking place. It seems inconceivable that there was no great ceremony. Perhaps further research of Persian language scripts may reveal the missing record and provide the explanation. Or is it the norm with great Islamic events to observe such only with great solemnity? Maybe someone will explain?

Sadly, the story of the 'Taj' seems so incomplete without details of all this saga of events. Today, even without the colourful guests and evidence of the myriad activity that regularly took place in the complex at the height of its fame, the spectacle is unique, tremendous and awesome. The multifarious scene in 1652 when the whole marvellous complex was in full swing would have been sensational. Imagine how we would have thrilled had we been privileged to view it during construction, and later when it was finally completed and in everyday use.

Usurped in 1658 by his son Aurangzeb, Shahjehan was imprisoned in Agra Fort wherefrom he could look down the Yamuna to his beloved's tomb. He grieved long for his departed wife, until in 1666 (the same year that London burned), he died and was buried alongside his beloved Mumtaz Mahal, in the Mausoleum of the Taj Mahal at Agra.

Sad to relate that upon the decline of the Mughal dynasty after Aurangzeb (d.1707), the marvellous complex of buildings created and built by Shahjehan suffered abuse and became dirty and dilapidated from almost total inattention. An illustration of the faded fortunes which followed in the next two hundred years, is evidenced when in 1790, not one hundred years after Aurangzeb's death, Thomas Twining, a notable British historian, observed, "When I visited the (Taj Mahal) complex it was almost wholly deserted".

How wonderfully fortunate then for posterity that in the late nineteenth century, dedicated men, supported by the zeal and mutual concern of the Viceroy, Lord Curzon, set to with a will and great devotion, to restoring and preserving the Taj Mahal complex, and very many of the other superb ancient monuments in India. Their work is carried on today by the Government of India to whom profuse and grateful thanks are assuredly due.

The "Magic of the Taj" once experienced, becomes forevermore a lingering loving memory, immortalised so graphically and so sensitively long ago by the same Thomas Twining. What he had to record indubitably personifies the sentiments of every visitor before or since, and in all probability, for all time.

Quote:

> "In the evening I walked about the noble terrace and luxuriant gardens of which I seemed to be the master. I saw nobody except a few gardeners among the orange trees. I rambled about every part of the Taj itself, enjoying a feast which seemed too great for me alone. Nothing can exceed the beauty of this structure".

Unquote

It is a phenomenal thing that the ecumenical spirit so ardently and democratically pursued by Akbar, the greatest of all the Mughal Emperors (a Muslim) is in present times so fortuitously and remarkably epitomized in the Taj Mahal a creation of his own grandson, Shahjehan. It is something to ponder on - a Muslim shrine set down in India's ancient heartlands, worshipped and wondered at by all Indians alike - Muslims, Hindus, Buddhists, Sikhs, Jains, Christians, by everybody, whatever their caste, creed or race - and by visitors from the four corners of the world. There has to be some magic present for this to happen.

To Princess Rosebody also must go our thanks for recording for posterity even the briefest description of happenings in the courts of the great Mughals, for surprisingly there are yawning gaps in Indian history, when for hundreds of years at a time, very little was officially recorded.

EPILOGUE: Visiting the Taj Mahal again in 1998, the whole scene was no less astounding than when I was first privileged to see it in 1954, and again on subsequent visits. Nothing moves me to change one word of the foregoing description. If anything, the first sighting of the Taj Mausoleum after entering the Taj Garden through the quite magnificent grand portal, the Taj Gate, was if anything, even more stunning. I rate the peerless and gracious Taj Mausoleum, the most striking and the most beautiful building in the whole of the world.

....as well, let me tell. Before and since I have searched every record in order to resolve what I (and others may) regard, as the non - celebratory 'Taj Mahal' enigma, without which the Taj Mahal story seems incomplete.

For the most wonderful, extraordinary and unique objects that grace our world (whether these be the works of nature *e.g.* sensational cloud formations and landscapes, or man-made) it is the inherent qualities embodied in the objects themselves, and the profound actions or the underlying reasons for their being, that 'does the speaking'. Man's greatest (and invisible) qualities and senses, allowed full play, are enough and more, and exceed every artificial device.

That this is so with Emperor Shahjehan's magnificent incomparable tribute of all tributes, to his beloved wife, is beyond all doubt, as unequivocally confirmed by the following accounts given to me, by two of India's most eminent Islamic scholars –

Professor Dr. Abdus Subhan - Calcutta

> ***inter alia*** **– "the building of mausoleums or tombs did not form part of orthodox (Islamic) religion. Pre- the great Mughals (1526), no great monarchs of former Muslim empires had any tombs in their memory. The Great Mughals brought to India prevailing Iranian culture.**
>
> **The wonderful architectural examples honouring (Emperor) Humayun, at Delhi and (Emperor) Akbar, at Sikandrabad, preceded Shahjehan's tribute to his beloved wife.**
>
> **In most respects the superb Taj Mahal complex, is a monument to a Monarch's excessive love for his Queen, which both wanted to be commemorated, for posterity. It represented a Ruler's personal and solemn tribute, ruling out any public celebration."**

Dr H B Maheswari 'Jaisal', The Heritage, Gwalior

> ***inter alia*** **– "The Taj Mahal ... was a memorial of a person. It represented for Emperor Shahjehan alone a personal endurable reminiscence of his beloved wife, Mumtaz. There was no reason to enjoy or celebrate the moment like happy times. While he lived it was (became) a part of his everyday life."**

End Note:

> **Despite the 'differences' between father and son, the next Emperor – Aurangzeb, the frugal nature of Aurangzeb mitigated against further significant expenditure from the 'public purse'. Hence, Shahjehan was laid to rest, alongside his Queen.**

8. A Memory That Would Not Fade

- Soamibagh - the garden of the Supreme Lord

Wherever we have travelled in the world, it would be a reasonable assertion that many of us have paid a deal of reverence to countless inanimate 'stone' memorials commemorating this event, or that person. Consider then, how much more wonderment and excitement could attach to 'rare living/thriving' memorials that we innocently stumble upon, along life's way.

For a very long time I had been stirred by the memory of a past occasion in India of being 'stood on my ear', not just in awe, but in thrall. It had happened amongst the labyrinthine lanes and by-ways of crowded sweltering Agra. Many years before I had been taken by Beni Ram Gupta, one of our upcountry Branch Managers, to a quite marvellous location on the northern outskirts of Agra, without me paying particular attention to how we had reached there. The position was compounded by the fact that I was a complete stranger and it was a crowded congested Indian town. It was akin to being taken somewhere blindfolded making it impossible on a subsequent occasion, to find the place.

Many times over the years I had recounted to others my earlier Soamibagh 'exotic experience' whenever the conversation had turned to memorable places we had experienced quite 'out of the blue' in our lifetimes. Now the chance had come again for me to revisit and to judge if I'd been carrying a fantasy beyond its proper due.

Nobody would dispute that the crowning glory of Agra is that 'wonder of all wonders', the magnificent Taj Mahal, that breathtaking incomparably beautiful white marble mausoleum, set in its quite superb compound and nestling on the west bank of the Jumna. It was perhaps nonsense for anyone, let alone me, a once only previous visitor to my 'special place', to suggest that the Taj Mahal could have a serious rival and one barely five miles away from it.

Yet, in my distant but still vivid memory, I knew that there was such a wonder, but of a slightly different kind. Surprisingly too, one which contained present-day connotations and which was within 'an horizon's view' of the redoubtable tomb of Shah Jehan's beloved queen, Mumtaz Mahal.

You may think I am referring to Itmad-ud-Daulah's Tomb, another exquisite marble structure, also to be found at Agra, and built only twenty years before the Taj Mahal. Or even perhaps, the marvellous Agra Fort. But no, what had captivated me was not something conceived by a King or a project funded by a bottomless national treasury. On the contrary, it was something quite different altogether, but nonetheless exquisite and uniquely funded by ordinary people.

Our coach from Delhi had just passed the mighty Akbar's final resting place at Sikandra, and Agra the companion city to Delhi in the Great Mughal days, beckoned just a short distance farther on.

The faces of my fellow passengers registered puzzlement when I got down from the coach some miles short of what seemingly was our common quarry - the 'wonder of wonders'. It couldn't be!' - they were probably thinking. 'I was making a mistake.' But there was no mistake, for the scent of a long remembered quarry was in my nostrils and nothing was going to put me off now.

Heading off on foot in the probable direction of my prospective goal I enquired my way from many people. A ricksha puller suggested to me that the objective I was seeking was probably to be found in the nearby district of Dayalbagh. When a little further along the way, to my enquiry in fractured Hindi, *"tum naya mandir malum kahan hai?"* a pan seller's face lit up understandingly, I knew I was on course. I was elated.

It was one of those all too rare moments we all long to experience and savour, when after striving against seemingly impossible odds and just about to give up the search, everything suddenly falls into place. The desired result simply materializes, and it is more than just relief, for we are exhilarated, and the feeling is good.

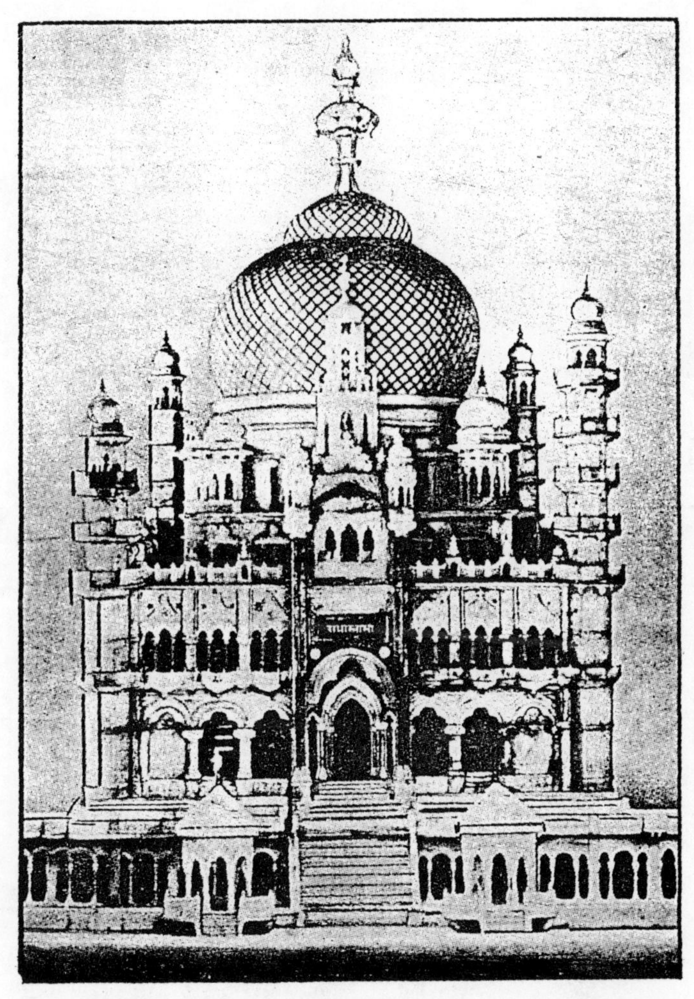

पवित्र समाधि स्वामीजी महाराज (निर्माण हो रही है)
स्वामीबाग, आगरा ।

11. The Holy Samadhi in the Garden of the Supreme Lord at Dayalbagh.

Through the din and clatter of pulsating life all around us, I quickly moved on towards my goal, a living temple of splendid proportions. Before very long I would reach the Holy Samadhi of Soamji Maharaj at Soamibagh, in the village of Dayalbagh, near Agra. The prospect was thrilling.

With summary abruptness I arrived, but it still takes a few moments to orientate myself, as it seems we are still amongst the hurly-burly. But it is true, for through the wall I can see my quarry, and even better than I had stored it away in my memory. There it was laid out before my disbelieving eyes. For me it was a feeling akin to unexpectedly meeting a dear friend again, after a long interval of time.

Our imagination can play tricks with everyone of us. We are either overwhelmed or hugely disappointed when reality happens. Whether we gain something or lose is determined according to how we set our feelings register. For myself I had asked myself would I be disappointed? Feel let down, or be thrilled? Memories can be so easily shattered. However, the unique ingredients contained in this extraordinary 'Indian pie' gave a predictable assurance, that everything would be much as I had remembered it.

Indeed, everything was very much as I had perceived it would be, for when the craftsmen's tools and methods owed their origins to times we in the West passed by eons ago, progress is slow and the scene not unrecognizably different, and any obvious change is almost imperceptible.

The garden surrounding the temple seemed hardly changed from what I'd remembered. It was still crowded with great blocks of white and pink marble that had been hewn from the Makrana quarries in Jodhpur. Myriad other building materials strewn around had been drawn from diverse regions elsewhere in India and some from places, now in Pakistan.

Artisans using ancient implements toiled all around us, many of them shaded from the burning sun by crudely arranged coverings, for scorching temperatures of 45° celsius and more, have to be endured for half the year and even longer every year; there is little respite. Crouched on their hunkers, a characteristic pose of Indians, to whom squatting down comes naturally, and for hours at a stretch, many artisans were painstakingly chiselling away with their age-old tools, fashioning ornamental capitals and architraves featuring intricate detail.

To saw through a block of marble using the same tools and cutting methods employed hundreds of years before, might occupy one man half a year. To completely fashion one door-frame might take three years of constant labour, chip, chip, chipping away. But there were no time constraints, for the building hadn't got to be finished by set dates. According to how long it may take to build, using the old tools with a limited labour force, and keeping up the necessary funds, there were no completion dates to be met here. I could not help thinking how Michelangelo might have wished for similar consideration from his wealthy patrons!

The Radha Soami fraternity set about building their own colony of Dayalbagh in the second half of the nineteenth century, to make a point to a sceptical world. So many of India's religious believe Karma can only be achieved by asceticism, by denial of material possessions, or by living the life of hermits. The Radha Soami fraternity takes the opposite view, believing that it is wholly possible to achieve the same goal, and more beneficially, if its adherents maintain quite normal lives, while at the same time contributing to the over-all well-being of their model spiritual community.

So much has already been achieved. The centrepiece of the community, the Holy Samadhi is ever so slowly being put together, financed by the voluntary subscriptions of members of the fraternity, and built by the community's artisans. Although most members are in modest or moderate circumstances, all regard it as their religious duty to give all they can afford to help the wondrous temple to final completion.

The marvel of the Holy Samadhi spread out before me for my wonderment, was its 'living' creativeness and the great inspiration behind the preservation of the old, but classical style and ways, of doing things. Perhaps it has been your experience also when looking upon some of the world's great architectural wonders, that you have longed for an instant perception of how it all had been possible to build, particularly in the times when it was built, sans all the modern equipment and devices nowadays available to constructors.

Regrettably, in most cases, we can only fall back upon our imaginations and may never accurately know how in fact things were accomplished, especially those tasks which even today call for exceptional technical skills and ingenuity, from architects and construction engineers. A case in point - an American documentary I recently viewed showing the planning and construction of a New York skyscraper set in a very busy location. It was fascinating to note the ingenious planning that was necessary to make it possible.

As well, with twentieth century thoroughness and wanting to display our cleverness to later generations, sometimes it happens that we now consign our drawings and photographs, through all the construction stages, to archives, or else bury these same records in canisters, for posterity to open later. It could be debated that by 'removing the mystery' we are denying future generations the same opportunities we have enjoyed and the mental gymnastics we have engaged in, when grappling with what went before us. The riddle of the Sphinx would be no more. It is something to ponder about, I'm sure.

Despite all this, I still find myself confessing that it would be fantastic to have at our disposal a complete picture gallery of the 'Taj Mahal plans, and a resumè of how all of the complex had progressively taken shape'. If we had this information, speculation as to who was its creative genius, would be dispelled. But on the other hand, with all the mystery removed, how much poorer might we be for knowing every detail. I'm sure readers will agree, that a retention of a modicum of mystery and of speculation about our world, can be no bad thing, for all of us.

But such a situation will never affect The Holy Samadhi (temple) in the Garden of the Supreme Lord at Soamibagh. We already know that the first loving steps were taken over eighty years ago and if the work so far completed is any criterion, it is conceivable that artisans could still be chipping away in another eighty years time or even longer!

With fifty storey high-risers common place nowadays in our society, and being built at a rate of a floor a week, readers might perceive the real significance of what is being carried out at Dayalbagh by the faithful followers of the founding Guru, Soamiji Maharaj.

Quite amazingly, and light years removed from western attitudes and methods, no change in the way construction is proceeding nor the purpose for constructing it is likely to occur, even should construction go on into the twenty-second century. However incredible all this may seem to us, we must also marvel at the unswerving attention being given to a decision made nearly one hundred years ago.

Worship already goes on in the completed ground level section. In due passage of time the whole wonderful project will be completed.

The completed temple promises to be staggeringly beautiful. There are plans to eventually clear the site for hundreds of metres all around the Samadhi and to flood the precincts, leaving the temple to 'shine' in the midst of it all, connected by a series of beautiful paths. Although it may never outstrip its peerless neighbour, the majestically superb Taj Mahal, everything points to it being a worthy addition to the earlier great Mughal contributions of the sixteenth and seventeenth centuries. Agra will have yet another 'wonder' to parade before its adoring public.

For me, the wonderful re-encounter was a great thrill. To have firmly logged, for all time, this spectacular living legend and memorial to mostly discarded or forgotten craftsmen's skills, was wonderful. It is my fervent hope that many others will also discover the great qualities embodied in the shrine which is happening before our very eyes at Soamibagh. I believe it should be on every tourist's itinerary, and that everyone who witnesses this 'living' memorial, will benefit from the unique experience in many ways. Dayalbagh the village, is a great experiment in selfless community enterprise, and although with a likeness to socialism as we know it, it contains so much more.

EPILOGUE: Last visited in early 1998, the building slowly takes shape, confirming the 'formula' for its construction and ultimate dedication.

Like many of the great Christian Cathedrals and religious edifices, final completion of the Holy Samadhi at Soamibagh will occupy several centuries (or more), exemplifying tremendous enduring dedication from the (Hindu) sect's faithful adherents, in India and spread around the world.

9. A Touch Of Class - The House Of TATA

- Jamsetji's great dream fulfilled

In today's world of such varying standards, it is a singularly tremendous and courageous thing for any corporation to loudly and proudly pronounce for all the world to hear - "We work with enthusiasm and with confidence in a spirit of togetherness, setting standards of excellence in everything we do. That is the basis of our success."

By dint of its consistent and unremitting magnificent service rendered to India for more than a hundred years, the world renowned free enterprise industrial organization of Tata can make this proud boast, unashamedly and with a sense of pride and exhilaration.

The 'Tata story' is unique and would have few parallels anywhere in the world. A very brief encounter (a motor tour of lovely green undulating Bihar from Calcutta thirty years before to 'catch some fresh country air') had left the writer with lingering memories of unique Jamshedpur, where the first steel mill east of Suez was established soon after the nineteenth century had expired. Jamshedpur or Tatanagar as it is just as often called, remains the pulsating heart of the now vastly expanded Tata enterprises.

But the real uniqueness of Tata and the source of its greatness lies not solely in the products they produce in their multifarious manufacturing enterprises, but just as importantly, from their deep and sincere concern for all their employees, a procedure instituted in Tata in an era when management/worker considerations were scarcely thought of, let alone practised by anyone, anywhere in the world. It is the pillar upon which their whole industrial empire has been built - a platform of mutual partnership and understanding which has spawned the co-operation that has enabled the Group to grow to the immense proportions it is today.

There is even more cause for wonderment and congratulations when the hugely tenuous times are remembered in which their great founder Jamsetji Nusserwanji Tata pioneered what was to expand and grow to be, India's largest and most prestigious free enterprise industrial empire.

When Jamsetji set about founding his first business venture, echoes from the Mutiny (1857) still reverberated around India. Indian efforts to create indigenous industry were given little encouragement and even less support from the British Government in India. Worse, little moral support was forthcoming from India's own intellectuals many of whom readily accepted foreign subjugation, being dazzled and even shamefully overwhelmed and 'paralysed', by the technological and administrative authority of their foreign rulers.

Paradoxically too, the opening of the Suez Canal in 1869, carried only mixed benefits for Indians themselves, for instead of opening new markets for Indian exports, it exacerbated the flood of 'finished European goods' (much of them made from Indian produced raw material) into India.

Such were the daunting and inhibiting conditions prevailing in the second half of the nineteenth century that assailed Indians eager to pioneer on the industrial front in their own country. To prosper, much courage and resolution was essentially needed by would-be Indian entrepreneurs. Enter Jamsetji upon the scene. Due to his extraordinary 'foresight' and driving ambition, he was destined to be one of the special breed marked for greatness. Strongly believing in himself and in his capabilities, Jamsetji embarked upon his new ventures, interesting himself especially in ones where he was confident Indians could successfully compete with British imports.

This display of fierce national pride and determination was to succeed against all the odds. The honest purpose displayed by the 'founder' over one hundred years ago continues to be exhibited today by 'Tata's men and women of 1987'. It is this characteristic which is so creditable and which puts the Tata Group in a special category of its own, when seen against the general deterioration in Management/ worker relationships, and the increasing militancy, which afflicts the world scene today.

There is no question that it goes much further than blind faith and of sticking to a system simply because it 'offers the best job security and continuance of welfare benefits'. Some cynics may suggest these factors are paramount and while this assertion probably makes a lot of sense in a country where permanent well-paid work does not grow on trees, to any objective and close observer, such an argument is belittling and can be wholly discounted. Innately, and in the ways of Indians, and especially the proud employees of Tata, there is much more to things than this. By any summation, the Tata method of successful labour relations is unique.

Job satisfaction and glowing pride in achievement amongst all of the members of the Tata workforce is plain for all to see, and this is coupled with a genuine desire by everybody to 'do one's best' to achieve the greatest harmony and results which benefit everyone. The whole community of the Steel Town of Jamshedpur exudes a wonderful spirit of goodwill, and consideration for others. That it rubs off is beyond all question of doubt.

Jamsetji Tata was a pioneering genius and endowed with considerable foresight. The high ideals and standards by which 'Tata' progressed its initial business are just as true and enduring today as when they were first conceived and introduced by the great man in 1877 in which year he launched his initial textile enterprise, "the Empress Mills" at Nagpur.

In the offices and grounds of every Tata enterprise in the land, and they reach into very many places throughout India spreading the 'Tata' message of goodwill and co-operation, the same fine strong face of the Founder (circa 1900) looks out and encourages everyone to give of their best. If ever there was an enduring and ageless 'father figure' it would be Jamsetji Tata.

The paternal benevolence of Jamsetji is still clearly welcomed and it continues to instil a great sense of pride and of purpose into every member of the organization. For such guiding spirit to have endured for over 100 years is absolutely fascinating, and the mystique and reverence continues undiminished as the various 'Tata' enterprises maintain their strong performance through the closing years of the twentieth century.

The Tatas are Parsees. Their ancestors originally hailed from Persia settling in India thirteen hundred years ago. A remarkable pure and resilient people, the Tata clan can trace its genealogy back to Sheriar who was five generations before Ervad (an honorific given to one who has gone through the ceremony of Navar, and can perform priestly rites) Zardoost (A.D. 1271). Ervad Jamsheed (Jamsetji) was born twenty-six generations later, in 1839, two years after Queen Victoria, as a young woman of eighteen, ascended the throne of England. It may come as a surprise to some people to know that Queen Victoria was not proclaimed Empress of India until 1877, twenty years after the Westminster Parliament took over responsibility for India. In the same year, Jamsetji opened his first textile mill at Nagpur.

Whilst he loved his country and its people, understandably Jamsetji also admired many things that the British had introduced in the modern world, and in order to broaden his education and knowledge of industry, he travelled extensively to many parts of the world. He was always on the lookout for anything which could enhance his Indian enterprises, whilst personally satisfying his insatiable hunger for more knowledge, for broader horizons. His interests were extensive and his curiosity led him into many areas of learning and of culture.

During these travels he visited the Paris Exposition (in 1889) made notable by Mr. Eiffel's fantastic iron meccano Tower. It has been conjectured that the connection between Eiffel's blatant but brilliant display of iron's possibilities (and its next stage - steel); and a viewing of a remarkable collection of ancient Indian weapons on display there, could conceivably have been the catalyst for Jamsetji's great drive soon afterwards to create a steel industry for India.

But to achieve this goal, Jamsetji first perceived the enormous and urgent need to develop technology and science amongst his own people. In his fashion, he immediately set to to foster and create the educational facilities which would provide these essential skills.

From these small beginnings ultimately sprang the vast steel plant that now graces Jamshedpur. It produces over 2 million tons of quality steel every year. In turn the steel mill supplies an array of materials for the Group's down-stream industries, also at Jamshedpur and elsewhere in India.

When the unsympathetic political climate of the times is remembered and the great odds that had to be overcome are taken into account, it is then that Jamsetji's immense native patriotism assumes truly noble and heroic proportions. The great circumspection that Jamsetji showed in wisely fostering scientific learning was also remarkable, for without such a highly skilled technical force, his great objectives for India had no way of succeeding.

Not satisfied with simply equipping men with the technical knowledge to carry out these tasks, Jamsetji was also to pursue with great zeal and determination the discovery of the essential minerals required for steel production. With remarkable sagacity he tenaciously regarded all the elements that would be needed to accomplish his great dream. It is now history that after much protracted and agonizing investigation by eminent American and Indian geologists, the essential rich iron ore deposits were found, together with limestone and coking coal.

With the discovery of these essential and cheap minerals in close proximity, a Steel Mill, India's first in modern times, (thousands of years before, India had in fact led the world in steel-making capabilities) became a reality at Sakchi a place adjacent to where the Kharkai and Subarnarekha Rivers meet, providing a rich supply of permanent water, essentially ancillary to steel production. The steelworks was built just a few kilometres away from the junction of the rivers.

Jamsetji died in 1904 but his dream lived on through his illustrious sons, Dorabji and Ratanji, and Jamsetji's cousin Ratan (R.D.). Aided as well by prodigious planning and exhaustive fund raising efforts, the first steel issued from the TISCO mill (Tata Iron & Steel Co. Ltd), in February, 1912.

Had he been present at such fulfilling event, Jamsetji's joy would surely have been beyond all description. I feel sure I am not alone in thinking that wherever he was, Jamsetji 'felt' some of the enormous elation experienced by those who were present, and relief too, for the project was not achieved without tremendous effort, even heart-break, on the part of so many, determined to keep Jamsetji's 'torch' alive (or alight).

Worker welfare had always been dear to the heart of Jamsetji, a man who also put great store in integrity and reliability. Additionally, job security for all workers was an integral part of management thinking and practice. As a consequence of this humanitarianism and consideration, the Steel Mill forged ahead to significant heights, particularly with the advent of the Great War (1914 - 1918), when everything that could be produced was needed to prosecute the war effort.

The Tata organization had voluntarily introduced the eight-hour working day in all its plants and mines as early as 1912, something that was not enforced by law throughout India, until 1948. Free medical treatment and educational facilities for children followed - in 1917. The attractive township that Jamshedpur is, was laid out along lines emphasised by Jamsetji before his death and remains a remarkable tribute to his farsightedness.

The orderly well-planned Jamshedpur of today is one of the best laid out and administered towns in the whole of India. As many as 650,000 people are catered for within the Company's orbit, and goes well beyond their prime responsibilities. With some justification, it could lay claim to being the most 'amenable' steel town in the entire sub-continent and possibly anywhere in the world. One could go further and say any town, anywhere.

Except for smoke belching forth from numerous columns dotted around the landscape, and viewed from the many beautiful wide tree-lined thoroughfares you could easily believe that you were in a garden city anywhere in the world, which is a splendid tribute to the planners.

The town is administered by TISCO in a most effective and praiseworthy manner. Careful attention is given to planning to avoid unwanted congestion. Scrupulous regard is also paid to the provision of clean and abundant water reticulation and sewage services. Excellent recreational and sporting facilities are available and their use greatly encouraged. A magnificent and very extensive medical centre provides the finest medical treatment for everyone - and mostly free.

It is a measure of Tata's generosity and concern for the wider community that they voluntarily extend their free medical services and some other welfare services, to areas adjacent to their own

12. One of India's greatest ever pioneers
Jamsetji Nusserwanji Tata (1839-1904).

establishments and to families having no connection at all with 'Tata' Companies. To all those who are deserving and who need these services, they are given freely.

TISCO continues to more than hold its own and surpass in performance the other cluster of new and huge steel mills in the public sector which have risen up in the last thirty years. Production levels at TISCO consistently exceed rated capacity which is a great tribute to its management and their technological skills.

The 'GROWTH SHOP' is another first by the Tata organization. An excellent investment in engineering skills it represents another unique 'homespun' concept pioneered by Tata. This engineering shop has succeeded so well, that it now exports gear boxes to M.A.N. in West Germany. There can be no better proof of Tata's precision engineering and skills than this achievement.

The Government Steel Mills and TISCO all draw their raw materials from the mineral rich regions of West Bengal, Bihar and Orissa. Most of these mines are State-owned enterprises, but as a mark of its particular skills and reputation, the 'Tata' organization enjoys the singular distinction of independent control and operation of its own coal mines, at West Bokaro and in the Jharia region. Iron ore is mined in southern Bihar and Orissa, at Naomundi and Joba and railed to Jamshedpur, a distance of several hundred kilometres.

The present day scene at Jamshedpur betrays nothing of the crucial events which happened in the Steel Company's early days when near disaster struck TISCO. When hostilities ceased in 1918, world demand slumped and brought great redundancy to the steel industry all over the world. As if this economic downturn was not enough to handle, TISCO had an additional problem, for buoyed up by the great advancement that had been made during the war years and confident of their own future, the Company had already embarked upon the 'Great Expansion'. They were committed and had to proceed determined to succeed.

A problem of crisis proportions arose but by dint of immense perseverance and determination to 'first survive, and then to succeed', TISCO prevailed. By their firm resolution and excellent leadership, and considerable personal generosity, the Tata sons, Ratanji and Dorabji, brought the Company through its darkest hour. The thought of failing and going bust had not been entertained, at any price. But it was a close call.

Climbing out of these dreadful troubles with renewed vigour and inspiration, TISCO went from strength to strength, overcoming on the way serious labour problems (experienced all over India) in 1920.

Careful and considerate rationalization had been carried out to ensure survival and in doing this, TISCO emerged from all these problems and vicissitudes shaken, but justifiably proud that in spite of everything, not a single worker had been dismissed.

The same respect on both sides of the fence continues right up to the present day, when morale and *esprit de corps* amongst the workforce (in all its enterprises the Tata organization employs over 350,000 people) are stronger than ever. Economic peace is extensively due to sensible Company/Union co-operation and understanding. Formulated in concept as long as fifty years ago principally by Mr. J.R.D. Tata and Union Leader, Professor Abdul Barrie, the same rules are respected and observed to this day. The continuing harmonious work environment is a great tribute to everyone, and whilst much is owed to its distinguished authors, their most worthy successors also deserve much praise. All in all, it has been, and continues to be, a victory for constructive union leadership and for mutual understanding, qualities all too rarely found at the negotiating table today.

Probably one of the founder's greatest attributes was his intuitive ability to choose the right people which capability took on even more significant importance with the introduction, under Mr. J.R.D. Tata's Chairmanship, of a 'PERSONNEL DEPARTMENT', a world first. The brain child of Mr. Tata, this new highly innovative step represented a development subsequently copied all around the world. And this happened over forty years ago and what is more, in India - conceived by Tatas for all the world to follow. The complete Indianization of TISCO and of most of the other Tata Companies in the early fifties, has resulted in great prosperity. The Group's fortunes have taken giant strides forward, in many directions, something not thought possible not so many years before, without the aid of foreign experts.

Mr. J.R.D. Tata's enormously benevolent and masterly leadership has played a great part in all this progress. As Group Chairman (since 1938) and Chairman of TISCO for 46 years, he put in place a system of trust and effective co-operation, that will ensure the Company's fortunes continue to prosper into the foreseeable future. The wisdom behind allowing people to grow and to thereby gain in self esteem has paid inestimable dividends, for Tata's staff themselves as well as for the Group's fortunes.

The Tata organization is blessed with many highly capable men, all of whom have made significant contributions to the Group's growth and success. One such is Mr. J.R.D. Tata's successor at TISCO, Mr. Russi Mody who has the 'Midas' touch in terms of humanitarianism and worker welfare. He is a 'natural' where it comes to people and the prevailing spirit and atmosphere at Jamshedpur under his hugely effective and remarkable democratic leadership sees a harmony, the envy of every other industrialist in the land.

Anywhere in the world TATA would be a fine show. In India it is superb, and the great example for all to copy.

The abundant capabilities, prodigious skills, human qualities and successes of Jamsetji and of his wonderful successors in providing exemplary industrial leadership, as well as in the fields of humanitarianism, represent a great national asset for India.

The Tata Story has filled many books. This article has concerned itself mainly with the founding of the great steel company TISCO and has barely touched on the great welfare work in India which has been initiated, and strenuously pursued by the Group, through its great philanthropic trusts, for the benefit of all Indians. Many more pages would be needed to portray the considerable and widely differing charitable works established and supported by 'Tata'. A considerable part of the great wealth created by this vast enterprise has been poured back again into great and beneficial public works, maintaining the founder's original credo 'CREATION OF WEALTH FOR OTHERS'.

EPILOGUE: Mr. J.R.D. Tata died in Geneva in November 1993 and his chosen successor, Mr. Ratan Tata leads the Group today. As well, Mr. J.J. Irani has succeeded Mr. Russi Mody at the helm of the Group's flagship company, TISCO.

The major Tata companies, TELCO (motor vehicles), TISCO (steel) and Tata Chemicals, presently rank second, third and seventh amongst Indian private sector companies, in terms of market capitalization.

When Tata Power Co., Tata Tea, and a score of other major enterprises are added, the Tata Group occupies a powerful and strategic position in the 1990's India.

Collaborations with respected world corporations - Daimler Benz, IBM, and others, will bring considerable benefits to India, and to all Indians, in the years ahead.

The Parsee community has indeed repaid its debt to India, for graciously and generously affording them a home and security, many many centuries ago now.

FOUNDER'S DAY AT STEEL CITY

The 157th birth anniversary of Jamsetji Nusserwanji Tata, the founder of Tata steel, was celebrated with pomp and gaiety in the Steel City. Elaborate floral decorations, colourful march past by school children and different organisations and processions featuring about 30 floats and tableaux presenting the various companies besides Tisco were the highlight of the programme. There were dance and music programmes based on national integrity and harmony as flower petals were showered on the mile-long processions. Mr Ratan Tata and Dr J.J. Irani, chairman and managing director of Tata Steel took the salute at the march past. *(PT1)*

10. Aboriginal Resettlement - "Birhore Basti"

- a human success story in Bihar

Fagu Soren is a remarkable man! A wonderful humanitarian, and humble to boot, he is ever ready to dispense love and trust amongst all his countrymen, but his particular devotion is to a group of primitive tribal people who have been resettled in the Hazaribagh District of Bihar, a State in eastern India.

Without this love, guidance and personal example, and help, inspiration and encouragement, these Bihores, literally "dwellers of the jungle" would likely have perished, and a section of another Aboriginal tribe in India, have slid on their way to extinction!

India has probably the largest tribal population of any country in the world. Tribals, or Aboriginal people, make up five, or more percent (35 million plus) of its total population, and Bihar has the largest concentration of tribals in the whole of India. Consisting of Birhores, Hos, Kharias, Santals, Mundas, Oraons, and numerous other Adivasi tribes, these aboriginal peoples fall into two linguistic groups - the Munda speaking and the Dravidian.

While most of the scheduled tribes live in six districts of Bihar, namely Ranchi, Hazaribagh, Dhanbad, Singbhum, Palamau and the Santal Parganas, there are also smaller pockets of other primitive tribes, elsewhere in Bihar, and in India. Due to their former isolated state and because of the alarming and wanton 'man-induced' changes to their environment and natural habitats (illegal deforestation and its consequences, figures high on the list), these 'peripheral' Aboriginal tribes need urgent help, if they are to survive. Literally fish out of water in any entirely different environment, unless they are helped to assimilate, their chances of survival would be minimal.

Great credit therefore reflects on the Government of India and on other community minded free-enterprise companies who readily see it as their patriotic duty to play a part in rescuing, resettling and instructing these people, who have been driven from their natural habitats, to adapt to a significantly changed lifestyle.

With so much happening in so many ways every day around India, affecting her vast conglomeration of people, it is not surprising, though regretful, that much of this wonderful humanitarianism amongst tribals, goes unheralded and unreported.

While foreigners err in regarding life in India as 'cheap' (so many poor people), this is totally erroneous, for great dignity and value is placed on every life, by all Indians, and in every walk of life. In a land where there is no fall-back on social security handouts the norm is that many mouths continue to depend upon a single breadwinner. The abrupt departure of such person can be catastrophic and destructive for the rest of the family group. Sharing of even the most meagre fare of life is common place throughout India, especially in the rural areas, where eighty percent of India's 900 million live. Inevitably, in such an exploding population and all so regretfully, troubles multiply daily. Very fortunately, and commendably, fortitude of only the rarest kind is a concomitant of most Indians.

TISCO (Tata Iron and Steel Co.) is one concerned free-enterprise company which regards every human-being as important. Wherever they operate in India, and particularly in their 'home territory' of Bihar, much attention is given to community affairs and rural development, and most importantly, generously supported with resources and money. The Tata Companies take their community responsibilities very very seriously. There is nothing token about their efforts to ameliorate suffering and assist development.

Sincere compassion for others is very evident but always wherever possible, with the emphasis upon self-reliance which, more and more, is the great 'catch-cry' in India (I was amazed to learn in Calcutta that there are 75,000 indigenous charitable organizations registered with the Government of West Bengal. Every State throughout the Union boasts many such community-serving organizations).

The virtue of 'mutual contribution' was seen long ago by TISCO and it is the very essence of all their community and rural development programmes. Providing something for nothing may alleviate the problem for the moment but in the long term, rarely achieves any worthwhile good. On the other side of the coin when appreciation and

13. Education for all - tribals at study.

gratitude goes hand-in-hand with basic training, progress is made, and long term objectives served.

It is in such a situation that our dedicated friend Fagu Soren performs his selfless totally dedicated service. A Tribal himself (an educated Santhal), he understands the ways of the Birhores and is also able to speak their dialect. His love for his small group is a joy to see as he moves amongst them. Essential trust and confidence in him is clearly evident. His complete sincerity is transparently obvious to all. In any times, and in any circumstances, these are precious commodities that should be nurtured.

I had come to West Bokaro to see a vast open-cut coal mining operation owned and conducted by TISCO. The fact that it operates so successfully and so harmoniously is due very much to the Company's long pursued and enduring welfare considerations. TISCO's workers (and there are thousands at West Bokaro) know the value of a warm smile and never fail to pass the time of day with one another, a splendid attitude emulated by nearly everyone, and one that is greatly fostered by management.

Whether TISCO scored a lucky 'bulls-eye' when they appointed Fagu Soren to 'look after the interests of the Birhores', (he has many other duties besides, not the least of which is the astonishingly successful reafforestation programme) or whether by natural selection he chose himself, I do not know. I do know that he is a winner and that he is doing exceptional things with the Birhores and for them.

Fagu Soren is understandably proud of his 'family' of nearly 150 Birhores who have been resettled as a community group, within an area of Dura Kashmar Village, about six kilometres from West Bokaro. Naturally suspicious of modern civilization, previous attempts by Government at motivating them to settle nearby had failed, for one reason or another. In 1981 TISCO decided to establish 'BIHORE BASTI', which in the light of previous failures was a brave though humanitarian decision, for another failure and the future of these particular Birhores would be seriously threatened. It is to Tata's great credit that their resettlement programme has been a wonderful success.

It was with much pleasure and keen anticipation that we visited 'BIRHORE BASTI'. As we drove into the village between the neat rows of brick, tile-roofed houses, the smaller children rushed from every corner to greet 'Uncle Fagu'. His extreme popularity needed no proving! Unlike the still developing smaller ones, the older children evidenced their growth and development by keeping on at their football. Soccer is an Indian national pastime and for the Birhores a game far removed from the kind of recreation available to them (if there was any?) in their former jungle habitat! One could readily believe that life for them was indeed now, very different!

It was Sunday afternoon and the men were all at home. Distilling home brew has been known to these 'men of the jungle' for many generations and who could blame some of them for 'having a drop' on their day of leisure? No one, I'm sure. In fact such conviviality perhaps added something to the friendly welcome we received.

Overcoming suspicions and used to practising customs learnt over centuries, the job of 'resettling' these Tribals into civilized community life could not have been an easy task. As an example, it is relevant to reflect upon the ancient lore and customs of the Birhores, and the carry-over from a former life lived in the jungle, and hardly more than yesterday. The transition has been swift and not without extreme shock.

Birhores had always been conscious of the need to preserve their native habitat and accordingly and literally, lived off the jungle. They carefully avoided any action which could reduce its permanence. They used fallen twigs and leaves to build their 'homes' doing nothing that would harm the balance of the forest.

They ate 'forest products' in the form of roots and shoots of forest plants. They hunted forest animals. When the food in one area was exhausted they would 'up sticks' and move on to the next.

They wore little or no clothes at all. They even shunned bathing believing in some superstition that their coated bodies afforded some protection and that they would endanger themselves if they removed it. They believed in strange spirits which decreed that wild animals would instinctively note any change, and as a consequence, eat them.

They were a self-sufficient people, and wholly self-reliant. Strangely though, Bihores do not dote over their children. Nature itself is meant to shape and nurture their children. Survival clearly required being part of the jungle and living by it.

Clearly a daunting task confronted TISCO and their appointed 'intermediary', Fagu Soren in overcoming such instinctive suspicions in their charges. As the record shows, gaining the full confidence of the Birhores has been slow and difficult work. It is important to remember that it was primarily destruction of their natural environment that had forced this group of Birhores out of the jungle, in order to obtain essential life-sustaining sustenance. They had not sought to be assimilated and had no notion of civilized life in the outside world.

It is therefore interesting that TISCO approached the problem through the children. Those still young enough not to have had tribal ways and customs wholly ingrained in them, could be shaped and nurtured in new ways. By steady application and through the additional process of playing simple games and having fun together, the children slowly came to have confidence in strangers and to reach out to their benefactors, after which their elders found it easier to break down their prejudices, and their suspicions.

The Birhores were completely new to modern housing, a simple thing, but nonetheless it was a very big hurdle for them to jump. Personal hygiene and sanitation were also strange things for them to handle, and to understand. Modern medicine also was very much taboo.

By dint of great perseverance, loving kindness and calm patience, the 'BIRHORE BASTI' dwellers had eventually come to accept and to trust in, the changed circumstances.

It was wonderful to see how they had absorbed their new situation, while still not wholly throwing off their old identity and certain of their basic and treasured tribal customs and traits. Their hybrid make-up would add an extra dimension to their attraction for others.

At this point of our visit, the youngsters pleaded with Fagu Soren to have a joy-ride in his Maruti Van. Good naturedly he agreed, when a mass of eager bodies clambered into the back and off they went, squealing with laughter, just like children anywhere.

But maintaining this progress depends very much upon inculcating in all of the Birhores the virtue of self-help. There is reason for confidence if the significant progress which has already been made is any criterion.

At Bihore Basti the Birhores have been introduced to cane basket making and to making clay cartridges and all of their output is put to positive use in the professional operations of TISCO. Book binding is also taught, together with training in animal husbandry and agricultural pursuits.

Additionally, for the women, there is training in domestic matters as well as instruction in health care and family planning methods.

Others again are engaged in working a four acre plot where the planting and nurturing of 'food providing' trees is being encouraged. A plentiful supply of Guava, Mango, Jack-fruit, Jamun, Lemon, Citrus, Coconut, Papaya and Banana is already coming forth. Pumpkins and other vegetables are also cultivated, and all of these items are contributing to a more nourishing and healthier diet.

Thousands of Teak, Bamboo, Acacia and Shisham trees have also been planted in the surrounding area. These are multi-purpose trees, which in years to come will supply most of the needs of the Birhores, for fuel and for other purposes. They have been educated to take care of this area themselves, and they are doing it with a new found willingness and enjoyment. All this, on the same plot of ground which years before had been abandoned by them as frequented by evil spirits!

Still others find remunerative employment assisting the Rural Development division of TISCO in the planting out of many hundreds of thousands of trees, all over the Company's Mine Site (10,000 acres) at West Bokaro. To TISCO's great delight, this revegetation of the huge dumps of overburden is succeeding beyond all expectations, and the whole area is now one of wonderful green hillsides. A great victory has been won for the environment.

Birhores do not hoard their money, never having been used to having any and never needing to save any (modern economics is something they would have to learn). Accordingly, the people in Birhore Basti prefer piece-work and like to get paid often and to dispose of their pay, equally quickly!

As another gesture of the Tata Management to boost confidence and goodwill, a Santhal, Kasturi Chand Marbi lives in Birhore Basti, with his wife and family, and provides on-hand medical service. He is doing fine work in weaning the Birhores from continuing with the use of ancient and oft times dangerous, even disastrous remedies, for overcoming illness.

As an illustration, the story is told of a boy Bala, eleven years of age, suffering from fever, a chronic cough, loss of weight and of appetite.

The tribal people, as had been their custom in their old life, turned to the Gods for help. They also made a sacrifice of chickens and a goat to their Goddess, praying for the boy's early (but natural) recovery.

The boy was suffering from Tuberculosis. Only when his condition turned grave did they seek the advice of the Medical Social Worker. By degrees, they ultimately consented to the use of anti-T.B. drugs. All active symptoms subsided and today Bala is leading a healthy normal life.

What does the long term promise? Excellent progress has been made and the previous primitive lifestyle of the Birhores has taken on new and encouraging prospects. They no longer depend on forest-products in order to survive. They are free to maintain their tribal identity without fear of outside interference. They have developed a lot of confidence without any loss of dignity. They now have a CHOICE!

We departed, wishing the Birhores well. To myself, I congratulated TISCO on its sensitive approach and for the wonderful results they had so far achieved in helping a small, but no less valuable, group of Tribals to avoid extinction, a fate which dangled very much before them if they failed to integrate with outside society.

What the future holds, no one can tell, but for these Birhores at least, they have been given a chance. I'm sure all of us wish that they survive and prosper, the forerunner of many other not dissimilar groups of 'bush people', driven from their former contented lives by the wanton destruction by others of their natural habitats, in the jungles of India.

11. Darjeeling - Mountain Playground Par Excellence

- beholder of the Five Treasuries of the Great Snow

As one looks out upon the great Himalayan mountain chain from Darjeeling, Frank Smythe's inimitable and marvellous impressions penetrate one's whole being. He said, *"No man has really lived until he has looked into the heart of Nature and has learned to appreciate the Magnificent World in which he has been created."*

Just as Frank Smythe, the famous Everest explorer and renowned author perceived this stupendous region, so have many others, fortunate enough to have visited the area. Darjeeling district offers so very much to its dwellers and to its visitors.

Even more than the pleasure derived by tea drinkers the world over from a 'cup of the finest Darjeeling', the awesome grandeur of mighty magnificent Kangchenjunga, at 28,141 feet the third highest mountain in the world, flanked by her sentinels Kabru, Jannu and Pandim, sets the seal unto eternity of this mountain district which has been so rightly dubbed - the 'Queen of the Hill Stations'.

Nestling in the mountains at an altitude topping 7,000 feet, Darjeeling in north-eastern India, is singularly beautiful. The 'hill station' occupies a long narrow ridge of the Sikkim Himalayas that descends abruptly to the Great Rangit, the river which weaves its course through the steep valley thousands of feet below. The famous town snuggles in the lower slopes of the greatest and best known, loved and feared mountain range in the world - the Himalayas - that almost impassable barrier in North India which was formed over 40 million years ago, when India torn loose from Antarctica and Africa, rammed into the under-belly of Asia.

To the west and south, Darjeeling is enclosed by mountains higher than itself. To the north and north-east, the view is more open, as the eye travels past fold after fold of mountains rising in ever ascending waves behind and beyond the cultivated slopes of the Sikkim hills across the Rangit river.

Beyond all this and towering up to the heavens, the prospect runs on and ever upwards terminating (for our view only, for the stupendous mountain chain in its broad sweep of over 1,500 miles, from Nanga Parbat in the west to Namcha Barwa in the east, is hundreds of miles wide as it reaches north into Tibet) in the distant snowy Himalayas with its vast, long girdle of snow capped peaks. It is a panorama unequalled anywhere else in the world. Its mammoth and majestic proportions dwarf everything else anywhere.

To the north-west lies Nepal. To the north-east Bhutan. Directly north of us lies the ancient kingdom of Sikkim, now a province of India. Fifty miles to the south begin the vast plains of West Bengal, which stretch hundreds of miles across the immensely fertile Ganges delta, to the Bay of Bengal on the Indian Ocean.

One of man's unexplained and enduring qualities allows him to hold an extraordinary lasting affection for his 'patch of dirt', however difficult or horrid it was or is, or wherever that patch is located. So it is also with the oldest known tribe of the Darjeeling region. The Lepchas known to have inhabited the region for over 1,000 years, have battled long and hard to eke out a livelihood from the rugged terrain but nothing - not deprivation nor extreme cold - has succeeded in wrenching them away from their beloved mountains.

Until barely 150 years ago, Kangchenjunga, or as it is reverentially regarded by the peoples of the region - 'THE FIVE TREASURIES OF THE GREAT SNOW' - thus peacefully tucked away from the populous world, had 'slept' undisturbed, from the beginning of time. The outside world hardly knew of its existence. Not so however the superstitious Tibetans to the north. They had lived for years to the accompaniment of great thunderous claps which attend the huge and frequent avalanches which tumble at great speed down the precipitous north-west face.

This great hidden 'Shangrila' might have remained lost to the outside world but for a quirk of history. The 'foreign colonialist' had found the hot humid plains of Bengal extremely enervating, and looking for relief from the oppressive heat, turned his attention to the distant hills, where he hoped to find cooler refuge, there to escape the fiery furnace of the plains.

Those other exquisite hill stations in north-west India, Simla, Mussoorie and Naini Tal had already been 'discovered' and settled. The mountains rearing up from the plains to the north of Calcutta beckoned. However, much intrepid surveying and engineering would be needed before a route was laid open and a British town added to the native village.

The customary route nowadays to Darjeeling is either by rail from Calcutta via Siliguri, or by scheduled airlines to Bagdogra and then by road or two foot gauge railway from Siliguri. Whichever route one takes the distance is about 650 kilometres. Given good seasonal conditions, coursing up the mountain road to Darjeeling nowadays is relatively easy, while adventure is never entirely absent, as many a traveller has discovered.

The coursing of the road up and through the mountains in the eighteen-fifties was a herculean task and took all the engineering genius and flair of many people including an engineer who was yet to achieve great fame as a soldier, Lord Napier of Magdala. He was then an energetic and enterprising young lieutenant serving Queen Victoria's army, in India.

Some years later, a better and less hazardous 'track' was constructed. A curse of the region, continual and prolific heavy rains, make travel by small bus or jeep by this same route today a harrowing 'cliff hanging' experience, as everyone who has travelled the route knows. Detouring by one of the longer alternative routes, which sometimes has to be resorted to, when landslides block the normal route, is even more spine-tingling!

But the initial thrills of the motor road up, are but a prelude to the main act! Until the Buddhist Monastery at Ghoom (2,500 metres) is reached, the great Kangchenjunga range remains hidden from view. Suddenly at the next turn, that great spectacle appears. As though suspended in space way way above you, one is introduced to the incomparable bulk of Kangchenjunga and her splendid guardians Kabru, Jannu and Pandim. This is a sight never afterwards forgotten. It is a truly breathtaking sight.

Only eight kilometres more along a now more hospitable road, the 'hill station' of Darjeeling is reached. Darjeeling derived its name from the Buddhist Monastery of 'Dorje Ling', or 'place of the thunderbolt' which once stood on Observatory Hill.

Apart from achieving renown by relieving Viceroyal brows fevered by the heat of the plains, Darjeeling became more extensively known to the world through the publicity accorded British attempts to scale Mt. Everest, the world's highest mountain.

Between the wars (1920 - 1940) British climbers unsuccessfully mounted seven attempts to reach the summit of Mt. Everest (one was a solo effort - considered suicide in 1934 but first accomplished by a Swiss climber in the 1970's). All of the British expeditions started out from Darjeeling.

Before 1949 and until Nepal eased its restrictions on foreign entry, all Everest parties tackled the great peak (one of over 40 peaks exceeding 20,000 feet in the Himalayan mountain-chain) on its north face facing out on to the Tibetan Plateau.

Although Mt. Everest is only 100 miles as the crow flies from Darjeeling, the march in from Darjeeling to base camp, entailed a journey on foot of five weeks duration, and a slog of over 300 miles. The walls of the famous Planters Club and the Gymkhana Club in Darjeeling are still graced by pictures of members of these notable Everest expeditions whose heroic exploits live on in history.

While the unsuccessful British efforts pre-World War II to climb Mt Everest spawned many accounts of remarkable human endurance and heroism, negotiating the remote mountain road up from Siliguri to Darjeeling also produced some hectic tales. One such concerned the same exceptional man, and climber, Frank Smythe. Proceeding by open tourer car of the 1930's and passing up through the dense jungle on either side of the road, the expeditioners made a brief stop to - 'spend a penny'. Seeking privacy, the occupants fanned out in different directions. While relieving himself, Frank Smythe heard the unmistakable growl of a tiger. Looking to the edge of the jungle he saw the tiger, partly obscured by foliage. Remembering the advice he (and others visiting India) had been given - ignore what you've seen and walk steadfastly away, giving no indication (to the tiger) that you know of its presence - Frank Smythe walked up the road. He afterwards recorded that the succeeding thirty seconds 'were the longest and most pregnant' of his whole life.

The Himalayan Mountaineering Institute since established along at North Point, also has a wonderful selection of mountaineering

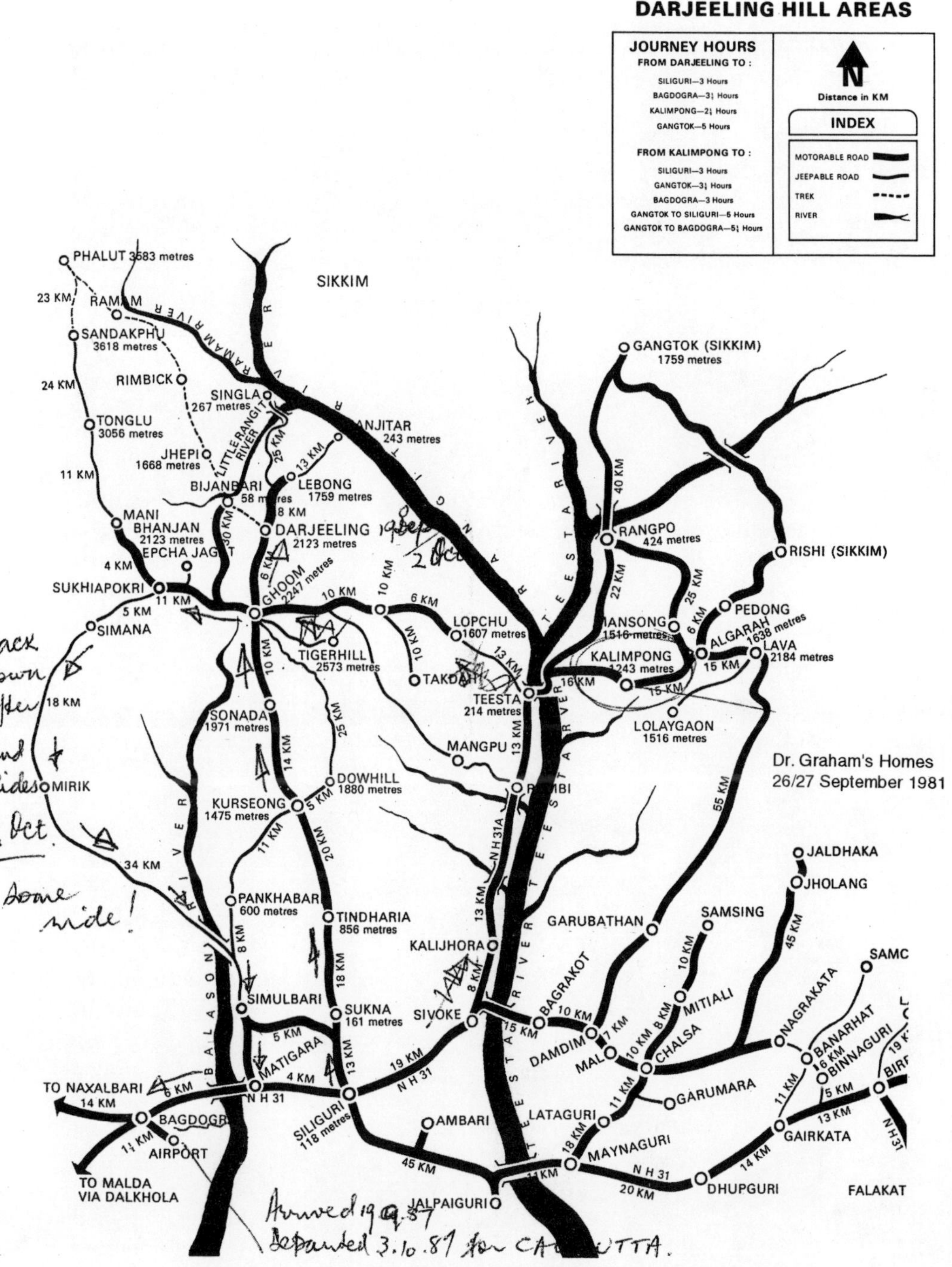

14. Darjeeling - springboard to the Himalayas.

artefacts and pictures, as well as an extensive library of irreplaceable books. Saving these books from the scourge of humidity and damp, is a never-ending task and expense.

Great and savage extremes of climate affect most parts of India. The proud settlement of Darjeeling at 7000 feet is frequently covered in rain-bearing clouds. These inclement weather conditions play havoc with most man-made constructions, requiring the attendance of constant, scarcely affordable maintenance, on them.

While over the mists of time some of Darjeeling's former splendour has diminished, in the 1990's a new era for Darjeeling may be dawning. Renewed vigour and interest is flaring up amongst its motley heterogeneous population, anxious to regain autonomy after playing a passive role to outsiders for so long. Restoration of pride should do much to bring about the revitalization of the region.

Alongside her great mountains and prime tea gardens, Darjeeling's great appeal to visitors lies in her colourful people. Once described as the 'Babel of tribes and nations', Darjeeling district is home to a great admixture of races, most of whom are of Mongol origin.

Predominating in the area today are the 'immigrant' Nepalese and their offspring through inter-marriage with Sikkimese, Bhotias, Tibetans, Lepchas and others. These small sturdy descendants of a hardy virile race are the most capable and adaptable of the whole population. They are born cultivators, resourceful and hard working.

A cheerful, alert and loyal people, the Nepalese were brought in in large numbers to the Darjeeling district by the British from Nepal in the 1860's to work the tea estates, when planting of tea on a viable commercial scale, first began.

Darjeeling's tea gardens hang precariously on to the sides of the steep mountain slopes, and are extremely labour intensive. In actuality, 'farms' of cultivated gardenia bushes, *Camellia sinensis,* each bush is skilfully pruned to create the maximum 'plucking' surface. Each tea bush may be 'plucked' as many as 30 times in a single year (if proper harvesting methods are faithfully followed, just 'two leaves and a bud' is ever taken from each stalk at a single plucking). It requires a big army of manual workers to undertake these tasks, which are beyond the capability of machinery of successfully accomplishing, because of the steep terrain.

Extensive seasonal rains, soil erosion and landslides, are the regular scourge of tea planters. Great slashes in the mountain-side on both the Darjeeling side and on the southern slopes of Sikkim left by horrendous landslides, provide stark testimony to the great and increasing problems confronting the tea industry in this mountain region.

The conglomerate and cosmopolitan peoples of the Darjeeling region speak many native languages. The lingua franca is 'Khas Kura', a kind of Nepali Hindi. Amongst the Bhotias, Nepalis, Lepchas and Tibetans as many as 20 or 30 different dialects abound. This possibly makes the community almost unique in the world, considering the constricted size of the area and the great diversity of race and language which lives harmoniously, together.

While 'Khas Kura' is the most widely understood language, many of the 250,000 inhabitants of the region know a smattering of English, particularly the shop-keepers and anyone associated with the tourist industry.

Whatever 'formal' religion is claimed by this marvellous cross-section of cheery people, it is an interesting fact that nearly all these hills-people veer towards animism!

Such culture would be difficult to avoid, affected as the people are by mighty nature in its most awesome abundance, all around them. Everyone is affected by the grandeur of the atmosphere, be they a practising Hindu, Buddhist or any one of many other beliefs.

The Animistic religion requires from its practitioners total prohibition from inflicting harm 'on any living thing'. Most of the people believe that there are malevolent spirits to whom the ills of life are due, and which exercise their malicious influence on the bodies and minds of men and women by demoniacal possession.

Religious ritual calls for regular propitiation of 'the mountain Gods and spirits' in order to escape their attacks. Often, the cure for disease is not medicine, but exorcism. It is the job of the Shaman, the village medicine man, (he who knows) to cure illnesses, intercede with the Gods and to preside over rites accompanying birth, marriage and death. It must indeed be a fascinating experience to be present when the Shaman is holding forth to a captivated audience of his going to

14A. The beautiful Kanchenjunga Range girdles Darjeeling - "Queen of the hill-stations".

another world to escort the soul of a deceased person to its new abode. Marvellous stuff.

A popular 'meeting place' in Darjeeling for making propitiation to the evil spirits of the mountains, is Observatory Hill where tall prayer flags ('the horses of the wind') flutter unceasingly to ward off the evil spirits. The Buddhist muttering of the mystic formula *'Om mani padme hum'* ("Om, the jewel, is in the lotus: Amen") goes on ceaselessly, craving protection from malignant Gods and demons. These words are the first ones taught to a Buddhist child, and the last uttered on the deathbed of the pious.

India supplies illimitable 'colour' in every shape and form and the contribution of the hills-people adds much to the great kaleidoscopic effect.

Everywhere in the mountains drama is in constant attendance. Life never stands still for its ebullient people, influenced as it is by the mass of the great mountains and the ever-changing weather.

Darjeeling's most famous son, Tenzing Norgay, a Lepcha, epitomizes the marvellous nature and character of these wonderful hill people. It was soon after 29th May, 1953 that news reached Darjeeling that Tenzing, together with the craggy New Zealander, Ed Hillary, had reached the summit of Mt. Everest. For the first time, the world's highest mountain had been scaled by man.

One of the band of marvellous Sherpas (those wonderful people from the Khombu region in Nepal adjacent to Mt. Everest, who are so much at home in the higher slopes) who have contributed so much to the success of nearly every Himalayan mountaineering expedition, Tenzing was a shy but happy smiling man. He was lauded all over the world, and it was due to his success and universal popularity that the Himalayan Mountaineering Institute was subsequently founded at North Point. (Nowadays, Tenzing's grave graces the Institute's grounds).

Begun in 1954, the H.M.I. has since produced many highly skilled Indian climbers and to it is owed the great successes Indian expeditions have achieved. Additionally, many Sherpas trained by H.M.I. have done great work assisting scores of foreign assaults on the great Himalayan peaks.

So Darjeeling is many things to many people. To countless people it revives happy memories of travelling up from Siliguri on the 'toy train' made famous by Lowell Thomas in his epic film "Cinerama Holiday" made in the nineteen sixties, the harbinger of the wide cinema screen.

The railway which has been in existence since 1881, still does a useful job in the 'dry' season, although its ageing tiny locos must be nearing the end of their usefulness, bringing to a close, another chapter of a slower, but more romantic age. The economics of keeping the track open are also a significant problem. Not a monsoon-season goes by, but extensive damage has to be repaired at prohibitive cost.

Whatever the future holds, the great mountains will continue to hugely impress themselves on the lives of everyone who has experienced them. People journeying to Darjeeling from every corner of the world and obeying the urge to visit the 'roof of the world', will continue to be overwhelmed by it all. It is an experience of a lifetime, not to be missed.

To Kangchenjunga, 'the five treasuries of the great snow' (these are the five tops of Kangchenjunga) and still the untrodden peak, (the only successful expedition to Kangchenjunga in 1955, led by Everest explorer Charles Evans, left the ultimate few feet inviolate - a wonderful gesture to Anglo-Sikkimese relations) must go the last praise, for it is it with its mighty satellites which dominate and glorify the whole region, now and always.

Referring to the Himalayas, and in particular, to mighty Kangchenjunga, a totally captivated devotee once observed -

> "the snowy mountains are magnificent beyond anything I can attempt to express; rising to a height in the heavens we have been accustomed to think nothing but a cloud can pretend to; and ever varying in their tints, and their hues; and their shades, at every change of the clouds, and position of the sun, but always above description. Glorious!"

12. "The Fire Worshippers"
- India's gifted immigrants - the Parsees

To see the celebrated maestro Zubin Mehta stand before an orchestra and conduct is a memorable sight, and the music he draws from the players is next to magical. He ranks amongst the world's most acclaimed contemporary music directors.

Zubin Mehta had his early introduction to music in Bombay, where his father Mehli was a noted violinist and conductor of the Symphony Orchestra.

He is also a product of a highly industrious and extraordinarily talented group of famous people, the ethno-religious minority group, the Parsees of Bombay, whose forebears initially came to India from Persia as long as thirteen hundred years ago.

While Parsees (literally men from Pars or Fars, Ancient Parsa, known to the Greeks as Persopolis, in southern Iran) are still numbered among the population of Iran, their main strengths in modern times have been in India from whence they have further launched themselves, settling in other parts of the world.

The transition to India can be traced to the downfall of the Sassanian Empire in 651 A.D., when Persia became a dominion of the Arab Caliphs. The Islamic religion was ruthlessly imposed on the vanquished Persians. They were subjected to extreme religious persecution and racial intolerance. The Parsees' Fire Temples were destroyed and mass conversion enforced.

Refusing to surrender their religious beliefs, many Zoroastrians (as the followers of the teachings of the prophet Zarathrustra are known) wishing to escape further persecution, withdrew to the mountains of Khorassan, in the north east of Persia, where they dwelt for a hundred years.

But even there they were not safe from the Caliphs, still hell bent on gaining more converts to Islam. Escape to a foreign land remained the only possibility of survival, and to a tolerant place where they would be allowed to practise their own religious beliefs unmolested. Setting out from Khorassan they temporarily halted at Hormuz, whereafterwards they left their homeland by sea for India. The Parsees eventually found relief and tolerance in Kathiawar, a town in what is now Gujarat Province.

Many years then passed relatively uneventfully for the followers of Zarathustra until, with the rise of British and Portuguese trading activities in western India (circa 1600 A.D.) a new phase of prosperity changed their fortunes. Quickly attuning to the new work environment created by the foreigners, they were in great demand as craftsmen, particularly in Surat, where many factories were established.

A further big lift in their fortunes occurred, when the Infanta Catherina of Braganza married Charles II of England. This event signalled the handing over of Bombay by the Portuguese to the British, as a wedding present (1661). Thus drawn to Bombay the Parsees rapidly capitalised on the great new opportunities laid out before them. Bombay has remained their principal stronghold in India, and in the world, ever since.

Considering their significant achievements and the impact they have had on affairs in Western India, it is surprising that the Parsee community nowadays represents no more than the minutest fraction of even one percent of the total Indian population of over 900 millions. In fact the percentage gets smaller every year, as 'official' Parsees become fewer in number. In fact it appears that if the religion's rigid traditional qualifications are not modified it could be inevitable that Parsee numbers in India will gradually decline and the community in that country, eventually become extinct.

The 1981 Census listed 71,630 persons as Zoroastrians resident in all of India. But this does not give a true picture of the total Parsee 'community'. Unlike earlier times, today marriage with non-Parsees is not uncommon when ancient Zoroastrian (eligibility) laws as they are still rigidly applied, discriminate greatly against women.

Parsee women who marry non-Parsees, and children of such mixed marriages, are automatically precluded thereafterwards from entering Fire Temples and from overtly practising or receiving the benefits of the Zoroastrian religion. This is a very sore point with 'liberated' educated Parsee women, and it is an issue which they are strongly contesting, even though tradition mitigates against their chances of winning sympathetic changes.

With statistics showing that fewer children are being born of 'Parsee' marriages, pressure is increasing for the Parsee ruling body to take some far reaching decisions. Except that the ancient religious rulings are relaxed to allow continued worship by families of Parsee women who have married non-Parsees, few doubt that the future of India's Parsees is gravely threatened.

Over the past two or three hundred years, the Parsee community has played a leading role in shaping particularly, the economic history of Western India. Overall, they have made major contributions in the educational, political, economic and cultural fields. To them is owed much of the credit for the Indian industrial resurgence from the late nineteenth century when, despite discouragement at every turn from India's colonial rulers, of all the subjugated races, the Parsees were foremost in initiating many significant new ventures.

The long history of Parsee enterprise and achievement may come as a surprise to many non-Indians, for, in colonial times, little publicity was accorded indigenous civic and industrial activity, misleading foreigners into thinking that India (for Indians), was little more than a land of myth and fable, and religious indulgence. Apart from sensationalism accorded Parsee burial procedures by foreigners, ignorant of the true facts, precious little else seems to have been related, or understood, about the Parsees.

Parsees follow a very unique religion. Zarathustra (circa 2000 B.C.) was possibly the first prophet in human history to preach of one God, Ahura Mazda, Lord of Life and Wisdom, a God of spirit and truth, of righteousness and justice, and love and compassion.

A cardinal doctrine of the Zoroastrian religion allows freedom of choice whether or not to follow one's parents, and become a Zoroastrian also. It is reasonable to think that most sons follow their fathers and become Zoroastrians but it would be a knowledgeable young Parsee girl indeed who delayed her decision until adulthood, perceiving and understanding the problems which could beset her in later life should she marry a non-Parsee.

A life of active good towards one's fellow men is the principal thrust of the Parsee religion. The ethics of Zoroastrianism are based on three cardinal principles, which are - Humata, Hukhta, Hvarshta, which translated mean "good thoughts, good words and good deeds". All good thoughts, words or deeds are the product of wisdom and a life directed towards these aims ultimately leads to heaven. (Noteworthily and significantly, these praiseworthy cardinal virtues are included in the Company crest of the great Tata industrial and philanthropic corporation, initially designed by and for, the Founder, Jamsetji Tata.)

The two great emblems of the Parsee religion are Hvare Kshaeta, the glorious sun, and Atar Khvareh, the radiant fire. Fire is an emblem of the Divine. It burns up any filth flung into it, but itself remains pure.

Parsees revere fire as a symbol of purity and divinity, replacing idol worship. Their shrines are called Fire Temples. There are three grades of Fire Temples: the Atash Behram, the fire of victory, the highest of all; the Atash-e-Adran, fire of fires, or Agiary or Dar-e-Meher, the gate of mercy; and the Atash-e-Dadgah, which is the household fire in a Zoroastrian home.

A properly consecrated and fuelled fire is believed to be the spark of endless light, the abode of the infinite, an epiphany of the realm of Ahura Mazda (the ultimate source of life itself) himself. These are lofty ideals, and call for great faith.

The sacred fire Atar burns day and night in the Fire Temples, being fed with sandalwood and incense. Wherever Parsees live Fire Temples are to be found. The entrance to Fire Temples is guarded by mythical ghodas or guardian angels.

While Brahmins (the highest caste in orthodox Hinduism) and Jews (the barmitzvah) are invested with the sacred thread among their initiation rites, Zoroastrians at their initiation ceremony, which is called the Navjote, receive the Kusti, or sacred girdle. The Navjote, literally 'the new birth', is the first important religious ceremony in the life of every Zoroastrian. This ritual goes back thousands of years.

The Kusti is woven from white lambswool spun into fine thread. Two threads of requisite length are twisted together symbolising the union of the two spirits. Seventy two double strands are then taken and woven into a long thin hollow tape. The number represents the seventy two chapters of the Yasna, the most important book of Scriptures. The Kusti which is wound three times around the waist to signify the three commandments of Zoroaster - Humata, Hukhta and Hvarshta, and worn next to the skin, denotes that a person by his or her own free choice, has chosen to embrace the teachings of the Zoroastrian religion. This event ordinarily takes place between the ages of 7 and 15 years, but in any case, before puberty.

Adherents are then entitled to also wear the other identifying garment, the Sudreh or sacred shirt, popularly called the Sudra.

Incorporated into this shirt or Sudra is a one-inch square pocket with a slit at the base of the V-neck. This pocket is known as the Kisseh-i-Kerfeh, or pocket of good deeds. Additionally, in order to signify equality between rich and poor alike (a teaching of the Prophet), three small tucks are featured at the sides at the bottom of every Sudra. Bound up with the tenet of equality, it is useful to comment here that while it may not be true that all Parsees are rich, there is plenty of evidence to show that hard work and application, and community bonds, ensure that few Parsees are ever allowed to go destitute.

After being invested, the worshipper wears the Sudreh and Kusti until death, except when bathing.

After the Navjote, the next most important ceremony in the life of a Zoroastrian is usually that of marriage, when again, very ancient and colourful procedure is followed.

The traditional Parsee wedding ceremony is recited in ancient Sanskrit. The bridal couple sit facing each other, when the officiating priests, one from either side, place a cloth in curtain fashion between them and tie the ends around the chairs.

The bride's right hand is placed in the groom's right hand and their hands are tied together seven times with a piece of twine. An attendant stands behind the senior priest holding the afarghan (sacred urn) while the prayers are recited.

At a signal from the priest the fire is fed with sandalwood and incense. The cloth curtain is then removed, and as the guests clap, the bride and groom throw uncooked rice over each other, symbolising prosperity.

Admonitions and benedictions from the Pazand and Avesta follow, after which parents throw grains of uncooked rice on the couple, evoking plenty and prosperity. The final blessing is given and the official ceremony is over. The bridal couple then visit the Fire Temple to pay homage to the sacred fire.

As related earlier, the history of modern Bombay up to the winning of independence by India in 1947 was substantially influenced by Parsees, who by their intellect and wealth and public leadership dominated the cultural and commercial scene.

Ample evidence of their significant contribution shows in Bombay's major thoroughfares which are dotted with statues to many great and colourful Parsee public figures. Sir Jamsetjee Jejeebhoy the first Indian Baronet; Dadabhai Naorji, loved and revered as 'the grand old man of India'; Sir Pherozeshah Mehta; Sir Dinshaw Wacha and others are publicly commemorated.

The story of Dadabhai Naorji is particular interesting. A leading Indian pro-active patriot, Naorji won much acclaim from his compatriots for his direct action policy in putting India's case for freedom directly before the British public. In 1900 he took the unprecedented step of taking up residence in England, and not only that, but he succeeded in getting himself elected to the House of Commons to secure the most public platform from which to put forward his pleas for self-rule for India. An unheard of thing, the mountain had gone to Mohammed! His courageous and enterprising act did not pass unnoticed. British political antagonists of the times derogatively referred to him as 'that fire-worshipping Asiatic'!

On the political front, many notable modern figures in Indian history have been Parsees. Among them was Mrs Indira Gandhi's husband, Feroze Gandhi. Not so surprisingly, as Mrs Gandhi's family (the Nehrus) were Brahman Hindus, yet nonetheless interestingly, neither of their two sons, Sanjay, nor Rajiv, embraced the Zoroastrian religion.

On the industrial front, the largest free-enterprise business group in India, (there are larger Public Sector Corporations – Oil and

15. Parsee nuptials.

Gas and Steel, amongst over 200 such P.S. companies), Tata and Sons, is as indicated above, a Parsee dynasty. Since before the turn of the century, and into this one, Tata and Sons have been India's leading benefactors. All Indians, whether rich or poor, Hindu, Muslim, Jain or whatever, are accorded equal respect and have benefited from Tata's charitable initiatives and significant endowments.

The Tata Philanthropic Trusts ('in their aims' absolutely unique at the time) gave India her first Institute for Social Sciences, her first Institute of Science (Bangalore 1911); her first steel works at Jamshedpur (also in 1911, and at the time the largest steelmill east of Suez), also her first Cancer Research Centre (1941), now part of the Tata Memorial Hospital for Cancer and many more. Their great philanthropy continues unabated to this day, assisting and nurturing many worthy causes.

It was Homi Bhahba, India's best known nuclear physicist, himself a Parsee and a relative of Tata and greatly respected by his peers the world over as a person and as a physicist, who set up the Tata Institute of Fundamental Research (1945), funded by the Tata Trusts. This same organisation has now passed to Government control, as India's Atomic Energy Commission.

Great works all of these institutions and all of them conceived, funded and staffed by many eminently qualified Parsees for the benefit of all Indians. In this most emphatic way the Parsee community has honoured the pledge it gave at India's Independence (1947), quote - 'it is our wish to completely identify with Indians and make ourselves indispensable'. This probably sounded obtuse and strange coming from a religious community which by that time had already lived over 1,300 years in India! An odd (but wonderful) thing indeed but India can supply many paradoxes!

So much for the story of the Parsees, the most westernized of all the communities in India. Perhaps no other single religious community with such small numbers ever did more for their adopted country. It is little wonder that their fame has spread throughout the world.

Next time you hear any idiosyncratic factors about them, you should consider the whole case and only then make your judgement.

A final word about Parsee burial rites. It was Robert Xavier Murphy who gave the name "Towers of Silence" to the Parsee cremation chambers. In the original Persian, Dakhma or Dokhma, it means 'a receptacle for the dead', and the round cremation tower is usually located on high ground.

The ancient Achaemenians (Parsee ancestors in ancient Persia) held sacred the three elements of earth, fire and water, which meant that a corpse could not be buried, burnt or immersed. Dead bodies were accordingly exposed on mountain tops, or else placed in towers specially built for burial purposes. The bones, after drying in the sun, were then collected and placed in ossuaries, or put into tombs cut into rock.

Perhaps the most famous of all the Towers of Silence around the world is the one situated below the Hanging Gardens, on Malabar Hill located in Bombay's foremost residential district. (It should be noted that Parsees had settled there long before their modern neighbours came upon the scene). It utilises more modern methods, although the results are the same.

If due respect and deference is paid and religious tolerance observed it will be recognised that 'the ancient command of not polluting the earth' has been faithfully kept for thousands of years by Zoroastrians, unchanged in its original and basic concept.

When that famous Anglo-Indian Lord Macaulay declared in 1835 that 'Indians would be educated in the ways of the English', he could not have imagined by any degree of his perception the zest and seriousness with which the Parsees would use his directive, not as a command, but as a means of educating themselves for the greater benefit of their adopted homeland, India.

13 *India's Man For The People

- A tribute to compassionate leadership of rare quality -
J R D Tata

** This article was written in 1988 after a pleasant chat with Mr Tata in his lovely office in Bombay House. Mr Tata, a splendid gentleman, and revered by everyone he touched throughout a long successful life, died in Geneva in November 1993. A great son of India's, his life story is an example to everyone, and bears telling again and again.*

J R D Tata, Chairman of the great Indian Free Enterprise Industrial Group, Tata Sons Limited, celebrates his eighty-fifth birthday in July. A renowned aviator, founder Chairman of Air India International right through its formative years up to 1978. Mr Tata has made outstanding contributions in many different areas of Indian affairs. In addition his wisdom and uncompromising attitude to anything but the highest business standards and ethics has earned him and the Group he leads, great respect from every quarter, everywhere in the world. This article is a tribute to him.

Fifty years of meritorious stewardship. That is the distinguished record of Jehangir Ratanji Dadabhoy Tata, the much loved and revered Chairman of the Tata Group of Companies, the giant Indian free enterprise industrial group, now in its second century of illustrious service to India.

Chosen to lead the "House of Tata" in 1938 at the age of 34, Mr J R D Tata has presided ever since over the Group's affairs, which read like a history of modern India.

Granted the first private flying licence in India, Mr Tata was the co-inaugurator (in 1932) of India's first regular air service, that later was to blossom into Air India International. Not long after, the same uncommon personal courage, integrity and leadership, was to bring great renown and distinction to the diverse Tata business enterprises. By grafting these extraordinary qualities on to innovative and far-sighted management and extraordinary 'people skills', Mr Tata's tenure of office has further enhanced the fortunes and good name of the Group in India and around the world.

Nestling in one of Bombay's quieter but congested quarters, not far distant from one of the city's most recognizable landmarks, the Flora Fountain (now renamed Hutatma Chowk), the Tata Group's principal office maintains a low profile, preferring to divest 'day to day control' to the major subsidiaries themselves, wherever the seat of their operations is in India. The confidence and trust vested in its operatives has built up a rare loyalty and produced enviable consistent results for the Group.

From his airy bright suite on the top floor, discreetly tucked away from the 'orderly' bustle in evidence on the lower three floors, "JRD" as he is affectionately known by every one of his hundreds of thousands of 'family', dispenses great commonsense, cordiality and graciousness to everyone he meets.

The imprint of the Chairman touches everything and everybody and all around him there is clear evidence of his (and the Group's) broad spectrum of interests and activities, and awareness of the world at large.

Spry and dapper (if attitudes temper ageing, then Mr Tata is a prime example of the great rewards of selfless thinking) and generally favouring white linen safari suits as a concession to Bombay's cruelly hot and humid climate, Mr Tata's eyes twinkle animatedly and humorously, from out of his crinkled countenance. There must be few people like him for his great devotion to a lifetime's singular direction, 'to serve others to the very best of one's abilities'. Even in advancing years his goals burn just as positively as they must have done, fifty years before. Mr Tata puts great faith in people's abilities to succeed, given the right guidance and opportunities.

The heartland of the vast Tata empire is at Jamshedpur in the centre of rural Bihar, a thousand miles from Bombay. There, over a vast area adjacent to the life-giving waters of the Kharkai and Subarnarekha Rivers, the multifarious activities of the major Group Companies, Tata Iron and Steel, Tata Engineering and Locomotive Company and the Tinplate Company of India are conducted. From its

16. A Great Indian Son - Jehangir Ratanji Dadabhoy (J.R.D.) Tata (1904-1993)

beginnings in 1877, the Tata Group had described the very first steel mill, east of Suez, producing the first steel billets in 1912, thereby carving out for themselves, a place in history and if cognizance is given to the political difficulties of the times, delivering up as well, an enormous achievement for indigenous Indian industry.

When in India, Mr Tata's great pre-occupation is with the greater needs of others. He has experienced a great deal of life and has encountered many different situations, moving as he has done not just among the rich and powerful of India, but also of the world. The welfare of the people of India has been his serious lifelong interest. Led by Mr Tata, the same humanitarian interests also govern the activities of the Tata enterprises, everywhere they operate.

Being able to draw from a vast fund of experiences, Mr Tata has a lovely knack of relating interesting anecdotes. His quick sense of humour and readiness to laugh (as much at himself) have clearly been valuable life companions and aids. Above all, and doubtless seen by his rare critics as inverted snobbery, he refuses to take himself seriously. He strongly believes that every person has some contribution to make and has an entitlement to be heard.

On the (rare) occasions that he laments his 'limited education', he emits a touch of sincere wistful sadness (his first 20 years were spent alternating between France, the country of his birth, and India, with all the attendant disruptiveness such comings and goings can bring). But if he missed out on a 'normal' formal education as we may interpret that condition, assuredly he has acquired an unsurpassed 'liberal and (big) business' education since. A known and considerable instinctive flair for perceiving and analysing problems and for providing solutions to them, allied to his genuine humility, peppers his long business record, marking him for greatness.

Very generously, Mr Tata attributes the Tata Group's continuous progress and unsullied reputation to the Group's consistent following of a unique set of beliefs, traditions and ideals originally expounded and initiated in practice, by the Group's great founder, Jamsetji Nusserwanji Tata.

Jamsetji was a man 'ahead of his time', endowed with rare and extraordinary foresight. A Parsee, he could trace his origins in India back 25 generations (his progenitors fled to India 1300 years before, to escape Arab persecution).

Even while 'liberated' India was still a very long way off, he (Jamsetji) uncannily perceived the essential 'tools' independent India would eventually have great need for - namely, technical education, electric power, iron and steel, scientific knowledge - and he made it his life's work to initiate these long-range objectives.

When, for possibly the thousandth time in his life, Mr Tata recalls his famous forebear's exemplary and rare qualities, genuine reverence fills his voice. Mr Tata is visibly moved when he humbly extols Jamsetji's greatness "for Jamsetji to have conceived these ideas, and more remarkably, clung to them - when India's aspirations for freedom were at their nadir (circa 1880), says much for the uniqueness of the man".

Mr Tata speaks proudly of Jamsetji's great concept of "CREATION OF WEALTH FOR OTHERS", with its basic tenet that those with the opportunities and the skills should use these gifts for the ultimate benefit of others not so advantaged. The same lofty considerations have conditioned "JRD's" whole approach to life and to success in the business field, when over eighty per cent of Tata Sons Limited annual profits go to philanthropic trusts, created since 1932, funding and supporting many and varied public institutions and causes.

Another initiative perceived and adopted by Jamsetji before the turn of the century and strenuously pursued ever since by Mr Tata, was 'worker welfare'. At the time it was voluntarily introduced in the Tata organisation, this practice was virtually unheard of, let alone practised, anywhere in the world. Humanitarianism rates highly with Mr Tata who says "We go to a lot of trouble and expense maintaining equipment, but by some strange quirk, people are apt to forget that our workforces are equally deserving of decent and essential treatment. Allowing people to grow and to thereby gain in self-esteem brings great dividends for everyone". In this regard, the Tata organization has unequivocally matched its words with deeds. How many people are aware that the eight hour working day was inaugurated in all Tata's plants and mines as early as 1912, and that free medical treatment and educational facilities for children, followed in 1917?

In his time JRD advanced Jamsetji's theories and practices many stages further. While careful attention had always been given to 'selecting the right people for the job', under his chairmanship a

PERSONNEL DEPARTMENT was introduced in all of Tata's enterprises, from 1944. The brainchild of JRD this new highly innovative step represented a development heralded all over the world. The complete Indianization of TISCO and of most of the other Tata enterprises in the 1950's has witnessed prosperity and advancement of the Group's activities.

One of Mr Tata's earliest and most distinguished mentors was TISCO's long serving Scottish Managing Director, Mr John Peterson, a man with insight who nurtured him 'in everything that was happening in TISCO'. Such was Mr Tata's preparation for the crucial leadership.

When he took over the mantle of Chief of Tata in 1938, the Second World War was about to happen and India's aspirations for freedom were also taking on an urgent note. He had the credentials for the job. He was youthful, well tried and tested, and he had the reserves of energy and vitality essentially needed to conduct the Group through to a time which was already showing the promise of new and spectacular things for the future, when India was free, and controlled its own affairs.

Mr Tata and other sensible Indian stalwarts, were conscious that much leeway needed to be made up if India's strenuously sought after freedom was not to be illusory - a danger envisaged long before by Jamsetji. Great challenges lay ahead, but equally certain too - extensive problems in finding and following, the right course for India.

Going on in a philosophical mood, Mr Tata marvelled out loud that - ***'of all the creatures God in his wisdom placed upon the earth, to walk, to crawl, fly or swim, it seemed that it was only members of the human race who found it difficult to live in peace and amity with each other'.*** It was Mr Tata's strong belief that to overcome suspicion and hostility between people, and for getting on (amicably) with people, three very important conditions must be present, to wit -

1. Communication. It sometimes will be frank. It will sometimes be contentious. But communication is essential. Issues should be discussed and be properly understood.

2. There should be total honesty and sincerity in all dealings between people.

3. If possible, one should trust and like the people with whom one deals. One should inspire a similar response in others.

Classic confirmation of these beliefs is there for everyone to see, in Mr Tata's own dealings in 1938 with a fervent Workers' Union at the Tata Group's great industrial complex at Jamshedpur. But let Mr Tata tell it in his own words ....

> "The Union Secretary, Mr Abdul Bari, was a man of violent emotions and liable to explode into equally violent anger. At talks one afternoon, as I listened to his angry and quite unjustified onslaught on our Management, I was somewhat upset, to put it mildly.
>
> Yet, when next morning I met him face to face, I found to my surprise that I could not help admiring and even liking this extraordinary man, uncontrolled but totally honest.
>
> As I greeted him with a friendly smile and shook hands with him, I saw a change take place in his face, which I interpreted rightly, as I found out later, as astonishment at finding not only that I felt no resentment for his violent attack on us the previous night, but was genuinely friendly towards him.
>
> We laughed together and when I gently asked him whether we really deserved his lambasting of the previous evening, he replied - 'Tata Saheb, I am sorry, but when I get on a platform I get excited and cannot control myself.'
>
> Mutual esteem blossomed between us at that moment, which lasted until his death in 1947, and that same friendship and mutual esteem has extended through Mr Bari's successors right up to today".

(TISCO has had a strike-free fifty years since, principally due to the unwavering observance to the principles espoused above and faithfully adhered to by all parties).

In his exuberant youth Mr Tata had felt impelled to work for the independence movement (in the late 1920's and early 1930's), but soon came to the sensible realization that politics was not for him. Not so differently from his great precursor Jamsetji, he wisely reasoned

श्री जे. आर. डी. टाटा श्री आर. के भसीन (दायें) के साथ विचार-विमर्श करते हुए

17 (1) Shri J R D Tata discussing with Sh. R K Bhasin (Right)

चित्रों में : बायो मास परियोजना के कार्य और प्रगति के बारे में श्री जे. आर. डी. टाटा को बताते हुए श्री दलजीत सिंह

(2) & (3) Shri Daljit Singh telling Shri J R D Tata regarding the development and progess in the Biomass Project.

लोगों से मिलते हुए श्री जे.आर.डी. टाटा

(4) Shri J R D Tata meeting with people

सभा स्थल पर श्री जे.आर.डी. टाटा का स्वागत किया गया, साथ में दिखाई दे रहे हैं श्री वी.जी. गोपाल (बांये) और श्री रूसी मोदी

(5) Shri J R D Tata welcomed at the meeting, accompanying him is Shri V G Gopal (Left) and Shri Rusi Modi.

that he could achieve a lot more for India and for her people by concentrating his attention upon industry, and by supplying goods and services. Increased work opportunities for Indians would be a flow-on. He acknowledged his heavy management responsibilities and correctly believed that the Tata Group's success would make a significant contribution to a free independent India, and in this, his decision was (subsequently) totally vindicated.

Some ten or so years later (in the early 1940's) his patriotism was to be publicly tested and attested, by another unique event. As a piece of inspired opportunism (but of a patriotic flavour), the BOMBAY ECONOMIC PLAN, initiated by Mr Tata and formulated by him in collaboration with a handful of other prominent business leaders, has a place in Indian history. These men put their great patriotic spirit before everything else in their anxiety to ensure that an 'independent' India got off to the right start. It was a desperate throw, noting Nehru's strong leanings to socialism and to public ownership and that at that stage Britain hadn't given any signs of relinquishing sovereignty over India, when hostilities did cease.

With typical modesty Mr Tata, the prime instigator of the PLAN (it looked at a fifteen year programme which might have signalled a model for later governments to imitate, for it is interesting to note that India has just embarked upon her eighth "Five Year [Economic] Plan"), reserves most praise and congratulations for others, who he says 'shouldered the lion's share of the work'.

The PLAN envisaged growth in the affairs of every Indian, but with the main emphasis upon 'raising the lot of the poorest, and those least able to help themselves'.

How different things might have been for India if the Tata inspired ECONOMIC PLAN had been accepted, can only be a matter for conjecture. At the time, Mr Tata and his colleagues were clearly conscious of the likely confusion (in the choice of prime objectives) which could occur in the euphoric atmosphere which would almost certainly follow the winning of Independence. They had (correctly) wanted to see sensible and balanced targets set and priorities put in their right order, prior to such mood engulfing the new nation.

It is salutary, albeit a touch distressing, to observe (allowing an 'independent' India has since achieved an immense amount against all the odds) that in those critical areas the "BOMBAY PLAN" most wanted to serve, least progress has been made. Mr Tata observed that - "Unfortunately in India, public interest and passions have been aroused more by political, religious, linguistic and philosophical issues than by economic ones, although it is on them (the latter) that the welfare of the people mainly depends". We find an echo of this very same thing happening in western societies today when a singular, often quite out of context 'nothing else except what we are espousing has greater importance' attitude is taken, by interested lobby groups, pushing their own barrows.

Besides being a veritable 'walking encyclopaedia' of much that had happened in this century, in India and around the world, Mr Tata occupies a unique position among Indians in that he has been in a 'highly involved' position to critically observe so much that has taken place in the forty years, since India won her independence.

He nevertheless offers his comments without rancour and is ever ready to forgive human foibles and weaknesses, as 'part of life' and to give praise where it is due. Mr Tata's quiet and deferential manner is an object lesson to all others on how to grow older, gracefully and graciously.

Alluding to India and to her great diversity and the fusion of so many different people of different cultures and languages into what is modern India (from 1947), he observes - "I think people (in other countries) make the mistake of comparing India with other advanced countries, where the assimilation of the various differences which once existed has already taken place, and over many centuries. In reality, India is not simply one nation but a federation of many nations fused together, and where this same process has yet to happen".

It is not everywhere known that prior to 1947 there was no such thing as one single "Indian" nation. While the 'one nation' notion arose out of the British dominion over India, at no time in thousands of years was 'India' under a single rule, a single overall domination, but consisted of many separate autonomous entities.

Mr Tata continues - "I prefer to think of India in the same terms as possibly another great amalgamation that is presently underway - a sort of United States of Europe. With this event the whole process of assimilation of people, language, race and cultures will very well have to begin all over again".

Viewed in this context, I am sure all observers (and less informed arm-chair critics too) will be constrained to regard India with greater tolerance and show more forbearance, realising the magnitude of the tasks before her people and the progress which has already been made towards achieving these objectives.

So much for Mr Jehangir Ratanji Dadabhoy Tata or JRD as he is universally known and respected. A man of humble demeanour he has performed towering deeds, in a country where perversity and adversity has cowered so many others around him. In an ever busy and fulfilling lifetime this man has counted his 'riches' in terms of deeds performed - during his life time, for his fellow countrymen and women. Whatever epitaph is subsequently ascribed to this splendid man, indubitably, in the honest opinion of a great body of his countrymen (and they will not be confined to just the Tata workforce) and admirers in many parts of the world, not only will he be deserving of every word of it, but he will have earned it by his uncompromising and unwavering efforts, for others.

14. Following In Saint Francis Xavier's Footsteps

- Goa, Portugal of the South

Mid-1997 found me again in India, my ninth long visit since 1987. Deliberately choosing to publish in India (I had toiled for nine years putting together a balanced sensible book on India, which I hoped many people in India would find acceptable and enjoyable, and others as well, elsewhere in the world, would wish to read) when one normally resides five thousand miles distant, introduces many uncertain factors not least keeping focused, at both ends!

Yet, it rarely happens (anywhere), that the full extent of any author's high hopes and serious objectives for his or her conscientious endeavours, are properly seen by anyone, let alone their Publishers. In this regard, India was no exception (Literary Agents with the marketing skills of Arundhati Roy's David Godwin, don't emerge very frequently, out of the woodwork. Worse luck).

After re-energizing my associates in Calcutta, Delhi and Bombay (Mumbai), I found myself temporarily free to transfer my thoughts and my energy to discovering and learning more about South India, territory that is largely untrodden and neglected by overseas visitors, and also to a very marked extent by northern Indians, who feel 'strangers' because of the language differences. This divorcement of north and south India, has prevailed for not scores, but thousands of years and Independence has really not brought the two halves of the (vast) country of India, any closer.

In the case of overseas visitors in the main, they head off more for the more publicized areas of India - in north India, to Delhi and Agra, to see the Mughal architectural wonders and west to Rajasthan, there to experience colourful Jaipur, Udaipur and Jaisalmer.

In consequence, a great part of India's superb cultural heritage is rarely experienced. Opinions of today's modern India, frequently,

and a tad regrettably, tend to revolve around Delhi and New Delhi (the latter the creation of the British in this century), Agra and Rajasthan, which in truth amounts to only a bare fragment of the bottomless treasures India enjoys herself and has to show others. Foreigners often cast the wrong description of today's India. It goes very much deeper and wider, and it has very many facets to it, most never experienced or overlooked.

Everywhere on the plains throughout India, June and the months leading up to it, are exceedingly hot and in many parts accompanied by high humidity. Visitors may delay their advent to India and so avoid these searing temperatures, but over one billion Indians suffer it out, uncomplainingly in the main, year in year out, whilst looking forward in anticipation, for the arrival of the south-west Monsoon.

The relief felt by the Indian people when the scarifying rains (in essence, the 'Kiss of Life') do arrive, is enormous. The wonderful rains are joyfully welcomed, a feature of the highly demarcated seasons so pertinent to every Indian's life (and 70% of India's many millions live on the agricultural estate). Every Indian's life is emotionally changed when the rains make their entry. They bring fresh hope to the millions.

The Monsoon has already broken in north-east India (Calcutta), but further north-westwards Delhi was still being scorched. Everywhere bore signs of a long hot dry summer (temperatures up to 45º C), and was parched and wilting.

India is a large country occupying over three million square kilometres (seventh largest in the world) where it is possible to experience all the different variations - of heat, of humidity and of wet (and in the higher climes, cold too) in a short space of time and distance.

Flying south-westwards from Delhi to Bombay (my one luxury in thousands of kilometres traversed by train and in inter-city buses and over many years of travel) I had caught up with the Monsoon, in Bombay (now also called Mumbai). But in spite of four days of consistent heavy and squally downpours, Bombay's fairer features had still managed to shine through, as enthrallingly as ever. It is an interesting city, and being situated on the coast adds greatly to its attraction, but above everything else, it is its star performer, the world famous Taj Mahal Hotel, close by the Gateway of India, which draws the people, and from every section of the population - even if only to gaze upon it in wonderment and with a good deal of awe and respect, remembering its very significant place in India's long struggle for Independence. The 'Taj' at Bombay is a huge magnet, for everyone. Deservedly so, for it is magnificent in all respects.

The short train journey to Pune (south-east of Bombay on the plateau above the Ghats) revived earlier experiences. The usual colourful motley of passengers who ride on all of the sectors of India's extensive railway network, ensured that my curiosity would receive plenty of stimulation on this run as had happened on every other one I had undertaken over the many years, in India.

It happened that my 'next seat companion/traveller' was an experienced bank executive who had served his Indian bank in Brussels. In the course of our short journey he regaled me with reminiscences of his time in that bustling (but extremely elegant) European city and of the opportunities it gave him and his family members, to see more of Europe, and to absorb some of that continent's (different) culture. It was an unexpected pleasure for me to meet such a pleasant interesting person, who had his stories to tell, also.

Arriving at Pune, I was soon whisked back down the line to Bhosari, there to join Indian friends manfully grappling with keeping India's vast public road transport network, 'on the road' and viable. The brief spell at C.I.R.T.'s splendid compound afforded a measure of relaxation before setting out for south India, largely to put that substantially less than widely known and understood tract of country into better perspective. Reaching down to the very toe of India (at Cape Comorin), I was destined to return to Calcutta many weeks later, a chastened but wiser man.

One does not experience the 'real' India, the infinite diversity of India, by only visiting major towns and flying between each of them. Putting up at 5-star hotels, although a grand experience (and perhaps some insurance against developing a rumbling tummy?), often can mean no more than meeting the same folks from home. It is only when one moves around on India's long distance trains and buses, and visits far-flung places, north, south, east and west, that the 'real Indian flavour' comes through. Impromptu, unrehearsed India, experienced at first-hand, allows an interested visitor to learn and enjoy so much more, enabling subsequent sensible comment on India.

It is the great variety of 'human activity' throughout India which contains the most sustaining interest and (abiding) memory of an Indian sojourn (memory of just the 'spectacular' - and at that, often exaggeratedly, though sincerely performed, runs into great competition everywhere, not least with India's predominant visitors, Americans, themselves fed a 'big and always yet bigger' diet, at home).

More deserving attention (leading to greater understanding and more lasting impressions), could derive from a little less of the overdosed publicity and promotion directed at just the 'glitzytrail' - the Delhis, Agra and Jaipur, and to a lesser extent Bombay and Madras, could have better and more beneficial outcomes - for everyone, visitors and Indians. Ordinarily shallow understandings would be honed, subsequently leading to more favourable and sensible, 'India-speak'. A wonderful step in the right direction, for everybody.

Every memorable visit to India, needs time and a deal of 'good value preparatory swot', of present day fact *viz* geographical, understand where you are; India's past cultural history - to provide better understanding of the considerable religious and regional differences; recent political happenings; and last but not least - attention to etiquette and the most important part it plays in India, just as it does everywhere. Giving of respect - especially 'when in Rome', is expected from all, no matter who you are, or where you find yourself.

While unplanned (at the very least, very sketchily made ones, full of 'unknown' gaps) forays into India by rank amateurs may (and inevitably does) produce lots of unusual spills and thrills, better to have some reasonably definite outline of what is intended *before* you arrive!

Heroic descriptions of the 'trials' and 'tortures' you experienced - and survived! may win gasps of awe from your hometown listeners upon your 'miraculous' return. However, an ability to draw their envy, from relating wonderfully unique and interesting experiences might be altogether preferable. Houdini is better left out of it, for India ordinarily deserves better from its visitors.

Millions of passengers ride daily on India's over 65,000 kilometres of rail track, covering many routes which bisect the country, one of Britain's greatest and most useful legacies to India. There are only 'full' trains. Millions more walk (in the rural regions, women especially, will walk many miles every day, collecting firewood; cutting and fetching grass for the family's cow or cows; going to the nearest river or tube-well or village pump, to wash themselves and their clothes, and to fill their clay or brass vessels with water, before lumping it back home, either balanced on their head, or carried in their (strong) arms).

Others travel by slow bullock cart or else pedal their bicycles, with the rider often totally submerged under an array of goods or farm produce. Most people of all travel by bus, whether privately or publicly run, many hundreds of thousands of them, daily. The strain on India's roads is enormous and getting greater, as traffic relentlessly increases contingent with the exploding population.

In many places, the town bus depot is the main focal point, bustling with activity seven days a week. Although bus and route numbers become etched in the minds (and memories) of regular travellers, because of the still high illiteracy in country areas, particularly amongst the older generations, it is customary (everywhere throughout India in fact) for every bus to have its 'spruiker'. The competition for passengers is vigorously contested. People want to hear the route followed, to know they are boarding the correct bus.

Invariably, each buses' one or two conductors hang in/out of every bus calling the names of the places it is proceeding to. Their other function is to 'signal', by hand slapping on the side of the bus, to the driver when it is clear to move on. An ingenious method, for otherwise his vision is usually totally obscured, and he would have no way of knowing when he could do so safely. Complemented by his 'navigators' little time is lost at intermediate stops. Few buses ever come to a full stop. Women struggle on, and off, as best they can. Little quarter is given, but the urge to 'get on with the journey', seems paramount with all bus crews.

But now it's all aboard for Goa and the prospect that awaits us - lovely fresh uncluttered beaches amidst a tropical paradise. That is the expectation. Reality would bring its surprises and its disappointments too.

Our Kadamba Transport Corporation's bus trundles on through the night, interrupted every few hours for occasional 'comfort' stops, and taken in what often appears to be in the middle of nowhere.

The road journey from Pune to Panaji, the capital of Goa and the erstwhile seat of the Portuguese colonists (up to 1961) would occupy fifteen hours.

Daylight, when it comes, is always a relief and so it was now. Our tortuous overnight journey through the hilly Western Ghats is nearing its end. Leaving behind the rugged undulating countryside, the narrow bitumenized winding road leads down to the flatter coastal strip, passing numerous sparsely populated agricultural communities as it goes. Every arable bit of country is used, and lush coconut palms, and *plantains* (bananas) abound, interspersed with plots of contoured rice paddies.

For much of this time it has been raining. Eventually, as we drop down from the last hill, the vast expanse of the broad Mandavi River comes into view. Goa, the smallest of the twenty five Indian states occupies just 3,702 square kilometres (one tenth of one percent of the total area of India). Most of its one million population is concentrated, along with its commercial activity, on the island of Ilhas which lies between the Mandavi and Zuari Rivers. Long dual parallel bridges cross the Mandavi connecting Panaji with the mainland. The older narrow bridge being replaced, had apparently to be kept in service, when it was found that the newer bridge was deficient in load-bearing capabilities.

Long before the arrival in India of seafaring Europeans, the west coast of India was regularly visited, for many centuries, by Arabian and Persian merchants. Their rakish-bowed dhows carried rich loads of commodities between India, Africa and Arabia and to other Persian Gulf countries.

Calling at Mozambique en route to India, Vasco Da Gama and his men were regaled with many stories from the Arabian seafarers (and as well were shown factual evidence) of the 'rich treasures' plentifully available in the India they regularly visited. It is easy to imagine the excitement of the Portuguese, contemplating the treasures in store for them when they reached their ultimate destination Kerala, on the south Indian Malabar coast.

The great Portuguese discoveries of the fifteenth century, which began with a period of gradual exploration down the west African coast, eventually led to the rounding of the Cape of Good Hope.

18. Beautiful beach of Goa.

Bartolomeu Dias named the cape on the extreme south-west tip of the African continent during his voyage in 1488, which reached farther east along the base of Africa to Algoa Bay, before he turned around and returned to Portugal. His reconnaissance paved the way for the voyage of Vasco Da Gama, the first (known) European to round the Cape, ultimately reaching Calicut (now named Kozhikode) on 20 May, 1498.

At Calicut, the weary but incredulous Portuguese stepped into a fascinating new world. The centuries-old market place was bursting with all the exotic merchandise they had been told about, and which they could only previously dream about, fine silks and porcelains; pearls, sapphires and rubies; gold and silver; and large warehouses filled with all manner of spices - cloves, nutmeg, cinnamon, pepper, ginger and other fragrant spices, which for centuries had only been available to Europeans, through Venetian and Genoese merchants.

The Portuguese could now put all that behind them. They had found a direct sea route to India, and could obtain the same riches at source, thus eliminating the Italian middle-men. The amazed Portuguese exhibited feelings of having discovered untold riches, making their long and arduous voyage worthwhile. They could even begin to contemplate the tremendous reception they would get when they successfully negotiated the voyage back to Lisbon, laden with all these marvellous goods.

Meantime, the Portuguese mariners were free to rejoice at successfully completing the first organised European voyage to the southern oceans via the Cape of Good Hope.

Buoyed by the hopes and expectations of their countrymen, the four-ship flotilla led by Vasco Da Gama in his flagship "Sao Gabriel" had sailed from Lisbon on 8 July, 1497. Modern day counterparts of this epic adventure, might reside in the first expeditions to the unknown North and South Poles undertaken in the early part of the twentieth century.

Great hopes and optimism, mixed with apprehension of the task ahead, must have been present in the hearts and minds of all who sailed from Lisbon. Such factors would have been heightened during the longest and loneliest leg of the entire journey – that bit after leaving the Cape Verde Islands and before reaching St Helena Bay in southern Africa.

Sailing on a 'never before taken' south-westerly course deep into the vast blue emptiness of the Atlantic Ocean, Vasco's four ships, were separated thousands of miles from all land and from all assistance, for over three months, which must have seemed (to the lone sailors) an eternity.

How very removed and different from today's position when constantly enhancing and improving communications systems of all descriptions keep a track of a ship's movements wherever it may be, out on the world's oceans. How Vasco Da Gama might also have longed for the 'yet to come' inventions of John Harrison (1769) and of Guglielmo Marconi (1899), both of which hugely reduced the isolation experienced by the intrepid mariners of yesteryear.

Great trust clearly reposed in Vasco Da Gama's immense (and instinctive) navigational skills and extraordinary seamanship and leadership, brought the flotilla safely to Calicut ten months after setting out from Lisbon.

As a 'trailblazer' of the greatest renown, Vasco Da Gama stands supreme and alongside, Drake and Magellan. The great Portuguese mariner made two more voyages from Europe to India, dying in Cochin, in 1524.

After early beginnings in Calicut (modernday Kozhikode), the first Portuguese penetration of Goa, situated several hundred miles to the north of Calicut, occurred in 1510 under Alfonso de Albuquerque.

Thrown out three months later, Albuquerque returned soon afterwards, setting in train Portuguese rule which continued (with minor Dutch intervention) until late 1961. Goa was incorporated into the Indian Union in 1962. Statehood was conferred in 1987.

A feature of erstwhile Portuguese settlement outside Portugal, and there is general evidence of it in every place they colonised in India, in Asia (Macau), and in Africa (Mozambique and Angola) - is or was, the 'stand-still' progress. Apart from trade aspects and most of all - religion, the Portuguese did little to advance the secular education and lifestyles of their subjects. Modern day 'Lotus Lands', life went on in very unhurried terms in all their overseas possessions, being perhaps a reflection in part, of a Portugal homeland exhausted by all its great enterprising ways and activity centuries before, in its former glory days.

Beaches aside (and Goa boasts a succession of them), the major factors governing the affairs of present day Goa, centre around several things - the Christian religion; the State's prolific and rich body of iron ore; and agricultural products, in particular, cashew nuts.

It is the influence of the great Spanish evangelist Saint Francis Xavier, which is all-pervading. Sometimes confused with St. Francis of Assisi, who founded the Order of the Franciscans about 1210, St Francis Xavier who was canonised on 12 March, 1622 by Pope Gregory XIII was a founding member (with St. Ignatius Loyola) of the Society of Jesus - the Jesuits, in 1534.

The Christian revivalist fervour which gripped the European mainland nations - Spain, France, Portugal and Italy in the fifteenth and sixteenth centuries was conveyed to the Asia/Pacific region, by the Portuguese (to south-west India, Goa and far down to Trivandrum), and Spanish (the Philippines) mariners. Zealously pursuing the conversion of the local populations, the spreading of Roman Catholicism ranked equally with spices and other commodities, in the hearts and minds of the Portuguese and Spanish, of that and later eras.

The ceremony and colourful display found in Hindu worship intrigued the original Portuguese seafarers, inhibited by the language barrier. What they saw they likened to a form of Christianity. In reverse, the Indian population greeted the Portuguese reverence of idols as not so visually different from Hindu religious display. Paradoxically, these reciprocal misinterpreted positions, shielded Vasco's men from belligerent reception and as well created the fertile atmosphere for the peaceful introduction of Roman Catholicism into India.

The then Portugal (and Europe) was a seriously religious society and conversion of their newly settled territories provided fresh fields to capture. Francis Xavier (he would not be canonized until 1622) began his mission in India - in Goa, in 1542. A Basque from a noble family in the Kingdom of Navarra (now a part of Spain), he had come under the influence of a fellow Basque - Inigo Loyola (later St. Ignatius Loyola), when they were both studying in Paris. The Society of Jesus, which they co-founded, today reaches to many places around the world.

Especially revered in Goa, the relics of the great missionary Saint repose in the Mastricillian Silver Casket which rests on the tomb in the alcove to the right of the altar, in the famous Bom Jesus (good Jesus) Basilica, the shrine dedicated to St Francis Xavier, ten miles off from Panaji, on the road east, to Ponda (old Goa).

The Basilica built nearly 400 years ago, and consecrated in 1605, is a vast imposing red structure, constructed from laterite stone blocks. An unusual material, formed by weathering of rocks in tropical regions, laterite blocks are widely used throughout Goa as a prime construction component, for fences walls and buildings. Extremely deceptive in appearance and looking very like flecked red spongy chunks, laterite stone has a surprising consistency. As heavy as lead, working with laterite calls for considerable physical strength.

The external walls of Bom Jesus Basilica show only minor signs of deterioration even after four centuries have elapsed, and after enduring as many wet and humid seasons, conditions which elsewhere in the tropics have caused havoc and reduced buildings to rubble. The same Bom Jesus Basilica seems destined to greet many more pilgrims and overseas visitors as they journey to Goa, to pay their respects to the memory of St. Francis Xavier.

Denial of self, the touchstone of Francis Xavier, Inigo Loyola, and Francis Bernadone, has been similarly demonstrated in more recent times on the other side of India, in and from Calcutta, by the lately deceased Agnes Gonxha Bojaxhiu (Mother Teresa).

To a greater extent than perhaps any other place in India, religion in almost equal proportion - Hinduism and Roman Catholicism - dominates in Goa. Keeping pace with the reverence shown to Bom Jesus Basilica and to the other ornate Catholic edifices in Goa, is the equal drawing power of the region's Hindu Temples. Two such splendid Temples, might be considered companion shrines to Bom Jesus Basilica, located as they are in close proximity.

One of these, Mangeshi Temple pays tribute to the Hindu God - Mangesh. The other is Mardol Temple, which with its magnificent brass lamps reveres the Goddess Mahalsa. The Goan respect for all forms of worship exemplifies the tolerance and community harmony that is followed by the majority of individual Indians, everywhere in India.

There has been a big spurt in recent years to promote Goa as a major tourist attraction. There is point and merit in doing this, in as much as Goa represents the newest (from the viewpoint of 'recovered' territory) piece of the Indian Republic. Isolated for centuries due to Portuguese occupation, not a lot of Indians know much about it, or have visited there, also due in part to its remoter geographical location.

While a mad rush of real estate developers have descended on Goa in recent years and despoiled the landscape to some extent, (rampant, uncontrolled, hectic development can bring unwanted/ undesirable results) all is still not lost if arrestation happens and properly managed development is substituted. As a quieter haven, still less congested than much else in India, its appeal will strengthen, but particularly for these attributes, for apart from its fame as the focal point for Francis Xavier's crusades, it contains very little else of historic interest.

Its hedonistic appeal for many will be its long string of beaches up and down the length of its Arabian Sea shoreline. Beyond commercial activities, yachting/sailing and sea bathing have never been significant pastimes of Indians. Hardly indulged in, even by those who live by the sea, for whatever reasons, Indians are not water people, beyond dipping their toes in the ocean. With increasing affluence perhaps more pleasurable (individual) pursuits will induce entrepreneurs to promote these kinds of activities. Seriousness still pervades most hours of an Indian's life, wherever he lives or whatever he does for his livelihood.

Leading up to its return to India (India has been taking back its own country for years, or acting in a *de facto* relationship the British did it for them - to wit from the Dutch, the Danes, The French and from the British themselves, and ultimately Goa from the Portuguese) many of the old Portuguese Goan dynastic families uprooted from Goa, settling either in Bombay or in other former or present Portuguese territories, elsewhere in the world.

Apart from old residential quarters (Portuguese style) in each of Panaji, Marmagao and Vasco, and several other ornate period administrative buildings, and churches, not much of hundreds of years of Portuguese occupation is in evidence. The Portuguese were neither showy nor energetically progressive colonizers, anywhere, or everywhere they went.

All the various colonizers around the tropics in the sixteenth, seventeenth and eighteenth centuries followed a tendency to introduce their own home-style living fashion in their foreign settlements. British settlements feature large manor-like constructions similar to what they knew (and which some) had enjoyed back in Britain. Less rich nations like The Netherlands, Denmark and Portugal, built their smaller semi-detached dwellings, wherever they went. Building replicas of home would clearly have stirred nostalgic feelings removed as the early colonists were (especially in the age of sail) from their homelands thousands of miles off.

Some of the foreign architecture suited admirably, (even if only by coincidence), but most of the small boxshaped dwellings transplanted for eastern living were originally designed to fit the less expansive and colder European conditions. Accordingly these sort of constructions were wholly unsuited to the tropics. Differing ideas on assimilation with local populations in overseas territories also formed part of the early decision-making of the various European colonists.

The ore-loading port facilities at Vasco highlight the importance of mining to Goa's economy. Exceedingly rich deposits of iron ore enable its major mining company Sesa Goa, to export over 32 million tonnes of ore each year. Visiting their active open-cut mines in the middle of the Monsoon season was a blessing - no dust!

The world-scale open-cut mining operations in the deep pits at Sonshi and Codli come to a stop during the wet season, a time also when large scale rehabilitation vegetation programmes on the used sites at Orasso, Dongon and Sanquelin, receive further extensive attention. Sesa Goa's deep commitment to environmental afforestation programmes has drawn much praise from many quarters around the world.

A unique feature of the iron ore industry in Goa, is the economic utlilization of its natural waterways to transport iron ore from mine sites and treatment plants to point of loading at Vasco. The Company's large fleet of massive barges has become part of the river scene in Goa. The largest ships to enter Indian waters, the huge bulk ore carriers using Goa, are loaded out to sea from smaller transhipper vessels.

From being a virtually unknown piece of the sub-continent, shielded from much, if any exposure at all, to the outside world (except for its alleged smuggling activities, especially during Maharastha's prohibition times - suggestions of there being a Johnny Walker factory buried in the sands of Juhu beach could be highly apocryphal?) by the neutral status of Portugal, in the several world wars, modern Goa, the newest of the Indian States, is slowly opening up to others - in India, and elsewhere in the world.

The exploits in March 1943 of the brave veterans from Calcutta's erstwhile Light Horse Club in silencing the German's destructive radio signals from their beleaguered ships trapped in Marmagao harbour, still faintly echo across Goa's placid inland waters.

But it is time now to repair to the wonderful old Portuguese hostelry - The Mandovi, by the estuary terrace, there to enjoy some *chorisum* and a Goan peg of the all curable and famous local liqueur, *feni* - smooth as aniseed and distilled from cashew pods.

Adios Goa

15. The Mystique Of Mysore

- Coorg (Kodagu) to Seringapatam

The modern realigned and renamed south Indian state of Karnataka has post-Indian Independence origins. Several stage changes, ending with the States Reorganisation Act, 1956 re-drew the composition and borders of the previous territorial boundaries to form the reconstituted and renamed States of Karnataka, Tamil Nadu and Kerala. In the new jurisdiction, the old states of Hyderabad, Mysore, Madras and Travancore, faded into history.

Except for those areas (of each of the three States) to the west of the Western Ghats and bordering on the Arabian Sea, the new States all suffer from inadequate all-year-round water supply, in the larger land mass to the east of the divide. So differently blessed to much of the northern part of India, due to the beneficial effect of the mightiest of all watersheds (with apologies to the Andes) the incredibly vast Himalaya Range, water is a crucial ingredient in the lives of all the people of these heavily populated States. There is clear evidence of this in the much poorer and tougher farming conditions found everywhere throughout Tamil Nadu, and particularly noticeable at the end of every hot, dry summer.

Needing to recognize the ever increasing problem of adequate water supply, and coping as well with the concomitant accelerating number of users, a new direction is emerging. New strategies are being engaged designed to deliver the optimum result, for all the people. As everyone will know, this is not just a problem for India, but similar concerns relate in many of the drier (more populated) countries around the world, where conservation and recycling becomes more urgent, more acute, as requirements multiply amidst ever changing weather patterns.

Agriculture requires a lot of water. India (and Karnataka State) contains a very high proportion of basic (subsistence) agriculture. In Karnataka State, and in many places everywhere, in India and in other countries similarly placed (relatively poorly blessed with water and with large increasing populations) urgent and positive measures are being introduced to take some of the load/the strain, off farming.

Besides water conservation and improved farming techniques, alternative investment in industry is a key priority for the Karnataka Government, to increase revenue and for the wider employment of its labour force.

Clearly seeing the problem, Karnataka (like its neighbouring State, Tamil Nadu, also beset with an abnormally high agricultural population) is hastening to develop substantial 'sunrise' industries, particularly in the services sector. Already, in the last 5-10 years, much progress has been achieved, especially in the burgeoning world computer industry.

The growth in this technical industry at its centre in India, Bangalore, has been phenomenal. Indian youth, long blessed with mathematical and scientific skills, has seized its opportunity and Karnataka's computer advances rank with the world's most prolific, and best. They are set to take over world leadership as the next millennium dawns. Already data for many of the world's leading companies - Siemens and many other European majors, as well as many of the world's top airlines, process their requirements in India, much of it around Bangalore.

So much for Bangalore's great strides forward. For us bus travellers the passing scene remains almost wholly rural. Having left Panaji (Goa) behind the previous afternoon, and travelling overnight up and through the hilly terrain–rain still accompanying us, bumpy narrow roads necessitating frequent slowing down and pulling aside to permit room for the endless succession of lumbering heavy transport vehicles to pass in the other direction (the condition of roads and their inadequacy denies India any hope at present of introducing on any scale, articulated semi-trailer transportation. Meanwhile, Tata and Leyland trucks do the work) - the awakening next day brings us to the plateau which surrounds Karnataka's capital, and by far major centre, Bangalore.

Extensive outcrops of Pre-Cambrian rock abound everywhere, in whichever direction one looks. In what would represent an unusual and very different scene anywhere, it all seems so pre-historic. One might easily believe one had entered upon another planet, for all around is arid, and a picture of desolation, and almost completely bereft of any thriving vegetation of any kind. It bears all the appearance of Flintstone country.

But we should not forget that we are in a land where necessity creates ingenuity, or if not always that, remunerable work, however small or unlasting, for its huge body of manual workers. And so in India where (nearly) everything has a use, or fills a basic need, or serves a particular function, the gigantic piles of huge granite boulders, many of them rising hundreds of feet into the sky, provide a source of material for construction uses and not least, hewn out stone fence posts, an article which is peculiar to south India.

Fencing material of whatever kind, -wood, wire, steel etcetera – is either not possible to supply or is prohibitively expensive. In consequence, the many tens of millions of individual farm holdings throughout India are mainly unfenced. A nightmare perhaps, for strangers, in identifying individual plots, but perhaps also an environmental blessing, considering the sheer extent of fencing which would arise and the (possible) hodge podge of different materials used. The orderly nature of India's vast farmlands is thus preserved.

Unlike the mess that is allowed to accumulate in cities and towns (and most Indians have become so used to the sight, that seemingly they've become oblivious to the presence of these nauseous junk piles), India's rural areas are neat, clean and well-ordered. It would be rare indeed to see on any agricultural plot in India, disused dilapidated and rusting discarded vehicles and farm equipment. This position is undoubtedly assisted by the fact that it was never there in the first place.

Karnataka's extensive stone quarries, and the chipped out rough-cast stone fenceposts they provide, appear all over the State. Besides its treasury of geologically famous Pre-Cambrian rock outcrops, Karnataka rates as one of India's foremost mining regions. Considerable quantities of chromite, magnesite, mica, bauxite and high-grade iron ore are mined. Importantly too, Karnataka is one of India's principal gold producers, from the Kolar Goldfields away to the east of Bangalore.

In Karnataka, one is in the deep south of India and in the heartland of Dravidia. Apart from the ancient cultures of Harappa and Mohenjo-daro, it is the oldest inhabited part of India, where the people are of a different ethnic character, and who speak languages, no way akin to those of northern India.

Brahmanical traditions are still practised and ritual observances more strictly maintained and followed, than happens in other parts of India. In today's nineties' terms, Karnataka is therefore unique, in that it combines some of the oldest and also much of the newest, that present-day India has to offer. Hi-tech industries centred on Bangalore, are on par with or ahead of the rest of the world.

As well, Karnataka has a very large and highly efficient, silk industry. Not something the British took much interest in (instead, looking to China for its needs), silk production was first introduced on a commercial scale by the redoubtable Tipu Sultan, one of India's earliest entrepreneurial 'businessmen', besides benevolent leader and revered fighter for democratic rights.

A twentieth century constructive thinker before his time, Tipu needing funds to buy arms (from the French) for his troops mounting a strong defence against, the forces of Cornwall and Wellesley, looked to develop a high-value low-volume exchange commodity, and hit on (sericulture) silk, which was highly sought after in Europe. By the time Tipu was defeated and killed in battle in 1799, the Indian silk industry was firmly established. It is now the world's second largest producer (after China).

Nowadays, producing and processing more than half of India's silk yarn, from four commercially viable varieties of silk - *mulberry, tassar, eri (or endi) and muga,* the Bangalore silk exchange and its extensive retail markets attract buyers from around the world. The great variety of magnificent silk garments made and displayed for sale, is stunning.

Known, not so many decades ago, as primarily retirees' territory (pleasantly cool all year round, on the higher slopes), Bangalore has metamorphosed as the scientific capital of India, with the computer software industry leading the way. Slow (or impeded?) in coming, a hundred years before, Indians themselves had begun the process, choosing Bangalore because of its congenial climate.

The great and illustrious Indian patriot and industrialist, the visionary Jamsetji Tata, had been chiefly instrumental in creating the Indian Institute of Science, in Bangalore before the turn of the twentieth century. Another great Indian, the renowned physicist and Nobel Laureate (1930), Sir Chandrasekhara Venkata Raman, was to become its energetic Director and huge promoter in India, of scientific education and endeavour, from 1933.

The I.I.S. together with other complementary, higher learning Institutes created also in Bangalore, foreshadowed the inevitable position now enviably occupied by world-standard computer technology-occupied, Bangalore, competing on equal terms with the rest of the world.

A city with a purpose (there can be no doubt about this) and eyeing major world goals, the Bangalore of today attracts the finest and best young Indians eager to acquire the learning and great skills, gaining kudos for India, and exciting and lucrative career opportunities for themselves (and not solely confined to India) working side by side with the best craftsmen and women in India, and elsewhere in the world, notably in the U.S.A.

The dreamy world of the retiree is indeed no more (or only a small part of Bangalore's present-day attraction). Contrarily, the business success of Bangalore will markedly contribute to India's progress, in the next decades, achieved through the minds, and metaphorically 'on the back' of India's big number of highly qualified service industry technicians.

Arriving at the bustling bus-station finding the 'next connection' invariably posed a problem. I am sure they won't mind me saying so, but after many decades in India, taking road directions from Indians is 'accident -prone' - a hundred metres extends to several kilometres, and ten minutes stretches to an hour. But at Bangalore a miraculously quick transfer is effected, and in just three hours we shall pull into the bus station in the town of Mysore.

Leaving the environs of Bangalore behind us, the rural scene right through to Mysore teemed with activity and interest. Although a Sunday (every day is just another working day for rural Indians), cattle had to be fed, fields needed to be ploughed ready for the 'expected' rains and the next planting, crops needed to be harvested and sent to market. Great fields of sugar cane stretched away into the distance. The whole scene was one of positive activity and promise.

The city of Mysore is a very pleasing place. Largely still uncongested, and in relatively recent times, well planned (the hand of M.Vishveswaraya in evidence) and laid out, the traffic moves steadily along wide streets and capacious roundabouts, in place at many major intersections.

The ruling Maharajahs of Mysore did a lot more for their subjects in welfare terms, and in providing congenial living spaces, than did many of their counterparts in the other 550 or so Princely - States around India.

Mysore also enjoyed the distinction of having some talented (brilliant, methodical, far-seeing) bureaucrats, allowed a fairly liberal hand at effecting sound works, for everyone, by the ruling enlightened Wodiyar dynasty.

Several of these distinguished Dewans (a sort of P.M.) did superb things for Mysore, notably Sir Mirza Ismail and the most extraordinarily accomplished man, Sir Mokshagundam Vishveswaraya.

Sir Mirza's most lasting (and wonderful) contribution are the superb Brindavan Gardens, a short distance from Mysore. The beautifully terraced gardens with their accompanying illuminated musical fountains, have given great pleasure to a great many people - local and visitors.

His successor Sir Mokshagundam put his clever hand and brain to many things. Chief Engineer of Mysore from 1909, the marvellous (and so strategically important and invaluable) Krishnarajasagara Reservoir, nineteen kilometres distant from Mysore, adjacent to the confluence of the three rivers - the Cauvery, Hemavathi and the Lakshmanathirtha, is the greatest and most lasting monument to his vast and lengthy public duty, to the people of Mysore.

Dewan of Mysore State from 1912, he exerted tremendous influence during his long and meritorious lifetime (he lived past 100 years, and was still very actively engaged in public works at ninety) across all topics - his speciality, water engineering of all types;

education; steelworks; town planning (his services were hugely sought after and used in many States of India, wherever there was a Civil Engineering problem - Hyderabad owes much to him for fixing their flooding problems); railways; the automobile industry; the aircraft industry, and there are many other areas where his skills and intellect, were co-opted.

Sir Mokshagundam's credo - EDUCATE: INVESTIGATE: ORGANIZE - holds just as true today, a beckoning shining beacon for India's budding youth, waiting to take their country into the twenty first century. He spurned ostentation and devoted his life to the betterment of his people and of his country, India.

Full of wonderful things, the most thrilling and appealing (to the senses, to one's imagination) of all, at least to your narrator, would be Mysore's association with one of India's greatest patriots and warriors, Tipu Sultan, himself a celebrated son of a great father, Hyder Ali.

To visit nearby Seringapatam is to step back into pulsating history. The majestic setting of the Gumbaz - the Mausoleum of Tipu Sultan, and of his mother Fatima Begum, and of his equally illustrious father Hyder Ali - is magnificent. Possibly on par as a wonderful spectacle with the superb Mughal offering, the incomparable Taj Mahal and Nur Jahan's beautiful testimonial to her father on the opposite bank of the Jamuna, the Itimad-ud-Daula, both at Agra in north India. An impressive square-shaped mausoleum with beautiful ivory-inlaid doors and black marble pillars set in a beautifully maintained garden-park, the Gumbaz was built by Tipu in 1784.

In between the Gumbaz and near Tipu's fort in Seringapatam, lies his smallish and quite humble summer palace called Daria Daulat. A wooden edifice, it is a striking example of Saracenic architecture. Its entire walls, inside and outside (along the covered verandahs) are covered with mural paintings of battle scenes and flowery designs. After Tipu's death, the future Duke of Wellington used the Daria Daulat, as his field headquarters. To Karnataka's credit, the whole complex is quite splendidly up-kept to the present day.

When Tipu's father was killed in battle in the Second Mysore War with the Mahrathas, the son came to an armistice seeking to allay more problems, with the British. But regrettably for Tipu and his people, this did not last.

Never wholly comfortable with such an alliance, and sensing betrayal, and that new political developments were occurring favouring total British control (of India), Tipu Sultan confronted the British Forces. His martial instincts and strong belief in Indian freedom, led his to his clear decision that liberty was more precious than life and that death should be preferred to dishonour and political servitude.

More bloody battles ensued, during the Third and Fourth (the last one) Mysore Wars. For a good part of this time Tipu and his loyal forces held their own.

But the larger and better equipped British forces now under the command of Sir Arthur Wellesley, (brother of the third Governor General of Fort William in Bengal, Richard, the Marquis of Wellesley. 1798-1805) and later to achieve lasting fame as the victor over Napoleon at Waterloo in 1815 as the Duke of Wellington, ultimately proved too powerful. Tipu Sultan was killed in battle at Seringapatam in 1799, and his once splendid Palace thereafterwards summarily dismantled and/or destructed.

Only remnants of Tipu's beautiful Palace and famous Seringapatam Fort remain today. The Fort's Mosque *Masjid-e-ala* with its two tall graceful minarets still stands and overlooks the town. Also carefully preserved in seemingly original condition, are the dungeons where particular English officers and others were held captive, in retaliation for the holding by the British, of two of Tipu's own young sons - the subject matter of a famous painting, in 1792 by a British artist, Robert Home.

A significant and fair minded observer of the final two (Third and Fourth) MysoreWars, and personally taken with the heroism and integrity of Tipu Sultan, Home's magnificently illustrated book, called *SELECTED VIEWS IN MYSORE, THE COUNTRY OF TIPPOO SULTAN; FROM DRAWINGS TAKEN ON THE SPOT; WITH HISTORICAL DESCRIPTIONS* and published in London in 1794 by Robert Bowyer, will captivate (if not-thrill) interested persons. Robert Home remained in India, dying there in 1834.

The dungeons (once all enclosed (?) but now, partly open to the elements) situated alongside the perimeter wall and the nearby river, retained meaning for the British for as long as they maintained their suzerainty over India (making political capital is no new modern

19. A herd of elephants feeding on bamboo foliage.

invention. It has been around for a long time, being especially used in most defensive situations), just as their preservation today serves the Indian retaliatory mind-set, in a non-physical and non-malicious way.

Pride is a valuable ingredient in the kit of every nation and today's Indians could be excused for 'putting their own spin' on the Seringapatam period, for Tipu Sultan was (and is today, very much so) truly adored, and held up as a great man, and a worthy son of an equally celebrated father, Hyder Ali.

In today's *'democratic - everyone is entitled to be heard, equal rights for the under-dog world'*, much that has gone before is being challenged. No one, no nation is spared. But giving proper and sensible regard to past actions requires some restraint and clear sense and judgement, taking in the whole circumstances of the times.

The glamorous and valorous aspects of colonialism (instance as well, post-Apartheid difficulties in South Africa) may no longer overwhelm the fuller picture. Everyone may agree that theoretically forgiveness is a wonderfully qualitative virtue. It is, but in practice, overcoming great hurt and suffering and the frailties of human kind do not always allow such to happen. The Holocaust is another never-ending situation for many people, whose horrific personal experiences and grief will never be assuaged while they live.

The ultra forgiving qualities exhibited by Indian people as a whole, are in many ways, unique. Often mis-read, and mis-interpreted unfavourably (frequently considered by some foreigners as a character weakness), this viewpoint appears to lack all validity.

The quality of forgiveness inherent in nearly all Indians (a lifetime of association with Indians in their country could never convince the author otherwise. There is too much proof of its real sincerity to judge otherwise) goes back to its origins thousands of years ago. Unquestionably, today's Indians should start challenging baseless foreign dogmatism based on superficial knowledge and non-existent personal experience, in India and widely, in that country.

Worn out, frayed anachronistic clichés have seen their day. Overworked outdated mass verdicts too. Time for all of us, to consign all stereotyped labels and opinions to the rubbish basket, where they belong. Only then can judgements have any value, any merit. We must all think for ourselves and rely upon what our own experiences tell us.

Coming to realistic (and truthful) grips with past happenings in colonial territories - in particular, the French still cling on tenaciously to many of theirs - understandably must present a poser, for current generations. Any serious-minded young Britisher wandering around India today might reasonably have conflicting thoughts and feelings, *vis-a-vis* past events that took place in India, during its occupation.

Putting in proper perspective the multifarious commemorative plaques and shrines that remain in place (within Christian churches and graveyards, etcetera, throughout India) which laud past gallantry of their own countrymen in *subduing* Indian resistance, to British occupation of what was 'their country', calls for much understanding. He or she may, as a result, think more deeply of the Indian's inordinate capacity to keep matters in their right perspective, and to forgive.

We may not be able to change a single thing that has happened or any of the many wrongs that were committed, but a better sense of right, and of responsibility, could be embraced by all parties. Astonishingly, even surprisingly (certainly disappointingly) nothing Britain initiated in celebration of India's 50 years Independence, contained even the merest suspicion of forgiveness. And the Indian people meekly accepted it all. Many of them, but not all.

Such is the message arising from Seringapatam, and Tipu Sultan. Interestingly the 1999 Edinburgh Festival intends featuring Tipu Sultan upon the 200th anniversary of his death, at Seringapatam, at the hands of the British. It will be intriguing to observe how they arrange (or re-arrange) history? Hopefully, bygones will be bygones, and the admirable patriotic qualities of Tipu will be given precedence. A hearty cheer for the Scots.

Between the old Fortress Palace (*Lall Mahal* - Red Palace) at one end of the island, and the Gumbaz, at the eastern end of the island, lies Tipu's summer palace, Daria Daulat. Built of wood and completed in 1789 and standing solitary in its own spacious grounds, it represents a fine example of Saracenic architecture. Its walls, externally (within an encircling verandah) and internally as well are covered with murals depicting - battle scenes of various campaigns fought by father and son.

One could dwell for long at Seringapatam, for the atmosphere (and what it all represents - for India) is so compelling. Heroic human courage is written over everything. Some Indians knew what was going on and did something about it!

Interest rich Mysore has many excitingly interesting treasures with which to fascinate and regale its visitors. The Palace compound is its prime jewel and drawcard. Visited in glorious sunshine it is a wonderful spectacle, in all its parts, and there are four particular segments, five if you count the splendid gardens and superb perimeter walls and gateways (as one).

The present Palace is relatively new, being completed only in 1912, replacing on the same site, a succession of palaces of much less flamboyance and size. At the time of India's Independence (15.8.1947), there were 554 so-called Princely States. Mysore was one of the largest, along with Hyderabad, and territorially it and Hyderabad, were initially left untouched in the reorganising/integrating process undertaken with the rest (the democratic part) of India. Changes to State boundaries were subsequently implemented - under the States Reorganisation Act, 1973, the State of Mysore was renamed Karnataka.

No 'Indian State' (*i.e.* Princely State) as such, existed after the Indian Constitution came into force - on 26 January, 1950. The former rulers lost their territories and the right to rule and administer them. They were left only a recognition of the original title, a Privy Purse, their private properties and a few privileges. From 1971, recognition granted to Rulers of Indian States ceased and privy purses were abolished.

The last (and twenty fifth) Maharajah of Mysore was Sri Jaya Chamaraja Wadiyar (b.1919) who had reigned from 1940. He had succeeded the most popular and the most benevolent of Maharajahs, his father Krishna Raja Wadiyar IV, who had presided during a most crucial time in British-India relations, from 1895.

The Wodiyar dynasty begun in 1399, by Yaduraya (Adi Yadurayaru), survived many turbulences to what pops up often in Indian (eastern) history, lack of male heirs and other problems, which influenced the manner and choice of succession. Deposed during the time of Hyder Ali and Tipu Sultan, and restored to power (by the British) in 1799, the glamour and fortunes associated with the Wodiyar dynasty will continue to entertain and enthral, well into the future.

The Western Ghats away to the west impede easy access to Karnataka's coastal ribbon of interesting country, dominated by the coastal city of Mangalore. Nearer to Mysore and nestling in the Ghats on the eastern slopes is the picturesque 'highland country' of Coorg, aptly named ' the Scotland of India'. Undulating topography and lush vegetation nurture a flourishing agro-industry of coffee, copra, cashew, cardamom, rubber and - citrus.

The home of *Kodavas,* these hardy proud sons of the soil are amongst the finest soldiers produced anywhere in India. Coorg (renamed Kodagu) district has earned the reputation of being 'the land of Generals and oranges". Marvellous retirement territory for India's soldiers, only sudden illness befalling the great man, prevented your author from visiting India's former Commander-in-Chief Field Marshal Cariappa, at his beautiful home in Mercara (renamed Madikeri). The Field Marshal has since passed on. A fine man amongst a host of good men hailing from Coorg.

Coffee from around Coorg, Hassan and Chikmagalur forms the bulk of India's coffee exports and is considered amongst the world's best. Today, on average, India produces 200,000 metric tonnes of the finest quality coffee - both Arabica and Robusta - annually. Visit any business establishment anywhere in India, and almost without fail, you will be invited to partake of a cup of tea or coffee. Besides the pleasure of extending this courtesy, Indians are great supporters of their home industries.

There are many interesting (novel) excursions one can take if one delays one's departure from Mysore - to the Biligiranga Hills to view the thick forests of teak and sandalwood, and the Ranganatha Temple, or to the picturesque Nagarhole National Park to see the animals, birds and reptiles, or to Sravana Belgola, a place of pilgrim - age for the Digambar sect of the Jains where reputedly a thousand years ago (AD983), the sect erected - or more correctly, chipped out of the living rock, of one of the hills - the colossal medieval image of the Jain Saint *Gommatesvara.*

Considered to be the largest monolithic human image in the world, the largely nude statue, fifty nine feet tall, stands bolt upright in a posture of meditation known as *Kayotsarga.* Feet firmly on the earth and arms held downwards but not touching the body, *Gommatesvara* smiles faintly as he looks out from the summit of the hill, amongst a profusion of shrines, pools and memorials combined in a single integrated monument, hundreds of feet in height. The statue is open to different interpretations, the one most favoured being that of a creature of the earth, whom the earth is pulling back. James Fergusson (c1820-1870) the historian of India's architecture declared the colossal statue of the Jain Saint "among the most remarkable works of native art in the south of India... Nothing grander or more imposing exists anywhere out of Egypt".

Nearer to Mysore a pilgrimage that is more often made, is to the top of Chamundi Hill. It presents a challenge to all devotees - one of either climbing up a thousand very steep and irregular stone-cut steps (and down again) or driving up (as I have done several times) and walking *down* the equally steep steps - a massive exercise, whichever way it is accomplished.

It represents a wonderful viewing platform from which to survey the town of Mysore and the beautiful country surrounding it in every direction (Chamundi Hill rises like a pimple from the plain). At the very top is the annexe containing the statue of the demon Mahishasura and below it, the very ornate and large Chamundeswari Temple.

Taking up the challenge and negotiating the thousand or so steep variously shaped rock steps down from the summit, one comes across the giant sixteen foot high rock carving of Siva's mount, the Nandi bull, halfway down the hill. Carved from a single black stone, Nandi is honoured with offerings given by devotees (accepted by the monk in attendance). Similar images of Siva's mount, though smaller in size, are to be found in most Saivite temples.

Away to the right as one descends, the Maharaja of Mysore's former 'guest house', now the luxurious Lalitha Mahal Palace Hotel, hovers into view. Positioned in direct line with the Mysore Palace nine kilometres away, the beautiful clean and graceful lines of the Ashok Group's dream hotel stand out majestically from its superb stand-alone setting.

My single regret was that I was too soon for Dussera, the colourful ten-day Mysore Festival (which usually falls in October). Formerly one of the most glittering events on the South Indian calendar (with the 26th January parade in New Delhi,.and compared with the tremendous Durbars conducted by the Raj), it involved as many as one hundred magnificently caparisoned elephants and thousands of gaily dressed musicians, dancers and other performers, drawn from all over India.

It also afforded people the opportunity of seeing and hearing the Court's tunic clad musicians (some of Palace attendants still wear the old heavy woollen British regimental-style tunics) performing on many of India's unique and musically remarkable instruments, ordinarily kept on display in the Jayachamarajendra Art Gallery - nearly all the string variety, *tambooras, veenas, the dilruba, sitar, sarangi, surasingar, dilruba tamburi combined, the double durdandi tambura and rudra veena*. Some amazing shapes; even more intriguing sounds.

A veritable klondike of wonders, Karnataka (and especially the part which was old Mysore) stirs the senses, and complements in a wonderful way, the store of treasures that abound everywhere in India.

EPILOGUE: It was only in the mid 1980's that India's forecasters, analysts and government policy planners came to understand the (significant) potential of Indian talent in computer software. A perfect fit for India, a country blessed with great mathematical skills and great depth of scientific manpower, (the second largest in the world), the software industry has since made phenomenal strides, particularly in its exports (of computer talent and software) to the world, predominantly to the U.S.A..

Software Technology Parks, receiving great support from Central Government, are now firmly established throughout India – Mumbai, Bangalore, Delhi-Gurgaon and Noida, Hyderabad, Chennai, Calcutta, Pune and others. At 11/1998, the number of companies engaged in computer software, totalled 430. Software exports now exceed $2 billion annually, estimated to double by the year 2000.

Huge investments are being made, with the Singapore Government being in the van of the international field, of collaborators. The 68 acre joint India/Singapore International one-stop Tech Park, at Whitefield (Bangalore) integrating office, production, commercial, residential and recreational facilities at a single (pleasant) location, and involving itself in information technology, software development, computer electronics and telecommunication, was recently officially inaugurated. The Chief Executive Officer, is a

Singaporean, Goh Kok Huat. It seeks to be regarded at the showpiece of the Indian Computer Industry, although Hyderabad (Andhra Pradesh) is making a very spirited challenge to this title.

Who would have believed (or even dreamt of the huge untapped, ready to be awakened Indian potential) such participation, of India even just twenty years ago! There are some marvellous surprises in store. How wonderful.

20. Colourful delight, contemplating Golconda.

21. A Group of splendid smiling faces (Darjeeling).

22. Pivot of Business activity, Flora Fountain, (Hutatma Chowk)- a magnet in the C.B.D. Bombay.

23. Christian India, the celebrated Bom Jesus Basilica - Shrine of St. Francis Xavier, at Old Goa.

24. Goats show their interest- Madras.

25. 10th Century Pallava art - the Shore temple and seawall-Mamallapuram.

26. A most venerable school setting amidst the marvellous 'rathas' carved out of monolithic rocks, Mamallapuram.

27. "Tiny tots, who sing like larks" - "Lucia King", Dr. Graham's Homes, Kalimpong.

28. A lovely bunch of housemates - growing up in 'Woodburn Cottage', Dr. Graham's Homes, Kalimpong.

29. Watching over the fortunes of Mysore, the Giant granite Nandi Bull adorns Chamundi Hill.

30. Regal roundabout - Mysore city, Karnataka State.

31. Looking ahead - the graciously curving Marine Drive, Bombay.

32. Enduring Indian ingenuity - Six roped baulks bring in the day's 'catch', S. India.

33. Vivekananda's unique Memorial - at Kanniyakumari, Land's End.

34. Prelude to greatness - the majestic Taj gate at Agra.

35. Shahjehan's ultimate homage - viewed downriver throughout his final years, from Agra Fort.

36. Plucking some of the finest brew - on the slopes at Darjeeling.

37. Immeasurable patience and skill - artisan at work, Radha Saomi Samadhi.

38. Towering gopuram - Ranganathaswamy Temple, Srirangam, Tiruchirapalli.

39. Very typically Kerala, Kovalam beach-side.

40. Sunrise at Pondicherry. Tranquillity itself.

41. India's southern extremity. Rock Temple at the meeting of the three seas - Kanniyakumari.

42. Hallowed chamber - birthplace ("The Chamberlain Cup"), Ooty Club, Udhagamandalam, South India.

43. In the style of the Basilica at Lourdes - the exquisite EGLISE de NOTRE DAME de LOURDES, outside Pondicherry.

16. Snookered At Ooty

- Where it all began

The run through shot, the stun shot, the screw shot, variously meaning hitting a little white ball either above centre, in the centre, or below centre, seem pretty odd terms to have 'begun' their lives in India.

But in a country which has spawned several distinct and old civilizations; many thousands of architectural wonders; people and languages in every dimension; the oldest and richest literary tradition in the world, art which is more refined, conceptual and grander than anywhere else in the world; the decimal system, algebra and chess - well? - everything is possible.

That necessity can be the mother of invention has been proven over and over again. And so it was to be in 1875, on the dry hot and sultry plains of Madhya Pradesh (then called Central Province) in the officers mess of the British Military cantonment on the outskirts of Jubbulpore, that the triple factors - boredom, inventiveness and chance, spawned the idea of a new version of the game of (black pool) billiards.

But it was not until seven years later, at the *pukka* Ootacamund Club high up on the slopes of the beautiful south Indian hill-station, that the first officially recorded game of Snooker was played in accordance with established rules.

A signal event, although many more years would pass before Snooker would 'take on' (or should it be 'take off') around the world and eventually surpass the older parent billiards, in general popularity. The first professional snooker championship was held in 1927, won by Joe Davis, the legendary British player who went on to take the title a record fifteen times.

While it is its connection with the universal popularity of Snooker that will ensure Ooty's place in the Hall of Fame, for most of the region's local population, it is its wonderful climate that is held most dearly of all and rejoiced about, along with its pretty rolling country-side. The nearest duplicate in India to the glorious Southern Downs of England, it is the special playground and retreat for southerners (along with Kodaikanal, not so far distant from it), pleased to leave behind them, for even a short while, the surrounding hot plains.

Enjoying pleasant weather all year round - never too hot, up to 25°, and never uncomfortably cold, down to 0° in winter - Ooty and its 'olde worlde' neighbouring towns, Lovedale, Kothagiri, Wellington and Coonoor, is situated in the Nilgiri Hills in Tamil Nadu, part of the plateau at the junction of the Eastern and Western Ghats. A blue haze is omnipresent over the Nilgiri Hills created by the floating wispy clouds which envelop the region, adding to the untroubled, unhurried atmosphere that prevails throughout these lovely hills.

To the north, heading towards Mysore and down the long winding approach road to Ooty, one traverses Bandipur National Park, formerly the game reserve of the Mysore maharajahs. One of fifteen tiger (preservation) reserves in India, the park also shelters elephant, Indian bison, gaur, sloth bear, chital (deer) and many different varieties of native birds. To get the best of the park requires a lengthier stay, although sightings of elephant and lots of deer, are not infrequently made, arousing the usual thrills associated with seeing animals in the wild.

A favourite holiday town, more inclined to restful pursuits than bayside frolics, Ootacamund unplagued by streams of vehicular traffic is a joy. Not much has changed in layout or appearance since the departure of the British Army fifty years ago. For a hundred years a chosen recreational area (a retreat from the hot dry dusty plains) Ooty and her satellites hosted many generations of British troops and their families.

Not so many years ago I enjoyed a chance meeting with an Englishman in Melbourne, who had lived as a young boy in Wellington and remembered going up the mountain each day in the famous Nilgiri Puff Puff to attend army school at Lovedale. 'Discovered' in the first half of the nineteenth century, all of the so called hill-stations of India, Ootacamund (officially now Udhagamandalam) in south India and Simla, Mussoorie, Naini Tal and Darjeeling, all located in the lower slopes of the Himalayas in north India, retain considerable vestiges of British influence.

Snooker was invented on a wet afternoon

Origin of a Great Game

By Compton Mackenzie

Here, for the first time, is the fully authenticated story of the origin of Snooker.

It is presented by one of the most brilliant writers of our time, Mr. Compton Mackenzie.

This historic article, which could never have been written without the co-operation of Colonel Sir Neville Chamberlain, is proudly published by us at a time when the game itself is being played in Great Britain by more people than is any other sport or game.

LAST year an article in "The Field" put forward the theory that the game of Snooker had its origin at the Royal Military Academy, Woolwich, where officers of the Royal Artillery and the Royal Engineers receive their training as cadets.

The theory was plausible, because a first-year cadet at "The Shop," as the R.M.A. is familiarly known, is called a "Snooker," the soubriquet being time's corruption of the original word for a newly-joined cadet, which was "Neux." It must be remembered that the R.M.A. was founded as long ago as 1741.

The writer of the article stated that the original rules of Snooker were copied out by Lord Kitchener from those at "The Shop," brought by him to Ootacamund, and there hung up in the Club.

This assertion was formally contradicted by General Sir Ian Hamilton in a letter to "The Field" of July 11th, 1938. In point of fact Lord Kitchener never visited India until many years after Snooker had become a popular game out there.

Investigation has established that, so far from Snooker's having originated at "The Shop," the game was invented at Jubbulpore in the year 1875 by Colonel Sir Neville Chamberlain, who is fortunately still with us and whose memory is perfectly clear on the subject.

On a wet afternoon . . .

It befell during the "Rains" that Sir Neville, then a young subaltern in the Devonshire Regiment, anxious to vary the game of Black Pool which was being played every long wet afternoon on the Mess billiard table, suggested putting down another coloured ball, to which others of different values were gradually added.

One day a subaltern of the Field Battery at Jubbulpore was being entertained by the Devons, and in the course of conversation told young Chamberlain about the soubriquet "Snooker" for first year cadets at Woolwich. To quote Sir Neville's own words:

"The term was a new one to me, but I soon had an opportunity of exploiting it when one of our party failed to hole a coloured ball which was close to a corner pocket. I called out to him: 'Why, you're a regular snooker!'

"I had to explain to the company the definition of the word, and, to soothe the feelings of the culprit, I added that we were all, so to speak, snookers at the game, so it would be very appropriate to call the game snooker. The suggestion was adopted with enthusiasm and the game has been called Snooker ever since."

Potted himself

In 1876 Sir Neville Chamberlain left the Devons to join the Central India Horse, taking with him the new game. A year or two later came the Afghan War, a more serious potting game in which young Chamberlain was himself potted.

However, fortunately for himself and the great game which we enjoy so much to-day, he recovered from his wound, and when at the close of 1881 General Sir Frederick Roberts became Commander-in-Chief of the Madras Army, the inventor of Snooker served on his personal staff, and was with Roberts when every summer he moved to the hill station at Ootacamund known to all and sundry as "Ooty."

There came officers from big garrisons like Bangalore and Secundderabad and planters from Mysore. All of them enjoyed Snooker as a speciality of the "Ooty" Club where the rules of the game were drawn up and posted in the billiards room, but *not* by Lord Kitchener.

During the 'eighties rumours of the new game in India reached England. One evening Sir Neville Chamberlain when dining in Calcutta with the Maharaja of Cooch Behar was introduced to a well-known professional billiards player whom he had engaged from England for some lessons.

This professional told the Maharaja he had been asked in England to obtain the rules of the new game Snooker and the Maharaja introduced Sir Neville Chamberlain to him as the best person to give him the information he wanted because *he* was the inventor of it.

In a letter to "The Field" of March 19th, 1938, Sir Neville regretted he did not know the name of the professional but thought he was probably a contemporary of

44. Pages from the The Billiard Player (April 1939).

John Roberts and W. Cook. A week or two later Mr. F. H. Cumberlege wrote to Sir Neville Chamberlain to say that the professional must have been John Roberts himself who came out to Calcutta in 1885. Mr. Cumberlege added that he remembered showing the Maharaja the new game of Snooker at Cooch Behar after a shooting party in the spring of 1884.

Famous people remember

Sir Neville Chamberlain has received from several other distinguished authorities confirmation of his claim to be the inventor of Snooker. Major-General W. A. Watson, Colonel of the Central India Horse (his old regiment) wrote:

"I have a clear recollection of you rejoining the regiment in 1884. You brought with you a brand new game, which you called Snooker or Snookers. There were the black, the pink, the yellow and the green. We all understood it was your own invention. We took to it very keenly."

Major-General Sir John Hanbury Williams (Colonel of the 43rd Oxfordshire and Buckinghamshire Light Infantry) wrote:

"I was always under the impression that you introduced the game of Snooker to the 43rd in 1884-5. Certainly the 43rd never played Snooker till you came and introduced it to us. Hope you will stick to the honour of its invention."

Field Marshal Lord Birdwood wrote:

"I remember well your introducing the game of Snookers into the 12th Lancers' Mess, when I was a subaltern in the Regiment at Bangalore in '85."

Complete

Sir Walter Lawrence, Bt., wrote:

"When we first met in Simla in 1886, when you were with Lord Roberts, the Commander-in-Chief, and afterwards when we served together in Kashmir, I always looked upon you as the inventor of Snooker, and I know that this idea was common to many of my friends. Quite recently, last year (1937) I was telling some of my friends in England who were discussing Snooker, that I had the honour of knowing very intimately the inventor of the game."

The testimony of these and other highly distinguished officers finally disposes of the theory advanced with some emphasis by the writer in "The Field" that the game of Snooker originated at the Royal Military Academy, Woolwich, and it has been a privilege for me to assemble in print such incontrovertible evidence.

There is nothing to add except that all the many thousands of Snooker players the world over will wish Colonel Sir Neville Chamberlain, who is now in his 84th year, many another year to enjoy the honour of being the inventor of a game, now 63 years old, which has added so much to the gaiety of nations.

My only regret is that he has not seen Joe Davis play it. He would feel still prouder of having invented a medium for such grace and accuracy of human accomplishment.

COMPTON MACKENZIE.

SNOOKER

There are twenty-two balls on the table at the start of a game of snooker: one white cue ball, fifteen red balls (value one point each), and one each of the pool colours — yellow (worth two points), green (three points), brown (four points), blue (five points), pink (six points), and black (seven points).

The game consists entirely of winning hazards, that is potting the balls. The player is obliged to pot a red before selecting any coloured ball to pot; the reds remain off the table after potting, but the coloured or pool balls are replaced on their spots until all fifteen reds have been pocketed, following which the colours must then be potted in order of points value, commencing with the yellow. The colours when pocketed now also remain off the table. It is always essential to hit the ball which is to be potted directly with the cue ball, otherwise it is a foul stroke. Penalties are awarded for various fouls; the minimum penalty is four points, but it is more if a ball of greater value is involved.

A 'snooker' is a situation when the striker cannot play a direct stroke on to the ball which he must hit. Thus one player will try to leave such a situation, where the opponent may fail to hit the ball, therefore committing a foul and giving points to the opponent who had caused the snooker.

The pedestrian mall in Ooty running off Garden Road (rather similarly to the Chowrasta and Mall in Darjeeling) allows easy strolling and window shopping down the gentle slope through the market area to the Bus Terminal and Railway Station at the bottom. The wonderful old retailers, Higginbothams book shop and the 'carry everything' Kishinchand Chellaram's General store still operate today with all their old world charm and courtesy. Great traditions are not left off lightly in India.

Going up the hill away from Garden Road and turning off at the Bank of India's premises at the junction (there can't be many Banks in the world where you proceed up a long flowered drive to reach the front door), the walk up the hill goes by the grand old buildings, the Art Gallery and Public Library just before one comes to St. Stephen's Church and clock tower. All quite delightful.

Around the hillside and along Sylks Road, one first passes the entrance to the Ootacamund Club and then further along at the end of the road, one enters the beautiful garden setting of the Taj Group's Savoy Hotel. Dining in the garden or in its resplendent panelled dining room, is another of life's memorable pleasures provided by an ageless India.

Several years ago I was privileged to stay for several nights at the Ooty Club (in the residential annexe) a memorable experience, and an opportunity to 'un-lock' the famous billiard/snooker room, and play on what might (I afterwards enlisted the aid of the E. A. Clare & Son Group of Liverpool - now Thurstons, first established 1799 in London, to trace and identify the original table at Ooty used in 1882) have been *the* table? Maybe not, but it was (and is) a very old table. My partner was a Mr John Carter, a member of the Royal Hong Kong Police. If he reads this 'tale of Ooty', John might remember the occasion in March 1988, which provided thrills for both of us, honoured to enjoy a teeny bit morsel of history.

Invented by Colonel Sir Neville Chamberlain while serving with the Devon Regiment and inaugurated by him and his fellow officers at the Ooty Club in 1882, the game of Snooker spread from one military station to another throughout India, assisted by the constant movement of personnel, who carried the game with them to all the towns and cities, and even to the remote frontier posts.

The game reached Britain via the returning troops. Because it carried a name, 'Snooker' familiarly known to the Royal Military Academy at Woolwich, (the term 'a snooker' was the tag applied by seniors to first year R A and R E cadets implying 'novice - still a bit wet behind the ears'. It stuck in the game's preliminary stages in Ooty, when most players were still 'pretty green', and yet to master the newly introduced post billiards game), for a long time it was thought that it had originated at the Woolwich Academy, later of course, conclusively disproved.

The game spread into the London Gentlemen's Clubs, and rapidly after the turn of the century, throughout Britain, and through the agency of John Roberts Junior, and that great exponent, Joe Davis, to its world epicentre, Leeds. The BBC's 'Pot Black' series stimulated great interest around the world, when today the game is played in many countries. The IBSF list supplied to me by the B&SCC, Leeds (in 1988) listed thirty five members, ranging from the Sudan to Negara Brunei Darussalam.

Indirectly spawned in India and custodians of the primary mould - in the pool room of the Ootacamund Club, on the wooded slopes above the town - I wonder if the Club Members realize what a potentially great treasure they have in their sole possession. Still wonderfully appointed, but showing evident signs of material dilapidation and hugely underutilized these days (as compared to the fantastic hunt gatherings of a former era), if it chose, the venerable Club could revolutionize and revitalize itself.

Shorn of its past riches and clientele and relying largely upon its tea-growing fraternity, it could become a 'true jewel in Ootacamund's and India's crown'. But will current prejudices and persistence in retaining the old and traditional condemn it all, or will sensible initiative and enterprise win the day? Nothing need be lost. Everything is there waiting to be gained.

It does not require much effort, to envisage the bi-annual staging of a World Championship Snooker Tournament at the Ooty Club. Its total uniqueness and indisputable right to put on such a Tourney would not lack for world sponsors. Beamed by satellite TV throughout the world, Ooty and India would reap great acclaim. Maybe some visionary entrepreneur will spot the promotional 'jewel' and ACT! It shrieks out for noting.

On a previous visit I had climbed the hill from Coimbatore to Ootacamund aboard the celebrated Nilgiri Express, ratcheted for a part of its journey up the steepest slopes (one in twelve from Kallar to Coonoor). The 46 kilometre journey by train from Mettupalayam to Ooty takes 4 ½ hours. From Coonoor, a little over half the distance, a diesel train now completes the run, formerly done by the old quaint steam puff puffs, for the remainder of the journey up to Ooty.

In a land where novelty can still provide unique pleasure, and where every second of every day is not vital and precious, it is sad that some of the more famous and pleasure-giving steam locos are not kept in service. 'Serving' contains many ingredients.

But to run down the hill by bus, in the early morning, still holds much interest. I wrote in my Notes "...17th July, up 5.30 reach bus stand 6.00. Away at 6.20. After reaching highest point 2440 metres, winding road drops away. Excellent driver, shows wonderful skill and judgement negotiating mountain road, hairpin bends. Much courtesy shown to everyone. Many tea estates passed on road down (South India produces twenty five per cent of total Indian tea production. Nilgiri, a bright brisk tea, is much prized for its delectable fragrance). We pass Coonoor, Lovedale and Wellington and to Mettupalayam - which revives memories of my close friend and colleague of Indian days, ASGS, who met with much adventure on the Mettupalayam Road".....

Soon the tranquillity and loveliness of the Nilgiris are behind us and I am aboard a fairly basic looking bus (which belies its capabilities) and we are off, hurtling - horn blowing continuously, sending the message 'move aside' - through the flourishing green countryside, bound for Thissar, and Cochin.

17. India's Idyllic South

- the beauty and serenity of Kerala

Tucked away, mostly on their own, in the farthermost south-western corner of the Indian sub-continent, the colourful diverse people and State of Kerala (formed by merging the separate areas of Kerala and Travancore) have managed to retain a large chunk of their own millennium's old culture/cultures, and as well, as further cultures were added, have succeeded in maintaining racial harmony amongst its many and varied parts more successfully perhaps, than elsewhere in India.

The bigger part of Kerala lies to the west of the Western Ghats (the mountain range which extends for a thousand miles down the lower half of the western side of India). Hemmed in between the foothills of these two and half thousand metre mountains and the Arabian Sea, Kerala gets the full force of the south-west Monsoon, with falls of up to 200 inches a year.

As the result of this extreme and regular precipitation, the long ribbon of very fertile land stretching three hundred and sixty miles from just below Mangalore southwards right down to and beyond Trivandrum (Thiruvananthapuram) - the Kannadan and Malayalam languages throw up some difficult tongue twisters! - is densely covered with vegetation. It was the combination of heat, precipitation and high rainfall which catapulted the region to world fame millenniums ago, through its prodigious array and prolific produce of many kinds, a food additive attraction which lured traders to its shores.

Kerala can perhaps boast more coconut palms to every hectare, than any other place on earth. The swaying, vital and curvaceous palm trees reflect peace and happiness felt by people everywhere, a natural blessing which probably accounts for much of the 'good-will to all men' attitudes which prevail amongst all of its people.

Palm-trees yes, but also water, water everywhere, something which is a natural concomitant of life there, making Keralans the prime water craftsmen they are, in numbers, greater than anywhere else in India. In these enlightened times the more progressive boat men have taken to diesel power, but confirmation that their skills and love of paddling their long slim wooden boats are zealously retained, is annually displayed at the many large and smaller boat festivals, for which Kerala is famous.

Kerala combines all the contradictions - a way of life containing the elements of ancient Hindu culture; many of the oldest Islamic mosques in the whole of India; remnants of Judaism going back nearly 2000 years reputedly visited by the disciple (Saint) Thomas in the first century A.D.; strong Roman Catholicism stemming from the early Portuguese and Dutch incursions, and on top of all this rich heritage, education standards, health measures, and literacy levels (mostly however in the local vernacular), the highest in the whole of India.

While largely left alone by the rest of (north) India, it was a different matter where it came to international trading, with foreign traders plying from Arabia and African east coast ports, to India, for centuries, going back to early Christian times. There had been a significant and regular interchange, enriching the south-western shores of the sub-continent. In effect, Kerala's advanced state was primarily due to its rich and exclusive agricultural products opening up to it other parts of the world, when without this, in its remote geographical situation, it could have continued 'in the dark ages'.

Situated three thousand kilometres from the nation's capital, New Delhi, Keralans have largely kept to themselves, not figuring very much in national politics. The appointment this year of one of their own sons, K R Narayanan as President of India, came in stark contradiction to Kerala's past minimal interest in national affairs, but the splendid qualities that reside in the eminent scholar for wide understanding, will serve India very well, and do much to bring Kerala closer to the rest of the country.

Kerala deserves much greater attention than what I've so far managed to personally experience of it. Three or four days spent in both Cochin-Ernakulam, and Trivandrum (Kovalam Beach) barely scratches the surface. But the little I've experienced, has whetted my appetite for a longer and wider foray and at the right seasons of the year. A few years earlier I visited Kovalam, in order to recharge my batteries after going full pelt all over India in the heat of summer.

45. Kerala boat festival.

THE ST. FRANCIS CHURCH

(CHURCH OF SOUTH INDIA)

COCHIN

KERALA (S.INDIA)

46. The St. Francis Church, Cochin (Kerala).

From 1503 - 1663. Portuguese Period
Roman Catholic Church
From 1664 - 1804. Dutch Period - Dutch Reformed Church
From 1804 - 1947. British Period - Anglican Church
From 1947 - Church of South India

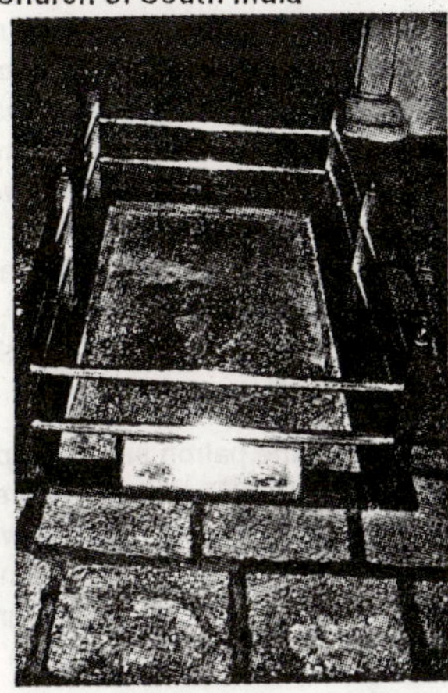

Vasco da Gama Tomb

Fort Cochin is believed to be the oldest European Settlement in India and St. Francis Church was the first European Church to be built in India. The history of this Church reflects the colonial struggle of European powers in india, from the 15th to 20th Centuries.

The Portuguese were the first Europeans to discover the sea route to India when Vasco da Gama landed at Calicut in 1498. Two years later, on 24th December 1500, Portuguese ships under the command of Admiral Cabral visited Cochin and the Rajah of Cochin permitted them to engage in trade. In 1503 Alphonso Alburquerque was given permission by the Rajah to build a fort at the mouth of the river which was constructed mainly of the stems of coconut trees bound with iron bands, whilst the rampart of stones and sand formed the inner defence. Within the Fort they erected a church of wood which was dedicated to St. Bartholomew and which occupied the site on which the more spacious structure of the Franciscans later arose. In 1506 Dom Francisco Almeyda, the Viceroy, was permitted by the Cochin Rajah to build a new city of mortar and stone. The buildings were roofed with tiles, a privilege hitherto confined to the palace of the local prince and to the temples in which he performed puja. The Portuguese vowed that, apart from the fortifications, the first permanent erection would be a house for Divine worship. The new Church, was completed in 1516 and dedicated to St. Antony.

Towards the end of 1524 Vasco da Gama returned to Cochin (Which he first visited in 1502) where he died on Christmas eve of that year and was buried in this Church. Fourteen years later his remains were removed to Portugal and deposited at Vidigveria where they remained until 1872 when they were removed to Lisbon.

The Church remained in the Order of St. Francis until the arrival of the Dutch in 1663. One of the first acts of the Dutch was to order all European Catholic priests to quit their territory, after which they demolished all the convents and churches of the place, except the Church of the Franciscans which they reconditioned and converted into their Government Church. On 8th January 1664 they celebrated their first service with a parade of all arms on the Anniversary of their entry into the city. During the reconditioning the stone alter and the wiring guilded screens were removed and taken to the Church of Vypeen, which the Dutch permitted the Roman Catholic to build in 1665, and the Communion table and rostrum furniture were installed in thier stead. A tablet over the west door indicates that the Church was renovated in 1779.

When the British captured Cochin from the Dutch in 1795 they permitted them to retain possession of the Church for a time. In 1804 the Dutch voluntarily surrendered the Church to the Anglican Communion when it was passed to the Ecclesiastical Department of the Government of India. But when the Rev. Thomas Norton came to Cochin in 1816 on his way to inaugurate the work of the Church Missionary Society at Alleppey, he found that the Church was just bare walls, the interior was very dilapidated and part of the roof had fallen in. The Building was sufficiently restored to enable Bishop Middleten, the Metropolitan, to use it for a confirmation service during his episcopal visit to the Malabar coast.

The change of name of the patron saint was presumably due to the Anglicans, for it was not until 1870 that any reference was made to St. Francis Church. The gravestones let into the walls of the church were taken from the floor of the nave in 1886. On the northern side can be seen Portuguese gravestones. The Dutch gravestones are on the southern wall. The Vasco da Gama stone is on the ground at the southern side.

Surfing at Kovalam was very pleasant, and perhaps the nearest any of India's east and west coast beaches come by way of comparison with the abundance of superb beaches, which bless my own country, Australia. One particular problem - keeping beaches and adjacent waters clean, is much easier when one's population is only eighteen millions. The refuse from thrown away packaging etc consistent with a population fifty times as great, presents a far more difficult effort and solution. Another significant problem India must begin seriously grappling with, is sanitary habits. From a community health viewpoint, it appears that greater discipline must occur, producing all round improvement for everyone. This really is a significant and increasing problem, which *every* citizen must begin to seriously tackle.

Cochin (Kochi) is water. Lots of it. Across the inlet (Vembanad Lake) from Ernakulam and accessible by regular ferry boats from the seafront, one can explore the group of islands that encircle and guard the ocean entrance - Bolgatty, Vallapadam, Gundu, Vypeen, Willingdon and Fort Cochin and Mattanchery.

Moving between the oil tankers and cargo vessels, the scene is enlivened by the constant presence of the native boats with their high prows fore and aft, criss-crossing hither and thither, laden with their catch of fish or prawns, or loaded with other produce. Intensive use of the waterways and canals besides ensuring safe two way carriage of living requirements not locally available - in, and produce whether tea, rubber, fruit and spices - out, often constitutes the only means of transportation. No intermediate roads means fewer cars, and a cleaner environment.

The high literacy rate among Keralans owes much to the equality of the sexes, a characteristic of Dravidian society, and to some degree as well, to the matrilineal societies, which survive there, in which women own and inherit land and are the heads of the family. Women are well represented in nearly every facet of affairs in Kerala, unlike in north India, where the old Sanskrit form of Hinduism, and the strict form of Islam preclude any real departure from male dominance.

In terms of the culture practised in south India, it is the usual custom for men to choose their brides from a narrow circle of relatives. The preferred type of union is that of a man with the daughter of either his mother's brother or his father's sister (cross-cousin marriage). Ordinarily people live in small, self- perpetuating clusters of families, a system which gives great stability to the entire social structure.

Ernakulam on the mainland, is the business-end of the twin-towns (of Cochin, and Ernakulam) and the most populated. Cochin – across the water, particularly at its northern end, is easily more Dutch and Portuguesy, and traditional South Indian.

To walk its narrow roads and lanes, and along its sandy tracts and absorb village life in its varied forms – amidst wonderful old churches and venerable educational institutions mingling with its intriguing prawn and net fishing, and coir-mat and rope making – brings much that delights and refreshes, in an atmosphere of calm and hastelessness.

Crossing over Vembanad Lake by ferry boat and winding ones way on foot up the Calvathy Road, partaking of delicious south Indian coffee on the landing of the plain but exquisite 'in feeling', Seagull Hotel, on the Lake's foreshore (two levels in very old colonial style - more like a barracks than a hotel), represents one of the cheapest, but most tranquil of life's moments. The unhurried extremely balmy atmosphere on Fort Cochin is totally removed from ordinariness and the hustle and bustle across the water. It is a wonderful tonic, highly recommended. Instead of the 5 star opulence on M.G. Road, a taste of the plainness exuded by the Seagull, would leave visitors with a far greater 'feel' for the Kerala experienced by the everyday Keralan. These words to some 'avid tourists' may sound heretical, but real delights are there for the taking.

Further north, close by Aspinalls (a nostalgic name in South India) the shrimp boats discharge their catches (mostly destined for export) from their interestingly compartmentalized long boats. Their tiny 'harbour' presents a mass of activity - no one seems to notice the putrid nature of the confined water, nor the colossal accompanying stench.

Along the channel extending out to the Lakshadweep Sea, the ancient and intriguing beach seine-net fishing rigs extend in a long line (something must attract the small fish, for these uniquely built contraptions have been fishing in the same place, day in, day out, for centuries) providing great interest. Out on the sands just inside the mouth of the channel, more fishing boats disgorge their catch in what appears to be an open-air instant market. From the melée emerge scores of native women carrying on their heads the heavy baskets of fish.

All this activity inevitably leaves the beaches choked up with litter. A shame, no one seems responsible for 'tidying up after them'. A world scourge, and not one confined to India. Difficult also to police, is the pollution spread by ships passing along the coast, despoiling India's beaches.

Religion affects practically the whole of Kerala's population in its very rich assortment. Many of the better schools are run by the Catholic Church, a strong influence dating back to the first Portuguese settlers, on the Malabar Coast.

The magnificent old church of St. Francis tells the ecumenical story of Fort Cochin and of the changing hands, from the original (Catholic) Portuguese period - 1503 to 1663, replaced by the Dutch and its Reformed Church for the next 140 years, followed by the British (Anglican Church) from 1804 until 1947, and now the Church of South India.

The first European Church to be built in India was St. Francis Church. In it reposed the body of Vasco da Gama from his death in Fort Cochin in 1524 until it was disinterred and removed to Vidigveria (Portugal), before, in 1872, being finally laid to rest in Lisbon. St. Francis Church retains its marvellous old-style punkahs, one row of three canvas flap flaps down each side. Hopeless for acoustics during the hot months, but otherwise greatly appreciated by the parishioners. A wonderful example of old time mechanical inventiveness, seen still in various parts of India, where the British saw fit to mechanize 'the traditional elephant's ear' either by replacing the manual rope puller or manual fan waver.

The nearby Santa Cruz Basilica dates back to 1505. The excellent girl's school attaching to it has provided wonderful instruction and training for good life, to many thousands of devout Keralans in an atmosphere wonderfully unique from what is accorded most Indians - uncongested, spacious, pleasant 'basic' surroundings -providing a wonderful learning environment.

Back along in Mattanchery more relics of Dutch occupation can be visited, while remnants of the very old Jewish fraternity continue to worship at the small Ardeshi Synagogue, which dates back to 1568. Today, there are very few Cochin Jews left, most having migrated to Israel (one of the author's staff in Australia, an Indian Jew, had followed this trail. Disenchanted with the rigid practice of Judaism there, so different from the wonderfully tolerant religious atmosphere he had left in India, he next migrated to Australia).

A visit to the much lauded Periyar Game Sanctuary where the elephant herds can be observed in complete safety from the placid waters of Periyar Lake, would have to be delayed, as also a call at Alleppey, home of the renowned Nehru Cup snake boat race, and of course - the coir industry. Beautiful Kovalam has been enjoyed before and so to proceed to the very bottom (the apex of the triangle) of India - and Kanniyakumari.

18. Southern Tribute To Religious Gods And Earthly Savants

- the meeting of the three seas

One of the great Hindu pilgrimages made on the sub-continent, is to the very bottom (southern) end of the country. But even more than this - to a huge granite rock island which stands (or is firmly sited) a mile or so offshore only approachable by boat. The more intrepid or zealously devout may elect to swim out to the rock. Seemingly, and perhaps sensibly, few do this.

As is the case with most Hindu pilgrimages (in India), some 'above the ordinary' effort is required from devotees, either because of the remoteness of the particular religious site or because of the considerable distance one has to travel to reach to it. The ruggedness of much of the terrain (nearing journey's end) often calls for extreme physical effort and taxes to the very limit, the capabilities of old persons, its main pilgrims entering the final phase of their lives.

Kanniyakumari (or Kanyakumari) sits right at the base of India, thousands of kilometres beyond where many of India's large population (predominantly Hindus) have ever travelled, or are likely to go to, in their lifetime. Kanniyakumari lies three thousand kilometres south of Hindu India's most northerly and perhaps most often undertaken and sacred pilgrimage of all - the pilgrimage to Badrinath high above Vishnuprayag at the source in the Himalaya Mountains of the great and sacred river Ganga.

Another extraordinary pilgrimage entails walking from Bharuch at the mouth of the Narmada River on the Arabian Sea, over a thousand kilometres, to the river's sacred source at Armarkantak on the Maikala plateau in central India, and - covering the same trail back again to Bharuch!

These pilgrimages undertaken by not insignificant numbers, are not for the faint-hearted. The *'Melas'* which regularly take place at the confluence of the Ganga and Yamuna Rivers at Allahabad, and at Sagar Island at the mouth of the Ganga below Calcutta, attract the greatest number of Hindu devotees. Benares (Varanasi) constitutes a less exacting, but no less sacred pilgrimage, for millions of Hindus.

Kanniyakumari's popularity has been greatly enhanced during the last one hundred and a bit years, through the visitations of two of India's most famous savants - Vivekananda, and Mahatma Gandhi. Both of these great figures enjoy a significant presence through 'memorials' constructed at Kanniyakumari to venerate and to perpetuate their teachings, and leadership of India, into these modern times.

Well served by good communications (road and rail) Kanniyakumari is approached from Trivandrum through a very thriving and productive region, and by way of a flourishing town, so rarely ever mentioned (outside India) or even known - Nagercoil.

A highly fertile area exhibiting marvellously abundant agriculture - rice paddies, *plantains* (bananas), sugar cane, palm oil and coconuts - as good as you will see anywhere (and in India), it leads on to a less favourable stretch of country notable for its frequent large granite out-crops *via* a passage through the last of the Western Ghats, to the joining of three seas - the Arabian Sea, the Indian Ocean, and the Bay of Bengal (so-named, even though Bengal is over two thousand kilometres distant) at Cape Comorin (Kanniyakumari).

Apart from catering to its transitory population, the main occupation of the permanent dwellers of Kanniyakumari is fishing. The shoreline is draped with the wooden dugouts (long, fashioned baulks of timber strung together with stout coir ropes to create a boat - in the same way as has been done for hundreds/even thousands of years) of the intrepid fisherfolk and their nets put there to dry and to be mended.

Breakwaters placed at various intervals break up the seas, creating artificial harbours. The influence of the Christian Church is prominently displayed by St. Mary's Church standing just above the fishermen's colony. Its creaminess and graceful architectural lines add lustre, and sparkle to the languid seascape. The single reducing factor along this section of the seafront, is the age-old but still indiscriminate use by the menfolk of the various strips of beach and rock breakwaters

47. Dedication to two of India's most renowned publicists - The Mahatma and Vivekananda, at Kanniyakumari.

for their body functions. This detracts from an otherwise colourful and interesting spectacle. A rudimentary understanding of basic health requirements, and as a last resort, the value of earthen pits, could work wonders.

Swami Vivekananda meditated, 'seated on the bare rock out at sea', when he briefly paused at India's 'Lands End' at the end of 1892, after a long soul-searching journey which had taken him throughout India, much of it on foot. A disciple of the mystic, Ramakrishna, and co-founder of the non-sectarian Ramakrishna Movement, Vivekananda was seeking answers. He was looking for inspiration that did not contradict reason and for a way to intuition through reason, being the legitimate extension of his total belief that truth and knowledge of individual self were essential ingredients of a fruitful serving life. It was his perception that India had fallen from the heights of (its former) glory. He was looking for ways of restoring it through the twin ideals of renunciation and selfless service.

A well educated powerful orator, he achieved 'greatness' in the eyes of his fellow countrymen during his short lifetime, enhanced to a degree by the huge and celebratory tour he made to America.

Greatly concerned for the sufferings and neglect of the poorer people in his country (ill considered by the successful and wealthier section of his own people, as well as by the British colonists), and conscious of the religiosity (and generosity) which permeated the America of that time, he was sent off to the Universal Exposition, held in Chicago, in 1893, by his great admirer, the Raja of Ramnad, as the representative of Hinduism (although non-sectarian in his actions, still he had been nurtured in the Hindu religion), at the Parliament of Religions, held in Chicago, at the same time.

Entranced by all he experienced and putting to one side any small concerns about his personal welfare in a strange (but largely friendly) environment, regarding such as of secondary importance, Vivekananda - probably the first of the modern Indian sages/mystics to find public audiences in America, and therefore something 'entirely different and even - refreshing' - ultimately found great acclaim there for his beliefs, patronage of which continues unabated to this day.

Through his Indian sponsor's great insight (intuition, or whatever it was that brought it about) the 'specialness' of Vivekananda was hugely highlighted. Vivekananda was costumed wherever he went, (or when he addressed meetings), in a long red robe, drawn in at the waist by an orange cord, the whole topped with a voluminous yellow turban.

The costume became Vivekananda's lifelong signature tune. If lifted him out of the usual conformity, giving him a most imposing look. The first appearance at such high powered world church gathering of a Hindu, and one so differently (strikingly) attired, complemented by fine eloquent speechmaking delivering an entirely new message, drew tremendous applause from his hearers. His unprecedented maiden appearance was telegraphed throughout America, resulting in crowds attending his public meetings everywhere he spoke.

Brimming with confidence, and buoyed by the reception he had received, Vivekananda achieved what he had set out to do - given spiritual guidance to Americans and in return had received generous, badly needed donations, from Americans for India's poor.

It is the strong belief of some American observers that Vivekananda's visit in 1893 inaugurated American giving to overseas charities, which have been substantially supported, all around the world on a large scale, ever since.

The Temple to Vivekananda on the rock at Kanniyakumari, closely resembles the Math at Belur, on the banks of the Hooghly River at Calcutta. Constructed at considerable difficultly and immense cost (from funds donated by admirers of Vivekananda and as an expression of thanks for the good works performed by the Ramakrishna Mission) the Memorial represents a fitting tribute to Vivekananda's great standing amongst his own people and with others elsewhere in the world.

Always unafraid of delivering home-truths to his own people, Vivekananda's no-nonsense admonition and rallying cry delivered to his own people many years ago still hold equally true and equally urgent today - "Indians, get off your backsides, and through your well-developed bodies, muscles of iron and nerves of steel, create a country and a people, worthy of your ancestors". Who will take up the worthy challenge? Great things could be won for India.

In many respects the life of Mohandas Karamchand Gandhi (1869-1948) was an incarnation of the beliefs of Swami Vivekananda. They are extremely 'well-met' together at Kanniyakumari. That Indian civilization is universal in the deepest sense of the term, is confirmed by the fact that this primordial civilization has survived intact and has not degenerated into a narrowly defined religion. India continues to produce men and women with a universal spirit. People of this calibre have shaped modern India.

Called *swadharma* in Indian philosophy, it is believed that every being has within them a code of growth, a principle that guides their evolution. Vivekananda went further when he said that each nation has one central theme in its life, which in India's case is its spiritual life.

It is this spiritualism that through aeons of time has evoked the highest devotion and the greatest sacrifices. The life of Mahatma Gandhi stands as the supreme example.

It is no exaggeration therefore to say the edifice, the Gandhi Smarak, built as a tribute to the Father of the (modern Indian) Nation contains great sanctity and importance, for all Indians. Indisputably ranking among the greatest men who have ever lived (an extraordinary man in his every part) no Indian did more than Mahatma Gandhi to give substance to the incomparable eastern qualities of morality and character. He will be spoken of throughout history, as the person who broke the stranglehold of the west over the east and restored spiritual values to their proper place.

Various events came together to shape this wonderful remarkable man who was a synthesis of the thinking of east and west, while his Indian heritage always surmounted everything else. Educated outside India, trained in *Satyagraha* (truth - force/soul-force) in South Africa amongst that country's persecuted Indians, such widely and deeply lived experiences, fashioned Mahatma Gandhi for his life's most important mission - successfully leading the Indian masses to their freedom from foreign yoke.

To this day it remains to one very famous person (himself - a good living man, and discerning Christian who had the distinction of intimately observing events affecting India, from the early years of the 20th Century, up to and beyond India's Independence in 1947) the

American evangelist E. Stanley Jones, to describe Mahatma Gandhi more adequately, more effectively, and more unerringly accurately - a trait also of the Mahatma ('great-souled one') - than anyone has done.

The greatness (amongst all his wonderful simplicity) of Gandhi, is encapsulated in what Stanley Jones wrote of Mahatma Gandhi soon after his assassination in Delhi, in early 1948 - quote verbatim:

> ***"Gandhi seemed very simple, and yet he was very complex. He was a meeting place of East and West and yet represented the soul of the East; he was an urban man who became the voice of the peasant masses; he was passive and militant, and both at one and the same time; he was the ascetic and the servant - aloof from and yet with the multitudes, and with them as their servant; he was the mystical and the practical come to embodiment - the man of prayer and the man of the spinning wheel and ten thousand other practical things connected with economic redemption; he combined the Hindu and the Christian in himself - Hindu at the centre of his allegiance and yet deeply Christianized; he was the simple and the shrewd; the candid and the courteous; he combined the serious and the playful - a man who could shake empires and who could also tickle a child beneath its chin and gain a laugh and a friend; he had poise, but not the poise of retreat and aloofness - he had power to change situations by a deep identification; he was strangely humble and strangely self-assertive; and last of all, and most important of all, he was a person who embodied a Cause - the Cause of India's Freedom."***

The fight he fought, and led, for India's freedom was never deceitful but open and frank, and certainly, where he was concerned, and something which he unequivocably acknowledged - by personally taking upon himself the unwanted and therefore, condemned violent impetuous actions of other Indians, united in the same cause - non violent. Gandhi had a huge task to perform, to dislodge the grasp of the greatest Empire the world had ever seen. He could not be answerable for the inability of his adversaries to 'read' his complex thinking. They held the guns, his weapons were of a mightier kind.

To glean a measure of Gandhi's unique character and greatness (and regarded in the stressful and volatile political climate, that prevailed at the time) every Indian today - and everyone else too, everywhere - would be improved by a reading of the proceedings of the Mahatma's first trial, and imprisonment by the British authorities, in early 1922.

There can be few finer addresses than the Mahatma's Statement given to the trial Judge, a Mr Broomfield, nor the response of Mr Broomfield, in bringing down his judgement. *(Pages 118-126 "Mahatma Gandhi", E. Stanley Jones).*

Anyone who wants to better understand the circumstances behind India's rightful quest for control over their country, and over themselves, could not fail to be impressed by the meaningful content of both statements. The dignity of the prisoner at the bar and also the noble utterance of the Judge, tell more about Britain's dominion over India and India's fight for democracy, than whole libraries of observations could possibly do.

A more astute and honest 'with the most honourable intentions' man, one could not find. Greatly revered by all Indians alike, but particularly by the poorer masses, still striving to be noticed and to be assisted to a less onerous life, Gandhi's message is as relevant today, (in fact more relevant, noting the state of the nation's current political disarray), as when he was leading India to its freedom. He tried to extinguish communalism. He implored all Indians 'to become scavengers - to help clean up their country, physically, mentally and morally'.

The Smarak at Kanniyakumari constitutes a powerful and constant reminder to all Indians, to 'live' the Mahatma's bidding, and not just sometimes, but all of the time.

<u>Epilogue:</u>

For anyone wishing to better acquaint themselves with E. Stanley Jones' interpretation and with Gandhiji's 1922 trial, the particular book is -

"Mahatma Gandhi"
Hodder & Stoughton
London (1st Ed 1948)

Final Note:

Curious to discover whether Judge Broomfield might have been 'affected' by his significant meeting with Mahatma Gandhi, I put my queries to the India Library in London. They responded saying that in their record of the worthy Judge, he left nothing (on record) to indicate he suffered any uneasiness or qualms, as a result of his unique encounter. Not unlike many other Britishers who 'served' in India, the Judge seemingly kept non-career matters at 'arms-length'. India/Africa/ Singapore - wherever, to many, it was all the same. I might easily have believed (J.B.) would have been otherwise affected. If he was, he kept it to himself.

19. Lately French

- intriguing lovely Pondicherry

The most southerly State in India is Tamil Nadu (the land of the Tamils - descendants of the Dravidian society which moved from north India, sometime during the second and first millennia B.C. to the 'Deccan plateau' south of the Vindya Mountains). It shares with Andhra Pradesh, its northern neighbour, the distinction of having the longest coastline (which includes the Coromandel Coast, from Point Calimere to the mouths of the Krishna River) of any Indian State, 900 kilometres from west of Cape Comorin up to Pulicat Lake.

While the peoples of northern India derive their basic characteristics from the numerous immigrant groups, who from the second millennium B.C. moved into the Gangetic plains, the darker-skinned inhabitants of southern India largely escaped any of this further dilution. The Dravidian cultural forms and its languages - Telegu, Kannada and Tamil, which uniquely have no apparent similarity or connection with any other language family, either in India, or in any other part of Asia, have been substantially retained, to this day.

In the south, and predominantly in Tamil Nadu, the purest and strictest form of Hinduism is still preserved amidst the great throng of magnificent temple complexes found throughout the State. The centuries old marvellously sculptured *gopurams,* (towering pyramidal tapering gateways) which distinguish them, are exclusively Tamil in origin. All of these architecturally thrilling temples attract vast numbers of pilgrims to worship at them.

In many of the places - Madurai, the twelve hundred year old temple town of Kanchipuram, and Thanjavur (with its architecturally superb thousand year old Brahadeeswarar Temple) - the towns grew from around their major Hindu complexes.

The magnificent Temple settings at Tiruchchendur (Senthilandavar Temple), and at Ramanathapuram (the

Ramanathaswamy temple at "Agnitheertham", together with the spectacular temple dedicated to Sri Ramanatha Swamy with its extraordinary 4000 foot long corridor of sculptured pillars which straddles the Pamban Channel on the isthmus which leads to the famous "Adam's Bridge" crossing over to Sri Lanka) stimulate and stir, in a tremendous way.

Other wonderful coastal gems are the superb Hindu complex at Mamallapuram, south of Chennai, with its eighth century Shore Temple jutting out into the sea (almost the scene of a terrible calamity for the author when his shoulder bag containing passport, all money etc. slipped down through the rock escarpment. Fortunately it stopped halfway down to the sea below and was able to be 'fished' out, A big relief!), the five 'rathas' named after the five Pandava heroes of the Mahabharata, and Arjuna's Penance. Another of a different religion, Christian this time, is the wonderful looking 'Our Lady of Health' R.C. Cathedral, at Velankanni. Its annual festival (in August) attracts people of all faiths from around the world.

All the foregoing dissertation is not simply to express the marvellousness of the ancient religious architecture, but as well to allow readers some absorption of the intensive emphasis and great focus there is on religious worship, an integral part of almost every Indian's life, and no more intensively than the practice and the commitment of devout South Indians, of every religious persuasion. The great and enduring wonders of spiritual India are forcibly projected within our senses and understanding, never to be afterwards forgotten.

The honesty of the religious fervour of the people is unquestionable and perhaps unquenchable, and inevitably has a marked flow-on to what we in the west, term 'progress'. Agriculture dominates, with all that state of affairs, brings in its train. A quiet, even serene life, in its most basic form and one subject to nature's best and sternest pressures. Religious attentiveness and faith provides the bulwark for combating any futility that could otherwise take charge. Accepting fortune and misfortune alike without complaint, dominates the Indian character, particularly that of the *kisan* (farmer), confronted as he has been for centuries by the vagaries of the elements which he is powerless to control.

Away from the lusher south-west, rice (the primary diet of most Indians) is the principal crop. Farming methodology and

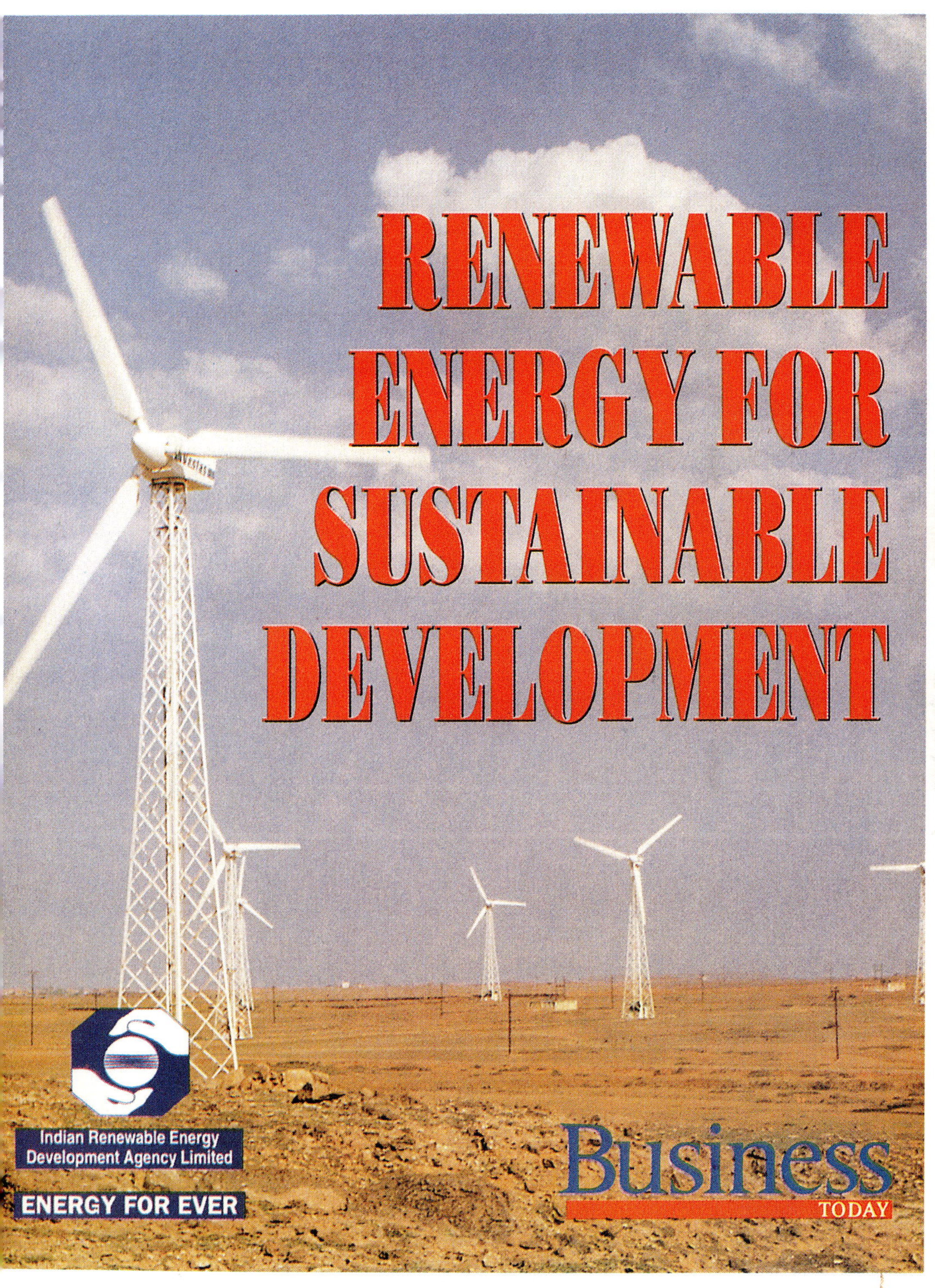

47 **A.** Wind farms-Renewable energy for sustainable development

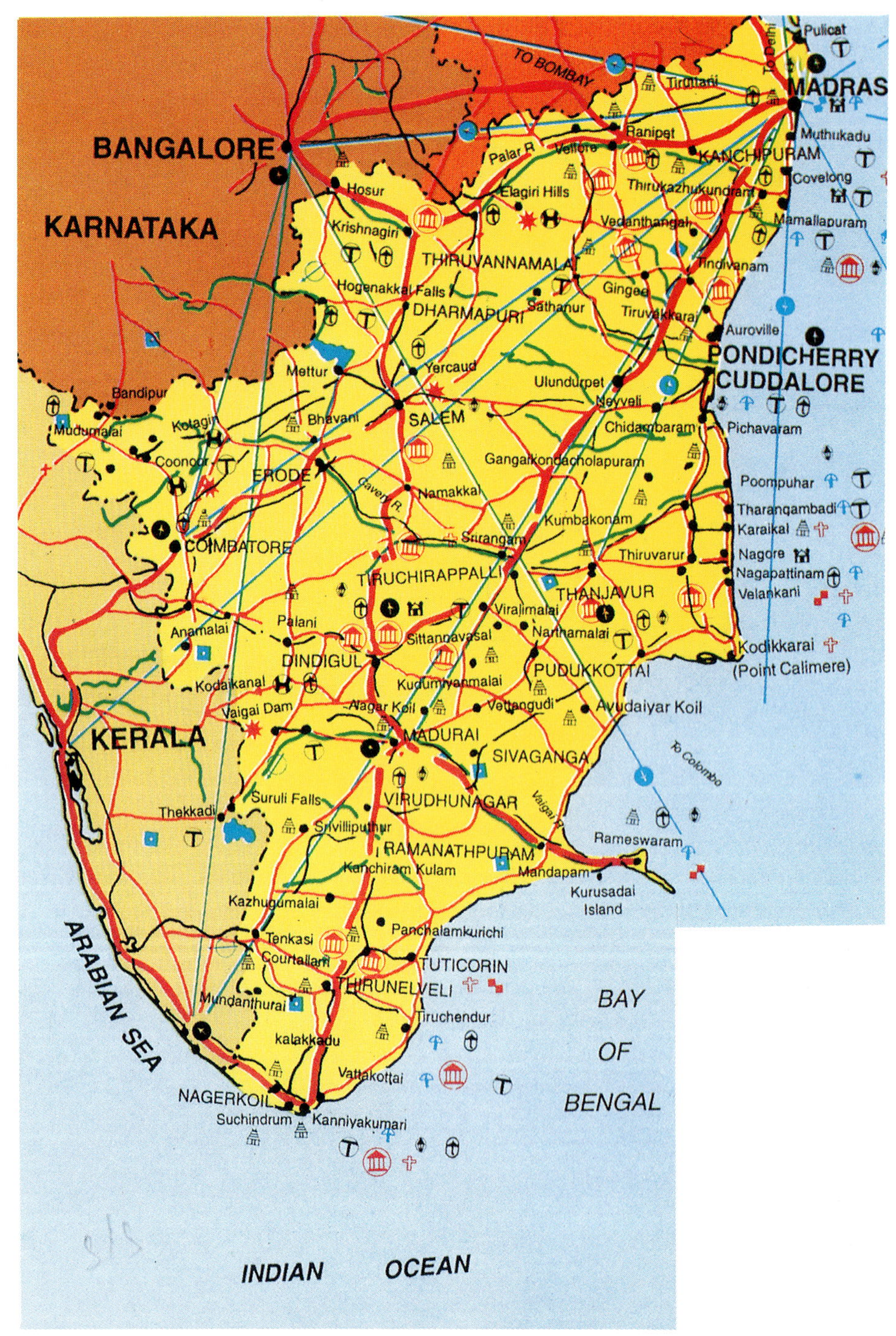

47 B. Colourful Map of Tamil Nadu, S. India

implements reflect older times, as does also the substantial use and reliance on bullock drawn transport incorporating the unhurried timelessness heavily a part of rural life. Population increases and generally dry and hot conditions, aggravating water shortage, identify difficult, frugal lives for many, a situation that is not readily remediable.

Departing from Kanniyakumari and resuming our journey, we re-enter the very fertile country that surrounds Nagercoil, as rich as one might see anywhere. But the effect of the Ghats shutting out most precipitation from the west, soon becomes too obviously (and distressingly) apparent, as one travels north. We have over six hundred kilometres to travel, over restrictive country roads, before we reach Pondicherry. We will break the journey at Trichy (Tiruchchirappalli - Trinchinopoly).

Leaving Nagercoil in our wake and before we reach Valliyar an interesting spectacle, "whirring propellers" atop hundreds (more likely there are many thousands of them) of slim gracefully tall masts enlivens an otherwise mundane run through farming lands, parched after months of hot, dry summer. Coming upon the wind turbines introduces a light-hearted happy wonderland atmosphere. Never seen on such density scale before, and in what could seem to be a fairly backward area of south India, my surprise is converted to pleasure for the rural dwellers, the recipients of the electricity which is produced. For them this 'gift' must appear like hurdling across centuries of time and space.

(It also causes the author to reflect upon the scene in his own country, Australia, where for most of the nineteenth century and much of the present one, farmers in the vast rural areas used windmills exclusively for drawing up underground water for their herds, whether cattle or sheep. Rainwater run off corrugated iron roofs and collected in 'tanks' served their domestic requirements. As well, for most of these people there was no electricity, and the only light was by kerosene or acetylene lamps).

Generating power from a renewable source of energy - the wind (and from other alternative sources, solar etc), is being taken up with great gusto by private as well as Government enterprises everywhere in India. Asia's largest power windmill farm in the private sector, is concentrated around one of nature's wind tunnels, at Muppandal, in Kanniyakumari District.

We have been privileged to witness this proud achievement which is a wonderful example for many similarly inclined private enterprise entrepreneurial companies to duplicate, wherever similarly endowed geographical regions exist, around India. While electricity extends to eighty percent of urban India, not more then thirty percent of rural households have electricity. The need, and the challenge to supply, is there.

Reaching the periphery of Madurai the whole scene changes to one of great congestion. One of India's (and Tamil Nadu's) most celebrated religious centres, Madurai is the oldest city in Tamil Nadu. The modern city, on the southern side of the Vaigai River, was literally built 'around' the great and beautiful Meenakshi Sundareswarar Temple, created and built by the mighty Pandyan King, Kulasekhara, circa 1300 A.D. With its magnificent sculpture, soaring *gopurams* and Hall of Thousand Pillars the Meenakshi Temple and the Mandapam (Hall), provide inspiring remembrances of Madurai - the so called 'Athens of the East'.

Tiruchchirappalli (or as it is affectionately formed 'Trichy') would add to the feast of Hindu architecture spread out before us. While the climb up the myriad stone steps to the top of the Rock Temple affords wonderful views of all the country around Trichy, it is the Ranganathaswamy Temple at Srirangar which invites more curiosity.

Crossing over the wide Cauvery and passing through the northern suburbs we come upon this very extensive Vaisnavite temple of Srirangar. The largest of all the Pandyan style complexes, the Ranganathoswamy Temple, featuring six inner walls, all with *gopurams* (towering gateways), is surrounded by an outer perimeter wall approximately a half a mile square. The comparatively modest proportioned shrine - the Golden Vimanam - sits amongst an array of superb sculpture.

Walking back to Trichy in order to absorb some of the local atmosphere, the Rock Fort (Vinayagar) Temple stands out as an unmistakable beacon in the distance. High positions, wherever located, possess great allure and the Rock Temple's worn stone steps (300 of them) evidence the passage of millions since the present shrine was constructed by the Nayaks of Madurai, several hundred years ago. There are signs that the giant granite outcrop has been 'inhabited' for several thousand years. Dravidian 'temple' architecture passed through many stages, examples of much of which can be found in excellently preserved state throughout South India, and very distinct from the chief cities of North India, where almost all traces of the architecture of the early Hindu period have vanished.

A land of small traders, menial workers and agriculturists, perhaps of much equality, typifies south India. Peaceful harmony seems a natural corollary.

The final leg of our journey to Pondicherry is uneventful. Transferring from one local bus to another at Villupuram market-place, the multifarious activity is fascinating and a scene that is repeated daily in thousands of places right across India. A study on its own, but something which we in western societies have largely relegated to a duty, instead of grasping and enjoying the pleasurable aspects it also contains, and dispenses, free.

A short run takes us through to Pondicherry, famous for the part it played in the modern colonisation of the Indian sub-continent. All of the foreign nations France, Portugal, Holland, England and Denmark (the seafaring nations of the 16th, 17th, and 18th centuries) entered into India - probably more correctly 'were welcomed into India' and never as belligerent invaders - with the sole purpose of funding a safe haven for their ships and for replenishing their supplies, particularly of fresh water. None originally had any intention of 'capturing' new territory. Unlike Australia (Capt. Arthur Phillip) 1788, or the "Mayflower" (Pilgrim Fathers in America) 1620, initially there were no flag hoisting ceremonies anywhere in India - not, at the beginning.

The changes that came about followed trade rivalries in getting the best from Indian associations, but most of all they were the result of international differences played out in Europe, in the various wars which regularly occurred in that part of the world during the eighteenth and nineteenth centuries. The rivalries of Europe were transferred to their fairly minor interests in India. The greater might and purpose of the English (after 1707 more correctly perhaps, 'British') ensured their survival, while the Dane and the Dutch interests, mostly just petered out.

While the bigger spoils went to the British, somewhat surprisingly several enclaves held by others were never seriously challenged. Portugal clung on to Goa and a few other small areas - until 19 Dec. 1961, while France retained Pondicherry and a few other tidbit possessions until post second World War (c. 1954). While all this was going on, and even more surprisingly, Indians themselves, the rightful owners of the country, could only be onlookers, but then they had filled a similar role since time immemorial. An extraordinary people, who with any justification could deny them their entitlement when 1947 arrived along. Their situation had no replica, anywhere on earth, other than Africa, and some parts of Central and South America.

The Pondicherry of today had its genesis with the arrival of the French, in 1673. The Dutch grabbed it twenty years later, then Portugal got it back six years later. During the Napoleonic wars Britain took control through to 1814, when they 'gave it back' to the French, who stayed on until 1954, despite the stoushes between the Frenchman Dupleix and the British, in the Carnatic in the mid-seventeen hundreds. An extraordinary series of events in a country which rightfully belonged to others. Such is history, none of which can be undone, satisfactorily explained, or altered in any way.

By all accounts, French influence in Pondicherry, suited many Indians. Substantial cultural links were forged, many of which continue to flourish. The Alliance Francaise and the French Institute zealously keep the French tradition alive. French missionaries did their work well, as evidenced by the significant church attendance in the three grandly embellished churches in Pondicherry - Sacred Heart of Jesus, Eglise de Notre Dame de la Immaculate Conception and the Eglise de Notre Dame des Anges, and the Eglise de Notre dame de Lourdes, a few miles away in its delightful setting, at Villianur. The spirited singing of liturgical music by the younger Indians is a highpoint, of their Christianity.

The sea-side strip of Pondicherry, the French populated piece, is bounded to the west side by the canal which runs from south boulevarde to Sardar Vallabhbhai Patel Road. This section retains its very 'Frenchness', even to the extent of the policemen retaining their little peaked redbanded caps *kepis*, like the gendarmes of old. The French Consul General's office and residence facing the northern seafront, might easily have been transplanted from Marseilles. The *Hotel deVille* (Legislative Assembly), is a small scale version of Paris' own magnificent City Hall on *Rue du Temple* by the Seine.

48. Sweeping view along surf beach and ocean Esplanade - Pondicherry.

Dupleix holds up the southern end of what is undoubtedly the best attribute of all in Pondicherry - the delightfully commodious seafront boulevarde along the length of *Goubert Salai*. Mahatma Gandhi surveys the passing multitude from his central possie opposite Government Place. High seas over the past decade have deprived Pondicherrans of most of their beach, now protected right along and beyond the New Pier, by a solid rock wall.

But possibly the main attraction of today's Pondicherry is the Aurobindo Ashram established in the early part of this century by the intellectual poet/philosopher Sri Aurobindo (Ghosh) a son of Calcutta. An Indian patriot Sri Aurobindo had run foul of the British and had moved to French controlled Pondicherry, in 1910.

The Ashram is attended by thousands of followers from around the world, who, when in residence in Pondicherry, must work at one occupation or another in the Ashram's various departments. The Sri Aurobindo Ashram strives for an all-around development of the religious individual.

Both during his life time and after his death, 'the Mother', French born Mirra Alfassa (Mrs. Mira Richard), was a tremendous influence on the affairs and advancement of the Ashram. A very beautiful and noble lady, her great teachings form a significant part of the Ashram programme.

The splendid Park Guest House on the seafront provides excellent (but spare) accommodation for short-term visitors to the Sri Aurobindo Ashram.

Another of Sri Aurobindo's dreams, a universal township where people from all around the world, irrespective of their faiths, could converge and find their inner spiritual selves, is Auroville, 'the City of Dawn', a city within (Pondicherry) city, substantially created and fostered by the Mother. The Matrimandir (literally Mother Temple) at Auroville designed by a French architect, and resembling a lotus with a globe-shaped sphere in the centre cradled by twelve uniquely shaped petals, must rank as one of the most unusual structures ever conceived and built.

At some time it will be intriguing to discover its effect upon Ashram devotees and to read of their experiences.

Au revoir. A votre santé.

Note for readers

- Pondicherry, a Union Territory with an area of just 492 square kilometres faces the Bay of Bengal on the east and is encircled on its other sides by the State of Tamil Nadu. Pondicherry, the original headquarters of the French in India, lies approximately 100 miles south of Madras (Chennai).

20. A Meeting With An Indian Gentleman And Hotelier Of Renown

- Rai Bahadur Mohan Singh Oberoi

The name Oberoi has reverberated throughout the hotel industry in India, and in the countries adjacent to India, for more than sixty years. More recent acquisitions, in Egypt, Australia and in London, and its Management of Singapore's Terminal 2, comfortably furnished Transit Hotel facilities, have further extended the very respected name amongst the business and tourist areas, of the Nineties' world.

'Oberoi' is synonymously bracketed with 'class' in its best sense, namely - the right degree of accommodation; the most respectfully delivered service, in all its facets; plus courtesy and efficiency of the highest order given by every one of its gracious well-trained, well-informed, and well-groomed staff.

For all this collective excellence, we have to thank the doyen of the Oberoi dynasty, Rai Bahadur Mohan Singh Oberoi, now in his ninetyeighth year, but who only a few short years ago was still playing a very active part in the hotel chain's affairs - as Executive Chairman of the Board of the Holding Company, East India Hotels Limited.

From his magnificent farm retreat at Bigwasen, not so far out of Delhi, Mohan Singh Oberoi, the wonderful trooper, can relax and enjoy his well-earned rest, and reward, knowing the tremendous job he has done for India, in gaining unequivocal praise and respect, not just from his countrymen, but from the highest pinnacles of the hospitality industry throughout the world.

The author has been intimately acquainted with the Oberoi Hotel chain throughout India for over forty years - where would Calcutta be without the wonderful "Grand" on Chowringhee? As famous an institution and part of its history, as Raj Bhavan or Writers' Building, and certainly - better known.

Ten years has passed since the Author twice visited the Oberoi father and son (Biki) at Bigwasen, but the continued progress and advancement of the Oberoi best traditions - keeps the Oberoi story evergreen.

In our less than perfect present day world, examples of unwavering consistent quality stand out, and deserve the accolades of all of us. Mohan Singh Oberoi's story would find a place near the top of any list of world renowned hoteliers - anywhere, and not just in India, where maintaining standards, the right scruples and the spirits of every member of staff, may sometimes require that extra bit of grit, of determination to succeed, while still preserving the highest ideals.

The description of my greatly enjoyed and vividly remembered call upon Mr Oberoi at Bigwasen, needs no redrafting, no retelling, for its message is as fresh and as wonderfully instructive today, as it was then. The Oberoi path (onwards and upwards) has never wavered, a tribute to its formation and operation, that employs only the finest and best, principles.

Mr Oberoi's story as related to me from his peaceful country retreat near Bigwasen follows -

Rai Bahadur Mohan Singh Oberoi is a man known far and wide and greatly revered and respected in India and in many parts of the world.

Any person who has travelled through India in the past fifty years has had cause to bless the name of Oberoi for its excellent hotels. The names Grand, Maidens, Cecil and Imperial (from the fifties and sixties) will spark pleasant memories for very many, for they provided excellence away from home, in times when, without them, the traveller might have lamented he had come - to India.

Throughout his long life Rai Bahadur Oberoi has been a tireless worker for the hospitality industry, and for India, and the fruits of his lifetime's labour of love are evidenced present-day by his splendid twenty-seven hotel chain, half of them outside India. Those in India are superb, you will not find cleaner, better kept hotels anywhere in the world. The Oberoi hotels are spotless. Those outside India are similarly excellent and in all of them, the public receive gracious service of the highest order. It is the 'badge' of Oberoi, exemplified by its

Chairman, Rai Bahadur Mohan Singh, a 'mine host' of rare quality and skill, known and admired everywhere.

From its tiny beginnings in Simla, the Oberoi organization now employs thirtysix thousand people in eight countries with an annual turnover exceeding 40 million pounds. Plans for expansion in Australia and to England and America can only enhance further the name of Oberoi.

It was my pleasure to see Mr Oberoi at his home, a little distance out of New Delhi and to learn something, however small, of himself, of his past and of his future plans - and all this from a still spritely, immaculately presented gentleman, of 87 years of age!

INTRODUCTION - Author to Mr. Oberoi

Good afternoon to you. Thank you very much for receiving me into your lovely home. It is an honour and great privilege to meet you.

Question: You have had a most distinguished business life. Do you regard the '1983 Man of the World' award from the International Hotels Association of the USA as the pinnacle of your career?

Mr Oberoi: Yes, I was thrilled to receive it. Perhaps more properly, it should have gone to the Oberoi Hotels Organization, for all my staff and my family too, have done much to provide hotels and service in India, up to a standard comparable with the best in the world. I am very proud to have helped make this a reality.

Question: World travellers pre-1960, had a lot to be thankful to you for - the "Grand" in Calcutta, "Maidens" and "Imperial" in Delhi, and in Simla, and Darjeeling too, "The Mount Everest". The name 'Oberoi' was then and is today, synonymous with 'good hotels'.

Mr Oberoi: Yes, I was lucky I suppose. I have always loved the hotel business and those were happy beginnings.

Question: Have you always concentrated your business activity upon 'the hospitality trade'?, i.e., running fine hotels, or did your working life have different beginnings?

Mr Oberoi: No, I only wanted to work in hotels. After finishing my schooling - it was in 1922 - I was in Simla and started work in Mr Clarke's hotel there as a desk clerk (now the Oberoi 'Clarkes'). I think my monthly salary was about the present day equivalent of US$5!

Question: As a young boy in the Punjab, did you ever dream of what the future may hold for you? Do you now believe you have achieved those goals?

Mr Oberoi: I always had strong ambitions, always! I felt a strong need to bring something to my life, to accomplish something. This strong personal 'urge' has always carried me through to my objectives.

Question: Looking around this lovely room, you are surrounded by so many happy family photographs. Seemingly, in an otherwise very busy life, you have always found time to keep your family around you?

Mr Oberoi: Yes, I've always thought it essential to keep strong family bonds. All my family (five children), live in and around New Delhi. For my birthday (15 August) every one of them (28) were gathered together in this room, except my son Biki, who was away on business.

Question: You started in the hotel business as a clerk. When did the opportunity come to you to own your first hotel, which event must have seemed the beginning of a great adventure.

Mr Oberoi: Well, in 1926-7, the opportunity was given to me by Mr Clarke to buy a part of the hotel. I had continued to work for an aging Mr Clarke when he made me the offer of his shares. Through the help of relatives, I found the deposit and became a hotel owner, which was a wonderful feeling. By arrangement I paid the rest off in instalments from revenue derived from the hotel.

Question: Did you ever doubt 'Clarkes' would be a success and lead you on to better things?

Mr Oberoi: No, I've always been lucky, everything generally came off, and successfully. I tried to give good service and good value for money, and it has never failed me.

Question: After 'Clarkes' at Simla where did the next opportunity arise to extend your operations?

"We believe our guests deserve the best the world has to offer."

49. Rai Bahadur Mohan Singh Oberoi - Founder and Chairman 'Oberoi Hotels'.

Mr Oberoi: Again, I was very lucky. The famous 'Grand Hotel' in Calcutta had been condemned and its doors been closed following some deaths attributed to unclean food or conditions at the hotel. That was in 1936 when there was a cholera epidemic.

I saw it as a great opportunity and in 1938 after negotiations, secured the re-opening of the hotel in a 'management' role. I had just one 'resident' guest.

But the war came along and accommodation became greatly sought. The C.O. British forces arranged with me to provide residential facilities for troops which we did, to the extent that at times 1500 persons slept in the hotel, ordinarily intended to accommodate just 200! People slept in the ballroom, in the billiard room, anywhere - just so long they were sheltered from the elements. The term 'buffet' too, came of age! It was amazing! and of course we did handsomely from it.

Question: I haven't asked, but generally every successful person can look back to a mentor; to someone who has encouraged them/inspired them, in their ambitions. Who do you believe helped you more than anyone else?

Mr Oberoi: Well, of course, I have to thank old Mr Clarke, for he did so much for me, and showed me much. His hotel was very famous and being situated in Simla, the summer capital of the Viceroy and his entourage, it got a lot of trade. Mr Clarke also helped me to my first proprietorship.

Question: It is a feather in your cap (and in your son Biki's also) that Oberoi saw a great need for a "Hotel School of Management' on Indian soil. What has this School achieved and prior to its being instituted, how did you recruit or train your executives and staff?

Mr Oberoi: Well, the last part of your question first.

Until the early sixties we employed expatriates in senior management positions for their international experience. We found our young executives in the high schools and universities. We interviewed candidates and made selections, then put them to training in our own hotels.

Since establishing a 'Hotel School' in Delhi nearly a thousand persons have graduated. Hotel trainees also come to us from those countries where we now 'manage' hotels. Of course, we don't retain them all, but other hotel chains make our graduates attractive offers. So, in a way, indirectly, we are helping to raise the standards of hotel service throughout India and elsewhere, and we are not unhappy about this.

Question: Nowadays you own and run (or 'manage) about as many hotels in overseas countries as you 'own' hotels in India. You run some very fine exclusive resort hotels in exotic places. Why did you choose to expand outside India and do you have any plans to further extend your orbit of 'fine hotels' around the world?

Mr Oberoi: Well, it all seemed to make good business sense to go into eastern countries for we are not so different people and we believed we had something to offer.

We earn good foreign exchange for India and have received much encouragement and financial incentives from the Indian Government, both in India (promotion of Indian tourism) as well as overseas.

Restrictive financial controls presently preclude our owning hotels overseas but some legitimate measures may yet be worked out to allow this to happen, for there are some wonderful opportunities available.

Question: You own and/or operate some superb hotels, mostly in near eastern countries, but also in Australia where Melburnians have particularly good reasons to be thankful for your excellent management, and for 'saving' the Windsor. The Windsor Hotel, 'the grand lady of Spring Street' has been magnificently restored to its original pristine condition and the service there is indeed 'Oberoi'. How did you happen to extend to Australia?

Mr Oberoi: Oh, we are always on the lookout for opportunities and 'The Windsor' came up for tender. After protracted negotiations our tender succeeded and we have a long lease. We too, are delighted with the renovations and value the sincerity and co-operation of the Australian people.

Question: For a long while, you have been likened to the famous American entrepreneur, Mr Conrad Hilton. I am sure Mr Hilton would not be un-delighted with this situation, your hotels having acquired world renown, and even at times, unscheduled fame.

Mr Oberoi: Well, it is kind of you to say these things about our organization. We simply try to provide high quality service and to do better and better. We believe our guests deserve the best the world has to offer.

Yes, our 'Aswan Oberoi' achieved fame unexpectedly, when the Shah of Iran and his family took up residence in the hotel after being deposed.

Question: We've talked a lot about the hotel business, but at 87 years of age you will have experienced a great many diverse things? When you have not been busy directing the destiny of your burgeoning hotel group, what other of your pursuits have given you greatest pleasure?

Mr Oberoi: Well, hotels really are my great love, they are my abiding interest! I have gone all over the world and stayed in fine hotels, to enjoy their facilities and to note how they do things. I have spent much of my 'free' time doing this.

I have been very lucky for there have been no adverse events in my life. I never was sick, always too busy, but I had a terrible sadness two years ago when my son Tiki passed away suddenly and unexpectedly. It was a great loss and I suffered a stroke as a result of it, which has restricted my walking.

Question: It is interesting that India's Independence fell on your birthday, 15th August (1947). While this is a nice coincidence, it must nevertheless always give you an added, good feeling, always celebrating another milestone, when all of India's millions celebrate theirs. You have served your country in both houses of Central Government - the Lok Sabha (lower house) and Rajya Sabha (Upper House) between the years 1962 and 1970. What prompted you to serve in politics?

Mr Oberoi: Well, I wanted to find out a lot of things and the best way to do that, was to get involved. I always stood as an Independent, but gave my support to Mrs Indira Gandhi's policies. I enjoyed it all and learnt a lot.

Question: Having witnessed many great changes and happenings within your lifetime, particularly here in India, down which path do you believe India should be seeking to travel in her relations with other nations?

Mr Oberoi: Independent India has played no 'favourites', but wishes to be friendly with every other nation. Non-alignment is best; that's what is really best for India, I'm sure of it.

Question: Besides your Parliamentary service you have made other valued contributions to the Indian commercial world through your

Membership of The Institute of Public Administration and through your representation of India on the Indian Council of World Affairs and as well, through your membership of The International Hotels Association. In the field of philanthropy have you ever sought to perpetuate the Oberoi name by setting up scholarships or by public association with philanthropic organizations?

Mr Oberoi: There is a Trust in my mother's name (Bhagwanti Oberoi Trust - 1980) which provides free medical treatment for people of Bigwasen (Charitable Dispensary - 1983) and gives other help as well.

Question: You established this lovely farm property (more, a beautiful park) outside Delhi twelve years ago, but still keeping yourself handy to your principal seat of operations. You've already achieved what many men might only achieve in many lifetimes. Do you ever think of retirement? And possibly in another of the lovely places you have visited, not necessarily in India.

Mr Oberoi: No, I like work, I love hotels, I want to do more. We have plans to go into London and New York and for another hotel in Australia, in Sydney. I want to see these things happen. Also, we are going to restore Maidens in Old Delhi and turn it into an exclusive superb 'olde worlde' hotel, just as it was, at its birth, and of course, it is very dear to my heart, as it was one of the first hotels I owned.

If I had to go anywhere (for a change) I'd go to Australia; I spent a year there when we acquired 'The Windsor' in Melbourne.

I love India, it is my home, and if I went away at all, my preference would be to Australia, a very friendly country.

Question: To very many people around the world, the name Oberoi means 'excellence in hotel service' and for 'recognizing the human touch', in your relations with your clientele. The 'public relations' practised with grace, charm and tact is most commendable and of course welcomed and appreciated. If you were to offer some words of advice to any young man or young woman starting out upon their life's journey, what would that advice be?

Mr Oberoi: You should tell them that their lives should be honest and they should create confidence in people and give a helping hand to deserving people. Love and get love!

CONCLUSION: Mr Oberoi it has been a great pleasure for me to meet you and to share a very little part of your distinguished and successful life. Thank you and very best wishes.

Post Script

Calling in late July at the 'Oberoi International' in New Delhi, (in my opinion among the finest and best of hotels, in all the world. It is superb in every respect) I learnt that Rai Bahadur Mohan Singh is keeping reasonable health at Bigwasen. Although not wholly removed from his great and long associated best love - 'his exceptional coterie of magnificently maintained and run hotels' - Mr Oberoi nowadays is mostly to be found at Bigwasen, rightly and deservedly enjoying there, the beautiful atmosphere it provides, among its lush vegetation. I'm sure I speak for every one of us, when we wish him 'all happiness' as he approaches his final triumph - a century of years serving many others, but most of all by unremitting effort heaping great credit on his land of birth, India.

P.P.S.

Visiting New Delhi several months ago, I was told that Rai Bahadur Mohan Singh Oberoi is now in his 103rd year, with another wonderful milestone coming up on 15 August, 2001. An amazing durable Indian gentleman, who has served India so well during his entire lifetime, inspiring so many others along the way. A most deserving son of India and like J. R. D. Tata, so commendably honest and modest.

Melbourne 5/2001

21. Bombay (Mumbai) In The Nineties

- A topical note for travellers seeking something more from a visit to India

For the unfamiliar (and even for those with a closer association) it will come as some surprise to discover that Greater Bombay, nowadays also referred to as Mumbai and one of India's four largest cities (in population terms - the others being Calcutta, Delhi and Madras. The latter also now called Chennai), is actually situated on a long narrow archipelago via a series of linked islands, which straddle the west coast of India. It is also by far, the largest and best-known Arabian Sea port.

Being conveniently located on the sea route to and from Europe, Asia and Australia, many sea-going foreigners have 'touched' on Bombay - for most of them however, it has been nothing more than a brief transit stop, permitting only the scantiest knowledge/association.

Bombay's modern era began from the time of its cession in 1661 to Charles II of England (by the Portuguese, as part of the marriage dowry of Catherine of Braganza). In 1668 Charles II transferred Bombay to the East India Company for an annual payment of ten pounds.

Since that time, and for hundreds of years up to the late nineteen sixties, most Britishers who served in the sub-continent (before, and after Partition, in 1947), entered India through the port of Bombay. The earliest British settlement in India had seen most activity take place on the east coast, initially from Madras and later at Calcutta, and back on the western side at Karachi (now in Pakistan).

The opening of the Suez Canal in 1869, provided a great spurt for Bombay. Being on the nearer "European" side, of India, has also played a significant part in Bombay's progress, something which has become even more evident in the last decade (the 1990's), as India has opened up to global interests and to the attention of 'western located' investors.

People will say that modern transportation and communications have negated geographical advantages/ disadvantages, and while this may be partly true, the facts still are, that geographical situation (from the viewpoint of economics, if nothing else) is an important ingredient and still tends to 'point' people and attentions, in a particular direction.

India has principally looked westwards and northwards for hundreds, even thousands of years, and predominantly it still does, look mainly to the western (developed) nations, but for ever so long, too long really, all too sufficiently adequately in the direction of its eastern cousins. India either put itself, or was put by others - 'out on a limb' and isolated from its own region.

Discerning observers put it down to the advent to India, of the British in particular, but as well to the other European colonizers - France, Holland, Denmark and Portugal - all of whom occupied slices of the sub-continent at various times, from 1600 right up to 1947, and in fact commercially British businesses still held sway, up to the mid nineteen-sixties. India's (likely) own *future* interests took second place, or no place at all, in the way of colonizers, of that age.

Before the arrival of the Europeans, India had conducted a thriving trade in cottage industries (textiles mainly) within India itself and also with Asia/Pacific countries, something which fell into serious decline, until withering almost completely away. For centuries this indigenous and regional trade had provided a steady supplement to family incomes, particularly for the people residing on India's agricultural estate. The loss of this source of income contributed to previously unexperienced wider poverty, aggravated in poor 'crop' seasons.

Under British rule (c. 1757 until 1947), apart from Indian migration to other colonized countries, in Asia/Pacific, and on the African continent, major trade, major relations and major attention - from the Indian sub-continent, was substantially directed westwards, reaching to today's difficult situation where India is a relative 'unknown' amongst Asia/Pacific countries, with very little influence of any sort, almost beyond Sri Lanka.

This huge 'gap' has historically 'distanced' India from the higher echelons of trade/security with its eastern neighbours, something its Government and its businessmen, are striving manfully to repair.

The combination of Britain's monopoly over Indian trade, plus India's own 40 year long introspection up to 1991 (when it believed its priorities totally belonged at home in India, sorting out its multitudinous problems, hugely unaided and aggravated by relentless population increases) has left a 'void' and India without any strong affiliations in the Asia/Pacific region. Becoming strong trading partners will be slow in coming, particularly since the 1997/98 financial meltdown will have introduced serious distractions enough to delay all new alliances. History can play some vexing unsuspected tricks.

But to return to Bombay, and that vast pulsating metropolises' position since it set sail on its upward course of prosperity. It seems possible that today's Bombay, very seriously constricted as it is, by its severely restricting geographical composition, could have avoided some of its present-day (and worsening) horrendous infrastructure problems (and this is not just my own personal opinion formed from observing the city's 'progress' over a long period, but the consensus of every responsible person, Bombay-ites and foreign experts, alike) if its builders had been more visionary. Difficult of course to work such into any positive long-term plans, when a colonizer's tenure is at best, uncertain.

Ad hoc or even *ad interim*, measures can be, and very often are, the villain. Other uncertainties apart, predicting future events and civic (people) requirements in its widest form, has defeated nearly everyone. The essential requisite 'the funds to do the work' which future generations will largely benefit from, are harder to procure, and the will to be beneficent, not (usually) there.

In India's case, the task is increased. Grappling with any accuracy, with uncertain population possibilities (and shifting populations) years ahead, with its many unknowns, defies most reliable assessments. India's cities, and particularly its four largest cities, are magnets for rural populations seeking succour/relief, whenever hardship strikes. Most of Bombay's accretion, in the present century has come from 'without' and not 'grown' from within.

But also, if earlier planning (although the 'mix' of the Indian population always skews public funding, with the greater numbers paying no direct taxes or rates and those who can pay, strenuously avoiding rightful dues. A burdening conundrum which India faces daily.) had pursued positive progressive plans and linked up with the mainland to the eastern side, with successive 'land bridges' (viaducts), instead of only doing so when saturation northwards was reached, Bombay might have enjoyed 'smarter' advances, and contained the strangling congestion it now must cope with - and find some urgent remedies for!

The size of the problem is now so daunting, that confidence is being sapped, that the money and the will to do it, is evaporating, or has already evaporated.

All the people must be conjoined to play some part, but few seem capable of getting the bit firmly between their teeth, and making a start. Yet it must be rectified, and - without further delay. Similar rectification of great magnitude, is also needed in other parts of India, whose problems and solutions are equally weakly approached.

In the circumstances, the 'progress' which is claimed for Bombay, remains hollow. Every day's delay brings greater congestion, as the population lives, and clambers 'one on top of the other', relentlessly filling up every available space, until only the Maidan (by the Gymkhana Club) and the magnificent boulevarde by the harbour wall, out in front of the Taj Hotel and the Gateway (of India) by Shivaji Park, are left to show off Bombay's glory. Hurrah, at least, for this 'mecca' for hordes of people, and for the enjoyment they get from it.

When the central Government of India introduced its new 'economic policy' from 1991, Bombay surged forward quite dramatically. It took the lead in attracting foreign investment to India.

While the Maharashtra State Government was quick to put alluring incentives before foreign (and indigenous) investors - multinationals and large-scale Indian Corporate Groups, in particular - it was Bombay's geographical position wholly bordered to the west by sea, which was a major attraction for many in first looking to locate in Bombay (Maharashtra State), rather than investigate the possible 'commercial' attractions of what initially suggested were less favourable locations, deeper in the heart of India.

As events have transpired, the initial glow reflected by Bombay (Maharashtra) has dimmed somewhat, due to a number of pertinent factors, namely - over congestion, the dearth of good accommodation (residential and business) and its attendant exorbitant rental costs, plus inadequate essential services and a changed political climate, and perhaps as well, tougher competition from other, now equally determined State Governments.

Also, many foreign companies too eager to 'jump in' failed to do their homework properly, completely overestimating the Indian domestic markets idiosyncratic nature. Their enthusiasm for prospectively juicy markets, huge ones (they'd been gulled into false thinking due to a non-understanding and complete mis-reading, of the Indian psyche, which favours spiritual not materialistic ends) was woefully wide of the mark, leaving one to question who it was who did their feasibility/marketing studies?

Any average Indian could have supplied more accurate business forecasts/predictions, than overblown inadequate foreign consultants, unconversant and with no (long) personal experience of India. Many untutored foreigners, successful in their own domains have since recognized the entirely different, real culture, and 'buying/selling culture' of Indians, in their home country.

After long personal experience of India and of Indians, I would wager that Indians recognize 'value' (for money) and the real essential need for whatever article (whether it is a basic food item, a household necessity or an item of clothing) as well as, or better than, any other native race on earth. Indians have learnt, 'how to exist', 'how to survive on very little', very well, and over centuries of need and hardship.

The careful nature of all Indians (rich and poor), would leave the proverbial Scotsman's penchant for frugality/for making do/for squeezing the maximum out of everything, in the shade. Superfluity (of virtually any kind), starts very far down the scale in the 'average' Indian household, where only basics and essentials have a place. Space (to put/to store) is at a premium. Crowding is the norm, and *not* the exception. Also, sufficient reliable water and power for household requisites, washing machines, etc is still very far off.

Every marketer (of consumer goods) *must* start from this premise. Few Indian businessmen make the mistake of not doing so. It comes naturally to them.

Probably the most significant change which has happened in Bombay State (Maharashtra) in the past couple of years, is the change of State Government. A big shift from the past occurred, when governance was won by the ultra radical right wing Hindu party - the Shiv Sena, led by controversial party chief, Bal Thackeray.

Another, has been the reversion to the ancient name for Bombay, for official purposes. Any overall swap over to the substituted name 'Mumbai' won't happen overnight, no different to what is happening all over India, as Indian nomenclature officially replaces Anglicised terminology. Habits and usage over many generations can not be put off by simple directive.

The Shiv Sena Government of Maharashtra, decided on the name change for their capital city, choosing that of the local Hindu deity, Parvati (in one of its numerous forms befitting most Hindu religious figures), the consort of Shiva, one of the Hindu religious triumvirate. The implications for non-Hindus might be seriously conjectured, through the divisive connotations it has (already, and seriously) produced.

Besides the influx of foreign businesses making Bombay their prime base in India (and many have already had a re-think), there has been a rush of people from the *mofussil* (adjacent country areas) consistent with 'normal thinking' that where the money is, there are (or will become) jobs. These kind of 'economic invasions' can not be prevented. Many of the skilled will be disappointed, whilst the bulk of itinerants to the city (a usual thing), will return home to their native villages, unfulfilled (until the next promise arrives along).

While being by the sea (a tremendous virtue for any large city, and especially so for a huggingly over-populated, congested city like Bombay, that can use every bit of breeze that blows) affords Bombay's population major advantages, the long narrow confined land mass (water on both sides, west and east up as far as Thana), also means inevitable serious restriction on adequate and convenient public transport.

Reaching from its two northerly situated Airports, Saha (international), and Santa Cruz (domestic), and proceeding by road to the CBD in the very south, entails tediously slow passage over inadequate and congested roads (except that one arrives at 2 a.m. in the morning as I have sometimes done). Squeezing in more multiple laned highways will not be easy. It seems likely that in Bombay they will have to go 'up', if they are going to solve their problems, and as well institute vastly increased ferry services.

Rail services are also necessarily cramped for extra space, putting more strain on road vehicles, buses and private cars - getting more numerous by the day, as recently inaugurated Joint-Venture foreign car manufacture clogs up already clogged up thoroughfares.

India has put the cart before the horse (even allowing that Indians are relishing the wider choice of new cars now available to them) in throwing open its doors to entry of foreign car-makers, before it has been able to construct better trunk roads. The upshot is that all their bigger cities have become inundated with cars that are rarely used beyond a ten or twenty kilometre radius. Parking too - business and residential - on streets has reached optimal limits.

The financial district of Bombay (Fort), in the vicinity of the Stock Exchange (the busiest and largest in India), is reduced to a crawl, and parking there is at an absolute premium (large 'pay and park' high-risers are not there).

Already tight for room, the Fort District suffers from too inadequate office space. Old, smaller, and minimally maintained (or renewed) buildings, have not been replaced, pointing up the special problems that relate to Indian real estate. Difficulties in vacating (existing) tenants; lack of large sums of money (no people anywhere in the world, know the value of money, better than Indians, or show the same reluctance to spend it - other than on essentials) or with the chance of making guaranteed profits, to re-develop, and sheer cramped space, all retard or inhibit major re-enhancement - in all Indian cities, and no more so than in severely restricted Bombay.

While office accommodation has been neglected, the same can not be said for high-rise, prohibitively expensive (to buy/to rent), apartment blocks, where most building activity has been concentrated. Of course, by the coast, and up on Malabar Hill, the views are grand. Developers are enjoying a huge bonanza, whilst poorer people are pushed further and further out.

Of the four major Indian cities all with populations hovering around twenty millions, easily the two most 'convenient in appointment' from a strict business viewpoint, are Bombay and Calcutta, with Calcutta easily the most compact and convenient 'to move about in' of all four of India's major cities.

While modern day Calcuttans hugely underutilize their wonderfully expansive and noble Hooghly River, incontestably, theirs is the best conceived and most compact city, in fact the most European - like of all Indian cities, which is not so unusual, being British planned and the seat of power for much of the British rule in India. Bombay was once almost idyllically open and pleasant, even delightful. Until it is opened up on the eastern side (by numerous bridges) to the mainland, there will be no return to its glory days.

But perhaps you are asking yourself - what has all the foregoing got to do with pleasure-seeking frolics in and around Bombay. Well, everything perhaps. Better knowing what you are coming to (*before* you arrive - amidst all the congestion and confusion) and being someways armed and prepared, than only getting your bearings when it is time to move on.

Complex India always reads/relates better, when you know something about it. Some travellers do amazing things, take amazing risks, all very innocently (naively?).

I recently read the 'horrific' account of two elderly English ladies who came to India for the first time (in 1996), both almost wholly ignorant of the ways of India, and who chose to head straight away to the back blocks of Gujarat and Saurashtra (some of the least known and least visited parts of India - by foreigners), and more than this, at the start of an oppressively hot and humid summer.

Visitors of this ilk, give India an undeserved bad name. Besides, they invariably exaggerate their experiences 'in the telling' of them to their friends 'back home', lauding their own personal courage, in surviving it all. 'Dining out' on India's misfortunate modern development, much of it due to 'economic standstill over the last several centuries', not authored by themselves, can only be repellent, and ungracious.

50. Various - including sweep of Chowpatty Beach and Marine Drive, Mumbai.

Memorable stays in today's India, where over one billion Indians command first attention, usually result from soundly prepared plans allied to big chunks of sensible (and sensitive) tolerance and understanding. Judging everything you encounter, in vast complex hugely diversified India, with your own personal habits and 'developed by constant gradual progress over hundreds of years general living environment, in your own country', is not only wrong, but a whole lot unfair and grossly mistaken, as well. I think Rabbie Burns had a word for it!

But, back to Bombay (Mumbai) and the lot of the tourist ('in transit' travellers rarely require 'extra' knowledge to see them safely on). I might think that most agree, 'forewarned is forearmed'. Improved knowledge (beyond tourist brochures?) of the local culture and local geography and something of the general atmosphere which may be encountered, ordinarily will result in better enjoyment of Bombay and its environs.

The business heart of the burgeoning metropolis of Bombay (Mumbai) is located at the southern end of the archipelago. Covering a distance of fifty kilometres, at the northern end, the long slim ribbon of extensive development of Greater Bombay, connects to the mainland across the Vasai Creek. On the northern bank lies a historic old Portuguese relic - Bassein Fort, a place likely to evoke interest with many tourists.

Below Vasai and running in a line southwards, one discovers some excellent sandy beaches abutting on to the Arabian Sea - Manori, Marve, Erangel, Madh and finally the best known of them all, Juhu. Before the former Portuguese enclave of Goa became part of the Indian Republic in 1961, Juhu was said to be more famous for liquor smuggling. The beach at Juhu was said to have unearthed many a bottle of Johnny Walker? In prohibition Bombay State, there was a great deal of truth in all this, something however which is no more, since Goa is now part of independent India.

ELEPHANTA Island, the mecca of tourists (possibly in part, because it is reasonably pleasant and convenient to reach) lies 9 kilometres by sea up the east (inside) channel, from the jetties by the Gateway of India, adjacent to that most famous and well known landmark, the Taj Mahal Hotel, the brainchild of Jamsetji Nusserwanji Tata, the founder of the industrial conglomerate, "The House of Tata".

Opened in 1904, it became part of the illustrious quartet of most famous hotels in the East. Its companions - Singapore's "Raffles", Hong Kong's "Peninsula" and Tokyo's "Imperial", all them, and still today, superb and superbly run super hotels.

The twin attractions adjacent to one another on the seafront - the historic "Gateway" which commemorates the King Emperor's (George V) landing in India in 1915, and the celebrated Taj Mahal Hotel, renowned and known around the world, are great magnets for tourists - Indians themselves and foreigners. In the days of scheduled ocean liner services, the first glimpse of 'the Taj' (in my own case when my ship 'STRATHAIRD' came by it during a tremendous Monsoonal deluge) was gained as one's ship moved up the harbour to Ballard Pier, a sighting which usually brought unforgettable thrills to every traveller, and ever afterwards remembered especially if one stayed on in India, and enjoyed it (that is, life in India).

For undiminished contrast and colour there is very little anywhere, to match the total offerings of the Taj Mahal Hotel. The world of east and west meets in its vast gleaming white marble and deliciously air-conditioned foyer, which is the personification of (achieved almost without trying) all one could ever imagine the East should be! The diversity of its clientele is captivating and completely fascinating, leaving one gaping in wonderment.

The magnificent foyer of 'The Taj' is unquestionably the finest 'meeting place' in the whole of Bombay. Lodging at the Taj isn't cheap (upwards of $200 per night) but everyone is able to patronize the hotel's restaurants, where the food needn't be expensive, depending upon what you choose to eat. Its great attribute and appeal, is of course, that its cuisine can be wholly enjoyed and depended upon - an important ingredient with all travellers. A timely tip for every itinerant traveller - go easy on the spicy food - mostly let your eyes do your eating! until your stomach acclimatizes.

The SHAMIANA restaurant (relocated and renamed "SEA LOUNGE", 2001) at the Taj is excellent. It is also quite informal (you can almost (?) wear what you like) and importantly - its prices are relatively moderate. Generally overseas, in eastern countries at least, it is the accommodation - if it's good - which is expensive, and not the food. Services are cheap, compared to Europe and as a bonus, most facilities are open everyday all day, and well into the night.

There are a number of other quite excellent - nay, superb hotels elsewhere in the City. On the opposite (western) side of the peninsula facing Marine Drive, the two Oberoi Hotels favourably compare with the best, anywhere in the world. For those who seek exclusive accommodation and the finest service - at a price, in an uncongested area looking across Back Bay to Malabar Hill, (where the well-to-do people of Bombay live in huge apartment blocks), then undoubtedly they will be attracted to Oberoi Towers and its exclusive twin next door, 'The Oberoi'.

The 'President' another of the Tata Group's hotels, and located on Cuffe Parade, also offers excellent accommodation. It too is fairly pricey although it suffers somewhat from being located in a less convenient situation, being a shade remote (not within easy walking distance) from the City's main attractions.

Nearer the hustle and bustle (just off Marine Drive) the 'Ambassador' offers good middle standard accommodation although I would recommend FARIYAS Hotel (25, Colaba just off the seawall and not far along from the Taj Mahal Hotel) to anyone looking for good clean accommodation at very reasonable prices adjacent to the Harbour.

"Fariyas" offers very good value at approximately $75 per night, board only, supported however with a good restaurant, but anyhow the 'Taj Mahal' with its splendid dining facilities available to everyone, is no more than a short stroll up the street. "Fariyas" is compact, well appointed and very popular with people visiting from all parts of the world. Additionally too, one can 'cool off' by their poolside, well away from the maddening crowd.

In fact there are many smaller hotels (charging around $40 to $50 per night, meals available but extra) situated on and just back from the sea front, in Colaba, all of them no more than a hop step and a jump away from 'the Taj Mahal' Hotel. Many new 'private hotels/ guest houses' are available on the seafront away to the west of 'the Taj', in the direction of the Radio Club.

Should you be on a tighter budget but are prepared to 'make do' in otherwise clean surroundings, the Chateau Windsor Guest House at 86, Veer Nariman Road, could do you quite nicely for a few days. It accommodates about 125 persons in 1, 2, 3 or 4 to a room, for quite modest charges.

The 'CW' is alongside the 'Ambassador' and there are many different food styles available at restaurants in the immediate vicinity, and of course there are always the 'Ambassador's' restaurants, right next door.

Random eating in Bombay (or anywhere in India for that matter) is not really recommended if you want to avoid the ever present bogey of travel in foreign countries - tummy problems. Bombay suffers from over-crowding and what reticulated water there is available is wholly inadequate for every (normal) need. There is no surplus left over for washing down footpaths and roads and 'Bombay tummy' is something one should try to avoid (Nature's "Hoover", the great Monsoonal cleansing rains, only operates during the Monsoon season - July/October).

Before it suffered the fate of so many other (beautiful) Indian cities, (ever burgeoning population growth creating tremendous congestion and overtaxed existing infrastructure), Bombay city too, with its (then clean) wide roads and superbly sculptured buildings (dating from the British era), was clearly a very attractive city.

The Indo-Saracenic Prince of Wales Museum (not to overlook the older though now resplendently refurbished section of the Taj Hotel too) and the quite magnificently architectured Railway buildings (interestingly Railways occupied a very special place in British times and possibly represent Britain's finest material legacy to India) of the old B.B. and C.I. headquarters at Churchgate, and Victoria Terminus, both most splendid edifices, are there to dazzle visitors and remind one of how very beautiful Bombay once was, and who can really say, may once again become?

Bombay may (and does!) teem with people, but try to profit from it, by pausing and making time to drink everything in - the enormous crowd scenes; the many faceted activities going on all around one; the attitudes of the people to the kaleidoscopic (bedlam) scenes going on everywhere one turns.

For the sporting types, the intensive activity on the maidan up by Bombay's Gymkhana Club, and a visit to Bombay's two top class cricket stadia on Marine Drive, the Brabourne (Cricket Club of India), and the Wankhede nearby, could be exciting, especially if India's current quite colourful and successful one day national side is playing.

A sight of Tendulkar and India's newest star, Saurav Ganguly would add greatly to your visit to Bombay.

Finally, never forget that the east is a wonderfully different concoction of dazzling, unforgettable, even bizarre sounds, sights and smells. You'll amaze yourself with your (very) different impressions and begin to understand many formerly not understood features of India - of eastern countries in general.

There can be no doubt that to the discerning visitor prepared to venture beyond the wayside bazaars, Bombay has some magical experiences to offer. A few hours spent swotting up 'on any place' can pay rich dividends. For you, Bombay and its attractions will almost assuredly be vastly improved by 'the knowing' of it just a bit more intimately.

22. Finding The Right Recipe For A Proud India

- Delhi's direction refocused

The apogee in the Indian firmament in relation to everything else Indian, must surely be Delhi, or to be more specific, those parts of the northern city, now particularly designated as New Delhi and created between 1912 and 1931 by the British Raj, under the guiding hands of Britain's then most eminent architects, Sir Edward Lutyens and Sir Herbert Baker.

Architecturally magnificent, and superbly crafted - in any setting anywhere, and sardonically described by one foreign commentator 'as the last great fling of a dying British Raj', it fills a paradoxical role in today's India, fifty years and more on from Independence.

A hybrid, and in its design and execution meant to be such because of the privilege which it engendered then, and fosters still today, (when Indians themselves are in charge of proceedings). It is debateable whether it sets 'the right tone/the right example' for aspiring Indians seeking to create (to restore) the conditions their fore-fathers once shared before 'western' influence unsettled far longer known and learnt and respected -'eastern' ways. The prevailing, less than seriously regarded situation, arguably neither one thing nor the other, gives off a Dr Suess 'push me, pull you' no win conundrum flavour. Seemingly, India ambles along, with no very firm 'formative overall plan' either on the table top or in (*or* not in!) the bottom drawer?

For a country thought to be (but often times, and invariably described by outsiders, as being) fixedly and doggedly absorbed in maintaining some largely controlled 'flow', of the status quo, without very much attendant advancement, the extent and magnitude and shape of what is actually taking place in India, would surprise many (including her critics).

Everything in India is relative, *i.e.* related to a population in 1998, nearing one billion people. This factor can never (and should not) be left out (1) of any equation, or (2) of any debate, or judgement, whatever is being compared, or discussed *etcetera,* which relates to India. Respectfully, dogmatic opinions should be avoided.

In particular areas, Indian technical progress and achievement equals, and in some cases exceeds, anything anywhere else. When comparing or interpreting India, all things or matters, require to be kept or to be seen in proper perspective. Regrettably such isn't always done, but don't expect Indians to explain, or to challenge – they won't! It is (just) not in their nature to do this.

New Delhi is a classic case of ready acceptance, of what a past invader/temporary occupier or ruler, has bequeathed to a country – of architecture, of town-planning. India has a penchant for keeping almost everything, (including what of the past the iconoclasts among themselves or their invaders didn't destroy).

A very distinctive, and very obvious trait amongst Indians, with very very few exceptions - amongst them, the burnings witnessed over a decade by the author, of trams and buses in Calcutta, during *bandhs* – is their enormous desire and capacity to retain and respect constructions, of all kinds, everywhere throughout their country no matter who built them.

They know the inherent value of pretty well everything (bottle tops, scrap paper etc, etc of everything, very little of anything is not recycled), unlike many people everywhere and not just the people of freed nations (Yugoslavia and Northern Ireland spring readily to mind).

Many invaders visited the sub-continent before the British came on the scene and much of what they built centuries/milleniums ago, is still there today (pretty odd now to recount that possibly more was pulled down in India, for clearing the way for constructing New Delhi, than in any other instance or time).

Hate the Great Mughals (and they weren't hated) and in revenge, tear down the Red Fort, the Taj Mahal? Never! So also with the imperial designs of the former British Empire – the splendid creations of Sir Edwin Lutyens and Sir Herbert Baker (who also had a hand in Pretoria), that adorn New Delhi today. Apart from Gandhi replacing – and only very recently – King George the Fifth at India Gate, very little else has happened, or is known to be contemplated.

Meanwhile, a piece of India unlike any other piece of India (the former British residential areas of Calcutta would come closest – of any other) is allowed to remain. One thing of course to permit this paradoxical feature, to go on unchanged, quite another altogether, if the 'privileged atmosphere' affects or influences the mindset of its current times residents, among the Indian hierarchy.

Perhaps (and it would be surprising if it didn't affect people, at least to some extent) those persons fortunate enough to partake and enjoy New Delhi's lovely atmosphere – bureaucrats, parliamentarians, wealthier Indian business-people and a host of foreign diplomatic representatives – are not fully cognizant of the considerable privileges accorded to them. Set down in such exclusive precincts, the plight, welfare and needs of the average Indian citizen, from the depths of Andhra Pradesh, Orissa or so, may not register as starkly or as urgently, or as necessarily clear, as good governance requires.

While it seems not wholly unknown, or acknowledged, or is it tangibly indicated that such disparities exist, gestures of magnanimity from the 'lofty heights of power', seem rarely to be (sincerely and positively) articulated. It is salutary for all to ensure that the right priorities are observed, and always preserved. Merely swapping buildings and seats, without much more, was far from the minds and intentions of the true patriots who won Independence.

Although Pandit Nehru resided in Teen Murti - a spacious home in beautiful peaceful grounds, it was otherwise most unpretentious. A true servant of the people, his spartan sleeping chamber exemplified the man. Nehru's simplicity (when leader of free India) bore strong traces of another great leader of people, who preceded him by over four hundred years - the incomparable and hugely compassionate and capable, Sher Shah c. 1530 - 1545, who when he exercised similar great power, never forgot the common man. Surprisingly (to note at this time) that in that era, living was so cheap that the small emoluments of the poorest labourer were sufficient to afford him a comfortable life.

What went wrong? to change the whole machinery of life, that had previously spread its favours more equitably. Soaring (a natural consequence of a base that keeps swelling) population is the favourite 'whipping boy', but changed economics; changed (neglected) supervision, has all contributed to skew matters, to the detriment of the vast numbers who particularly dwell in the rural districts (many of whom also make up the poorer itinerant populations of the larger cities).

Joining in and adding another voice to World Conventions on population control is in itself admirable, but perhaps Indian leadership needs to conduct its own 'much more pertinent discussions' relative to its own burgeoning population. Any solution that guarantees a reasonable life to everyone born, can only come from within. The huge bank of intellectual talent available in India could do the job, or at least make a start, in conjunction with other parallel governance from New Delhi.

One thing is very certain - an 'Indian way' is needed, and one that puts modernity and the technology age/the electronics revolution, into (sensible) perspective. As the sated western world is learning, going full pelt in the worship of consumerism is not the way to contentment and happiness. Necessity, the mother of invention (and source of resourcefulness), has sagged noticeably, in recent years. Doing things oneself, built pride. Leaving it to others has reduced self-esteem and self-confidence. India should be happy to note the mistakes of others; not envy them.

But you ask -"what has all this to do with New Delhi?" Well, everything in fact. Keeping up with the Jones's of the world, should not be a priority. As well, the comfort and privilege which oozes from the detachment induced by the sterility and spacious precincts of New Delhi could very well have the effect of distancing its servers from the 'real' India.

Canberra, Pretoria, Washington D.C. and Brasilia, all suffer from the pretence of artificiality. New Delhi too. All of them quite distinct from say London or Paris, where Parliaments are made to operate cheek by jowl with the 'real world', where the vibes are more felt, understood and regarded affecting their decision-making. No 'artificial curtain' is allowed, or can, get in the way.

In reality, Delhi is a lot more than just New Delhi, which in the first instance was just that area of Delhi proper which was 'cleared of everything' - the whole planning and execution and *cost,* must have been prodigious - to make way for British India's new capital (moved from Calcutta, in 1911-12). Shades of Baron Haussmann's *carte blanche* in Paris.

Remnants of past empires can still be found - the oldest of them on the very outskirts of present day Delhi.

Started by the first Muslim Sultan of Delhi, Qutb-ud-din Aibak, the unique 100 metre Qutb Minar (tapering tower of victory, featuring four projecting balconies and still in amazingly good order) was completed by Firoz Shah Tughlak, builder of Delhi's third city TUGHLAKABAD, in 1368.

In the same compound as the Qutb Minar are the ruins of what was one of the finest Mosques ever - Quwat ul Islam Masjid, built 800 years ago. In the courtyard of the Mosque is the fabulous seven metre high Iron Pillar. Belonging to a much earlier age and consisting of 98% wrought iron, it provides proof of ancient India's knowledge and skills in metallurgy and is rust resistant.

The third city was followed in successive eras by Jahanpanah and then Ferozabad, when the finest yet administrative system was instituted by Sher Shah (whose skills and humanitarian feelings have already been mentioned) who built the city of SHERGARH upon foundations which had been originally commenced by the second of the Great Mughals Humayun.

One of India's fabled great modernists, the comparatively young Sher Shah's unscheduled death in battle in 1545 changed the (probable) course of Indian history. Hugely popular with his people, his death allowed the Afghan leaders to reassert their dominance, when the weak Humayun was restored as Emperor, to be succeeded by his son and the greatest Mughal Emperor of them all, Akbar.

Up to this time the Great Mughals had set down at Agra. Akbar oversaw the move to the Agra Fort, the magnificent complex on the bank of the Jumna River where the Court resided, except for a sixteen year period (1569-1585) when for lineage purposes Akbar dwelt at Fatehpur-Sikri (literally the 'City of Victory' and enduring monument to the greatness of Emperor Akbar, and situated twentythree miles from Agra).

Akbar's grandson and creator of one of man's greatest architectural masterpieces, the Taj Mahal Complex, at Agra, Emperor Shahjehan, years subsequent to his wife's death, moved his capital to Delhi - to what is now often referred to as 'old' Delhi, the part in reality which constitutes the biggest section of the whole metropolis of Delhi/ New Delhi.

The biggest numbers of people and all the major commercial markets (bazaars or *chowks*) are located in the old part i.e. 'old' Delhi, beyond the new part the British Raj put together, almost wholly for (their) own exclusive use, for administration and residential purposes and which has since been joined by lots of other commercial and residential areas (beyond the unique circular complex of Connaught Place/Connaught Circus) and the diplomatic enclave of Chanakyapuri.

Although we have rapidly skirted by it, the Lodhi dynasty (A.D. 1414 to 1526), which preceded the advent of the Great Mughals, is still prominent in the eyes of Delhi-ites, through the Tombs scattered around the lovely Lodhi Gardens in Jor Bagh district in South Delhi. The Lodhi Colony close by and the area adjacent to the Gardens, boasts some very fine garden bungalows, occupied by senior Civil Servants and prominent business people. The renowned and prestigious India International Centre, graces this part of Delhi.

But despite the capaciousness and majestic environment of British 'new Delhi' on the southern side of town, perhaps the most interesting aspects of Delhi and also its most intriguing side, lies to the east of Barakhamba Road and right along Bahadurshaha Zafar Marg (the domain of many of its leading newspapers) northwards to Delhi Gate and Emperor Shahjahans' old city Shahjahanabad.

It is in this very heavily congested part that the 'real' Delhi lives and breathes (many critics say 'foul air', but if it is so, it is nonetheless remarkable the huge amounts of energy which are expended right through the seasons - and Delhi can be very oppressively hot in Summer, and in the extreme, particularly [but not too unbearably] cold during the winter months, December/January - by millions upon millions of hard working people over consecutively long days relieved only by religious holidays and festivals).

Once fully enclosed, the Mughal city of Shahjahanabad's major focal points, are the stupendous Red Fort (Qila Mubarak), the equally

51. Wonderful setting - 'Wazir, Safdar Jang's Tomb, New Delhi.

glorious Jama Masjid and Chandni Chowk, possibly the most varied and the most heavily 'shopped' of all the bazaars in the whole of India, if not the whole of Arabia and Asia outside China itself.

Western nations pride themselves in being the creators of the ubiquitous supermarket, bringing centralized convenience to western shoppers. For thousands of years another type of system has been followed in all 'eastern' countries - the bazaar (in the old European system the nearest equivalent, was, and in many places still are, the town squares/the village market days).

During my regular working days in India, I 'inspected' many of these bazaars situated all over India, including several visits to Delhi. I recall going to at least five major bazaars in old Delhi including Chandni Chowk. Each of the bazaars caters for particular things/goods, whether it be food, household appliances and furnishings of every conceivable kind, engineering articles, clothing, or foodgrains or you name it - everything for home and farm and industry.

For convenience (amazingly no one minds the intensity of competition thus created, side by side) all one type of goods is kept and sold in the same area - hundreds and hundreds of ten foot openings on to the street - forget pavements, there's little or no room for such or even road space, for that matter. Each of the great towns, Delhi, Mumbai, Calcutta, Chennai, Bangalore, Mysore, Cuttack, Bubhaneshwar etcetera all over India, acts as a major supply point for India's surrounding *mofussil* - where seventy per cent of her approaching one billion people work and live. Point of trade, greatly aids access and convenience.

Delhi's Chandni Chowk is probably the 'daddy of them all'. Utterly fantastic to wander through, as I have frequently done and again not so many months ago, from the Lahori Gate opposite to the Red Fort, through its lanes and byways emerging at last, at Turkomani Gate.

Shahjahan built his new capital city (in reality a great walled fortress city, perhaps in order to keep people in, as much as to protect them, and to keep invading armies, out - and they had repeatedly foraged across the northern plains of India until 1800 when the British forces maintained practically full control) between 1651 and 1658.

Covering an estimated 1500 acres the Emperor's Palace compound - *Qila Mubarak* or Red Fort, occupied (occupies) a site midway along its eastern perimeter between its south and north-eastern corner, with the rear wall of the Palace looking eastwards upon and across the parklands to the Jumna (or Yamuna) River. Seven gates or entrances were let into the massive walls at various intervals, each bearing names redolent of famous Muslim strong-holds - Kashmiri, Mori, Lahori, Kabuli, Ajmeri, Turkomani and Akbarbadi.

Still regarded as a marvellous edifice and synonymous with traditional Indian power (Nehru spoke from its ramparts on 15 August, 1947, and on every Proclamation Day since, the current Indian Prime Minister addresses a huge throng at this venue) the Red Fort was seen as a marvel when it was first constructed - and of course, it was! No one who looks upon it today,.is unmoved by the experience.

However many people lived (and worked) in Shahjahanabad in the seventeenth century, the fact is that millions do so, in 1998. Both the Red Fort and the large and exotic Jama Masjid face west towards Mecca.

Going one day just a few months ago to New Delhi Railway Station along Chelmsford Road, I afterwards decided to keep walking north along Qutb Road, hoping to eventually end up at the Mutiny Monument, high up on the hill overlooking Civil Lines. It was probably the most fantastic and illuminating walk I've ever done in an Indian City, perhaps in any city, anywhere in the world. It featured nearly everything - life and commerce in most of its forms.

My walk took me in turn through the ultra crowded bazaar areas - of Sadar Bazar, Naya Bazar and Azad Market, where successively a vast cornucopia of goods was displayed and sold - all of them wholesale markets, markets for people in the (particular) trade. Hand carts, bullock carts, bicycles, trucks, rickshaws, coolies with baskets balanced on their heads, and all of them going in both directions (in parts fortunately, along exceedingly narrow and congested roads, with concrete dividers down the middle). The hurly burly of human-kind was utterly prodigious, a tad frightening perhaps, but also always enormously exhilarating.

Turning right from Azad Market Road into Rani Jhansi (a great Mutiny patriot highly revered by all Indians) Road, afforded more breathing space as I tramped on and up the hill to the Mutiny Monument erected there by the British. It recorded some exceedingly poignant events, particularly happening to British (British and other Indian soldiers serving in what was the Army of the time in India. Things changed after the Mutiny) troops.

One such plaque reads as follows -

List of Actions fought at or near Delhi
by the Delhi Field Force from 30.5.1857
to 20 September, 1857

Battle of the Hindun	May 30
Battle of Chazeeoodeenucur	May 31
Battle of Badlee Sepai	June 8
Breaching and bombardment	Sept 11, 12 & 13
Storming of Delhi	Sept 14
Capture of Magazine	Sept 16
Capture of Palace	Sept 19
City eventually evacuated by the enemy	Sept 20

Casualties 30.5/20.9.1857

Strength		7275
	Killed	820
	Wounded	2179
	Missing	29
		3028

In typical (and wonderfully generous) Indian fashion, the Mutiny Monument commemorating an event terribly awful and distressing to both the British and to the rebelling Indians, still stands on Civil Lines hill overlooking old Delhi (to the east) and Kamala Nehru Park (to the west), undisfigured and unmutilated in any way.

On 28 August 1972, a plaque was placed on the lower front side of the Monument the top quarter of which is in Hindi, the one beneath it, in Urdu. Beneath that is the English translation -

The 'enemy' of the inscriptions'
On this monument were those
who rose against colonial rule
and fought bravely for national liberation in 1857.

In memory of these immortal martyrs
For Indian freedom, this plaque was unveiled on the 25th
Anniversary
Of the Nation's attainment of freedom.

28 August, 1972

The lower fourth of the plaque records the same message in (another) Indian script.

I felt quite humble amongst these historic, though tragic, memories of the bitter conflict which took place one hundred and forty years ago.

Overlooking one of the great Asoka's famous pillars located just a little further along Rani Jhansi, and retracing my steps downhill, I set off for St. James' Church, located near to Kashmiri Gate. Old Delhi twists and turns all over the place, and very few places are not heavily congested. Asking one's direction elicits some amazing (and very often, extraordinarily inaccurate) responses. But everywhere all around India is the same. How many times I've been told — "go straight". There aren't a lot of long 'straight' roads, they turn and twist madly, but my helpers are nearly always right, for - my goal is invariably in that 'pretty rough direction'.

Finding Kashmiri Gate was indeed extraordinary, but finding myself as well alongside the celebrated Skinner's Church was a joy. Built by James Skinner, Persian scholar and soldier of fortune, in fulfilment of a vow made on a battlefield (in north India) some thirty years earlier, St. James', Delhi's oldest and most historic Christian Church, was consecrated in 1836. Its Baroque architecture and cupola is mindful of St. Peter's in Rome and St Paul's, in London, on a smaller scale.

Skinner's Horse, an irregular Corps and Regiment composed of 1000 cavalrymen was first commanded by James Skinner from 1803. It became one of the best known and most valorous units in the whole of the British army, in India. Known as the Yellow Boys from the colour of their uniforms, and commanded successively by heirs of its first commander, the Persian motto of the Regiment was *'Himmat - i - Mardan, Madad - i - Khuda'* which translated means 'the valour of man, the help of God.'

James Skinner is buried below the Altar. The rest of his clan are laid to rest in a delightfully small and private graveyard in the grounds of St. James', a unique tribute to the celebrated Skinner's Horse, since absorbed in India's own forces, after 1947. James Skinner's mother was the daughter of a Rajput Zamindar.

Being in the path of most invaders of the sub-continent (the only ones who didn't *tramp* into India were the British and the rest of the modern Europeans), the Delhi region is alive with past history.

Its population hails from all corners of the land, whether to lobby, whether to settle, or whether to take up a position in the Government Administration (Secretariat) or to take their seats in Parliament, in either the Lower House *'the Lok Sabha'*, or in the Upper House 'the *Rajya Sabha'*, both of which are accommodated in *Sansad Bhavan* (Parliament House) near to the Raj Path and on the road to the Anglican Church of the Redemption. Delhi caters for all religions and denominations in some quite beautiful structures, many of them non-Hindu and or Muslim ones, dotted around New Delhi.

Gateway to the north and to the colourful north-western regions of India, most foreign tourists make a bee-line for New Delhi. The wide and quieter thoroughfares of New Delhi boast many beautiful modern buildings, foreign diplomatic residences and very very lavishly appointed hotels, and provide many hours of interesting hiking for visitors prepared to hoof it, when you see so much more.

Coursing down (or up) the Raj Path from or to India Gate and to the President's house (all 340 rooms of it) Rashtrapati Bhavan, has its rewards. In every respect the great metropolis of Delhi/New Delhi abounds with interest, whatever your purpose may be. What happens there, or from there, in the next fifty years (or less), will have a marked bearing upon the world, nothing is surer.

23. The Nizam's Treasure Pot, No.2

- all systems 'go' in Hyderabad (A.P.)

I had never been to Hyderabad. A chance meeting a short while before in Pune, had elicited an invitation to *"look-in on us, and fill in the gap"*. I had been assured.... *"you'll enjoy it"*.

But any great incentive was not there. Whatever it was - the strange sounding 'elongated' name; the virtual dearth of any more knowledge about the State (the City) beyond notoriety for mean-ness, widely proclaimed in respect of Nizam VII - in my mind's-eye, I could only envision illimitable sandy wastes, and camels, camels, camels.

Perhaps too, my problem (interest-blank) had something to do with differentiating between the Hyderabad, in the State of Andhra Pradesh in India and the other Hyderabad (Sind), in Pakistan, where indeed you may find plenty of sandy wastes - and camels!

My 'second' strong chance to visit Hyderabad (Andhra Pradesh) and fill the serious gap in my education came about in a fairly unorthodox and unexpected (certainly unplanned) way. I had spent several months 'investigating' south India and refreshing my knowledge and enjoyment of 'that different part of India' the bit that is much less frequently traversed by north Indians, and foreigners too, more drawn to the better known northern half of India.

Provided the opportunity of regularly reading the south's excellent English language daily newspaper *The Hindu* - established well over a century ago - I was very much taken by its excellent quality, and strong emphasis upon dissemination of very well presented 'continuing education' for everyone. The scope, consistency and variety (and thoroughness) of its articles, and its borderlessness - it takes in the best on offer in the world - is on par with anything, elsewhere.

One contribution from a reader particularly grabbed my attention. It might have been composed by the great Mahatma Gandhi, for it replicated (and resoundingly echoed) Gandhi's recurrent pleas and admonitions, made to India's people, during his lifetime, but which seemingly have gotten lost, or else been flung aside as having no current value (Gandhi abhorred selfishness of every kind) in more recent years.

The correspondent's article was aptly entitled *PROPAGATING INDIAN-NESS*. I felt that it was brilliant, being obviously very thoroughly thought out and formulated. As well, it was also timely. Great countries, large diverse populations, require very strong, 'broadly life experienced', able and credible leaders.

In Mahatma Gandhi, (so tremendously 'life equipped' to undertake his so enormously arduous but successful 'against all the odds' victory for his people), and the equally undaunted, unflinching Pandit Nehru, and a handful of other grand stalwarts, all of them patriotic 'Indians' to the very core, Independent India had them. There are none such identifiable in these same terms, present day. For too many and tragically for India, any leadership, of whatever kind, is no more than a lucrative job and a path to (personal) riches.

The Hindu correspondent's heartrending message was a fervent cry to all his fellow countrymen and women, to put to one side their personal and selfish desires, and instead to give first and unqualified priority to the pressing needs of their country, and all of the people, not just some of them. An exhortation to be 'Indians - made in India', and not some Anglicized ill-fitting hybrid version.

At no time in the past, or in the future, was there a need for adopting such a persona, for India already possessed (and still possesses) a vast human treasury of her own, built up over thousands of years and one suited to her people. Any transition (enveloping India) has always been slow, no matter that at the present time, her computer literacy has achieved a quantum leap of enormous proportions, and leads the world. Proper absorption, across the spectrum is a slow process, and in the broadest terms, can not be hurried.

Fine yes, for Independent India to borrow and integrate the better bits from anywhere and everywhere (no single system is perfect in its own form), but *not* to replace or supersede on any wholesale scale, the 'nuts and bolts' that over a long period have kept everything together for what are probably, the most ethnically and religiously diverse people, populating a single country, on earth.

The shock from trying to inflict a large dollop of British ways and traditions on the vast nation of India, would be immense. Why was it even attempted? Conscience perhaps? A bit thick too that India has been castigated, or even reviled and scorned - for not successfully managing such an impossible exercise. A different 'custom tailored' properly fitting model was always the way to effect change.

Prior to the advent of the Europeans, history shows us that the Indian original skills and order, and its generally harmonious culture moulded over thousands of years, survived every foreign incursion, and amazingly assimilated everyone and everything. But not so the Europeans - more particularly, the British.

Even the most simple analysis provides the reasons. Britain progressed far swifter than any other nation from the sixteenth and seventeenth centuries on. She outstrode the rest of the world, in modern thinking, in modern learning, in effecting change. The 'clash' of cultures with India, a wholly different country, could only be explosive (Gandhi saw this very clearly).

Light years removed from Indian specifics, integration on any wide scale could not happen, was never going to happen. Quite inimical to Indian culture, a carbon-copy of British life, of British ways, could never (should never have been contemplated) occur. The current 'hybrid' model has no real place.

A small elitist group of Indians, representing only a minuscule percentage of India's nearly one billion population, may 'affect British', and just 'partly' British ways, but the Indian plan for everybody, could take a very different outline.

I might have thought that many Indians would rejoice with me, that *The Hindu* contributor's article was a gem of profound and sensible thinking and be worthy of deep contemplation and positive consideration, by 'the powers that be'.

Whatever its impact among *The Hindu's* readers, I felt that the author was due much congratulation. But more than that, that his message (clarion call) deserved to be broadcast across the length and breadth of India and very seriously debated.

Greater cohesion is called for. Opinions on everything are tossed into the ring, by Indians of every shade of thinking, but politicians seem unconscious of 'the big points affecting the social structure of all Indians'. The best minds, divorced from the 'hurly burly' of everyday politics, could ponder these questions, and seek results attuned to the consensus of the ordinary people. Political parties ignore their responsibilities and selfish ambition thwarts the best outcomes for all Indians.

Upon my return to Australia months later, I passed my whole-hearted and sincere congratulatory advices, to the (un-known to me, just a name, no address) author, through the newspaper's Editor in Chennai (Madras).

Imagine, if you can, my unheralded surprise when early one Sunday morning several weeks later, the phone in my living room in Melbourne rang, and the voice at the other end requesting ....."*take this call from Hyderabad please*".

Although all the praise was due to the author (for his courage and sincerity in composing and delivering such a strong declaration to all his compatriots), here he was wanting to share some of his reward with me, at this point a foreigner and a stranger. But such an attitude, while not embraced by all Indians, is nonetheless symptomatic of most basic Indians, those sharing the most populated rungs of Indian society. Why is it then, that the upper echelons of power (in politics and in industry), unlearnt so soon the voice they should never have stopped heeding - the Mahatma's?

A return to the real Indian qualities and virtues, more in tune with the wishes and the wants of all Indians, rents the air, pleading, pleading to be heard, but so wilfully ignored by those who could do something. Why has commonsense and humility deserted those who populate the corridors of power? Only when India projects itself, its true self, will true independence, for all its people, be achieved.

On my next visit to India, some months later, it was a great pleasure for me to honour the author's remarkably spontaneous invitation to go to Hyderabad and spend a short time with him and his family and wonderful band of relatives, friends and workmates. The hospitality and sincere hand of friendship extended to me was indeed overwhelming, from everyone I met.

Alighting at the twin-city of Secunderabad's (the former older settlements of Hyderabad and Secunderabad are now so interwoven, that virtually, it is all one very large metropolis, with two heads and two hearts, and two major central districts and two large railway stations) busy railway station after a tedious twenty seven hour train journey from New Delhi, it was quite a thrill to be greeted by 'wholly new and beaming faces' - those of my host, and two of his charming daughters and an equally charming girl-friend. Receptions like this, in otherwise completely unknown places, leave one with a glowing feeling - of delight, and a harbinger of pleasures to come. And so it was to be.

It was night-time and a clear sight of my new surroundings would have to wait. Meanwhile, whisked along to Habsiguda, an emotional interlude followed - *'so this is the foreigner who'd so entranced our Dad'* - *'hmm, how interesting to be treated as a long-time friend of the family'* - a meeting of the races, and all so convivial.

Indian households spring into life very early in the morning - for respectful (personal) prayers, and if there are children, to ready for school or college, all going in different directions. Reliant upon road transport (and in Hyderabad/Secunderabad there is no subsidiary train service, or any tram system) and people are moved by huge numbers of public and private buses. However, the road-network is excellent. Wide roads, well-maintained surfaces, are undergoing a wonderful uplift, as a dozen or more flyovers and overheads are currently under construction.

If I thought Pune held the record for three wheelers and motor scooters, I obviously didn't know Hyderabad - let's call it H/S for Secunderabad. Over one million (*10 lakhs*) motor scooters are said to be registered - they weave in and out of queuing traffic, ridden by men, women, young and old.

On my first morning a Sunday, my thoughtful host, a local businessman and as well, a very organised gentleman, felt it useful to take me for a spin around H/S to enable me to get my bearings. So different to many of India's other bigger cities (Calcutta, Delhi, Bombay, Chennai), H/S presented a lot more space/a lot more room, better layout, wider thoroughfares, not very many skyscrapers (in fact, there are surprisingly few of them), and all of it much cleaner, less rubbish indifferently strewn about.

In fact, the only blemish anywhere appeared to reside in the dreadful smell emanating from the Musi River, in the vicinity of the *kachha*-built squatter camp (probably a milk colony, from the numbers of buffaloes receiving their daily ablutions in the nearby receding still water-sufficient section of the river, months after the skarifying Monsoon rains had passed) occupying the bed of the river channel near the Sardar Patel Road bridge. So it was only temporary and like so much that happens in crowded India, allowances are made for higher (human value necessities) priorities.

A wonderfully convivial afternoon/evening followed, when scores of relatives and friends stopped by, with impromptu renderings of song and instrument, all topped off by squeals of great delight (after the growing tentative agony) when the Indian one day side scored a marvellous close win over Pakistan, in the Dacca Triangular. What better tonic is there, than a sea of smiling faces.

Further orientation followed next day, when joined by my host's charming youngest, *Surekha,* we sped off at 6.45am to join a group tour going to the famous Golconda Fort, as well as to other quite marvellous Hyderabad 'jewels' (aptly synonymous with Hyderabad, and the alleged but true, propensity of Nizam VII, to amass precious stones).

A flying brief look at *Charminar* (literally the four minarets) the legendary centre of old city, and Hyderabad's best known landmark, sometimes referred to as the *Arc d'Triomphe* of the East, then away west to be entranced by the *Qutb Shahi Tombs* set down amidst the *Ibrahim Bagh* and situated just to the north of Golconda Fort, on the very outskirts of Hyderabad.

A tremendous 'garden', set on a hill, the variously sized tombs, from moderate to very large, are domed structures built on colonnaded square bases. Some are single storeyed, the larger ones are two-storeyed. In the centre of each tomb is a sarcophagus which overlies the actual burial vault in the basement below. Celebrated together in death, the Tombs of the seven monarchs form a fitting tribute to Hyderabad's fame and growth.

The history of Andhra Pradesh, the northern-most State of south India, is dotted with rulers, settlers, invaders and survivors. The greatest influence was wielded by three powerful dynasties - the

Veiled Rebacca (Salar Jung Museum)

Hyderabadi cuisine

Mecca Masjid

Buddha Statue, Hussain Sagar

Qutub Shahi Tombs

Golconda Fort

52. Where Islam and Hinduism are well met - Hyderabad (A.P.).

first of them in the first half of the fourteenth century - the advent of the Vijayanagar Empire, marked a new chapter in the history of South India. Not just of political significance but also the symbolic expression of a vigorous cultural movement.

In an age of frequent Islamic aggressions the Vijayanagar Empire rose as the defender of Hindu *dharma* and institutions. That South India retains today its individual cultural complexion, is substantially due to the defence and protection afforded to Hindu culture by the Vijayanagar Empire.

The *Qutb Shahis* followed. Initially ruling from the rock - citadel of Golconda (from 1512), the fifth great king of Golconda Muhammed Quli Qutb Shah (1580-1612) founded the city of Bhagyanagar in 1591, later renamed the city of Hyderabad.

The last and seventh King of the *Qutb Shahis,* Tãnã Shah was deposed and taken prisoner in 1687 by the forces of the last of the six great Mughals, Aurangzeb, when the last Bahmani succession state became a part of the Mughal Empire.

Founded originally by the Kakatiyas in the thirteenth century, the great hill fortress compound of Golconda was restored and expanded by the *Qutb Shahi* kings into a massive fort of granite with walls and ramparts five kilometres in circumference.

Much of it still appears awesomely rock solid, while other parts now display some deterioration. But without doubt, it breathes history and maintains the glory and grandeur of the *Qutb Shahi* dynasty. Around the old hill fortress today, the busy activities of the villagers who live adjacent to it, provide a wonderful contrast, and in essence relieving the Fort from being just another piece of isolated old history.

But the name Golconda is still, and has been for centuries, universally emblematic of great wealth and riches. Often thought so because of 'gold mines' in the region, in reality it was diamonds which spurred Golconda's 'exciting' fame. It was an early centre of the diamond trade, and reputedly the shaper of the famous Koh-i-noor diamond, which now resides in the British monarch's crown.

Hyderabad-Secunderabad, twin cities fused into one, is a city where north meets south, Islam meets Hinduism and conservatism meets cosmopolitanism. The constantly changing scenery is always absorbing, and most often excites the senses. There has been a very positive effort to merge or to give equal merit to all groups. The magnificent large Arts building at Osmania University incorporates both Islamic and Hindu architecture. While Telegu and Urdu are the principal spoken languages, room is made for sharing with Marathi, Kannada and Tamil, as well.

Conscious efforts are (obviously) made by all the people to avoid conflict and to respect all beliefs, leading to constructive and progressive partnership. Isolated to a degree from the rest of India (sitting in the middle in the lower one third of the sub-continent), perhaps it is cushioned from the radicalism with affects Calcutta and Mumbai, and from the extreme conservatism and parochialism of Tamil Nadu and Kerala, below it.

Evidence of a unique cultural amalgam exists everywhere one goes. The giant statue of the Buddha erected on the Gibraltar rock in the Hussainagar Lake provides another example of the union between peoples, further illustrated by the placing of thirty three life-size statues of various Telegu personalities along the Tank Bund (of Hussainagar Lake) as part of the Buddha Purnima Project.

Andhra Pradesh is currently blessed with a wonderful civic leader (Chief Minister) Chandrababu Naidu, who is the most computer literate C.M. amongst his counterparts, in the whole of India, and perhaps the most (widely) respected, by political friends or competition, and by most of the people of Hyderabad-Secunderabad. Given such climate - progress can be made and is happening. It is being noticed elsewhere and a point of considerable promise and attraction to many.

The Asaf Jahis whose dynasty followed a period of Mughal control, were Muslims and much beautiful Islamic and Indo-Saracenic architecture abounds in H/S. The superb Legislature building; a large hospital by the Musi River that must surely be one of the most unique and exquisitely gorgeous looking hospital buildings anywhere, and there are very many more superbly architectured buildings in the twin-cities, of H/S.

The spelling of Indian names, confirm the extensive and colourful ancestry of the country. Variations abound and those associated with Hyderabad's history add more confusion (although not, for India's scholars), with their Turko-Islamic origins. Every historian adopts his (or her) own version.

History records that the City of Hyderabad, (the State was merged in 1956 with Andhra Pradesh to form Andhra Pradesh), was founded in 1591, by Mir Qamruddin Chin Qilich Khan. He was the son of the Emperor Aurangzeb's General, Ghazi-ud-din Khan Feroz Jang, who traced his ancestry to Abu Bakr the first Kalifa (Caliph - Sultan of Turkey).

In 1713, Emperor Farrukshiyar made Mir Qamruddin Viceroy of the Deccan, with the title of Nizam-ul-Mulk Feroz Jang. Later (c.1720), Emperor Muhammed Shah conferred on him the title of Asaf Jah, by which title the dynasty became known, down to (and beyond, by one) Nizam VII, his exalted Highness Mir Usman Ali Khan Bahadur, who succeeded to the *gaddi,* (officially recognized succession by the paramount power), in 1911, reigning until his death in 1967.

Of all India's Princes (and Princely States - V.P. Menon says there were 554) Nizam VII of Hyderabad was probably the best-known of them all throughout the world. But not for his polo playing skills (like Jaipur and Cooch Behar and others), or Kashmir (where the Hindu Maharaja ruled over a predominantly Muslim people), but for other reasons, some accurate, more of them however, exaggerated and beyond true fact.

Nizam VII 'stuck to his guns' with the British administration. Hyderabad occupied a strategically important and pivotal position in the heart of India. It was the premier State in the country. Nizam VII rarely given much praise for his toughness and generosity to his subjects (his critics preferring to castigate him for his personal frugality - seeing it as mean-ness), along with another large and rich State - Mysore, stood outside and aloof from the Chamber of Princes, inaugurated by the Crown in 1921. A Muslim ruling over a predominantly Hindu State, he and his people occupied a unique position, which caused the British not a little 'heart-burn' right up to Independence.

The real test of a ruler comes from his people. Today, under excellent leadership the 'separateness' of Hyderabad (extended to take in overall, Andhra Pradesh), is acting to their advantage. No 'hangovers' from reputed Nizam-induced backwardness are apparent. Many tongues, environment, for all to share. An air of confidence permeates everything.

The extensive complex occupied by Hyderabad's wonderful Osmania University exemplifies the 'condition' of the State. The magnificent original core of the University at the present location, the Arts College Building, at gift from Nizam VII, was opened in December 1939. A translation of His Exalted Highness' speech, "VISION OF OSMANIA" seems entirely appropriate -

> I remember very well that about four or five years ago, I laid the foundation stone of this building and thanks to Almighty that this gorgeous edifice is now complete. This structure has perhaps no parallel in the whole of India in its architectural beauty, grandeur and nobility. As the Osmania University is one of the greatest achievements of my reign, the Arts College too will be a grand monument of my period reminding the future generations for centuries to come, of the culture, civilization and architecture of this age. The foundation laying of this edifice and its inauguration have alike given me great pleasure.
>
> The most distinct characteristic of this University is that its medium of instruction is Urdu - a language born of the commingling and friendship of two great peoples, the Hindus and the Muslims, and Urdu is their common heritage which is widely spoken and understood throughout India. It is most gratifying to note that this language has been enriched by the Osmania University in such a manner that today it cherishes the treasures of both oriental and occidental knowledge and learning and has acquired capability of expressing difficult ideas and can be used for imparting higher education. Though the medium of instruction and examination in this University is Urdu, yet its educational standard is no less than any other Indian university having English as medium of instruction.
>
> Now I would like to say in this connection that the architectural style of this building is like Urdu language a manifestation of fusion of the Hindu and Muslim styles. Its pillars, its portals and its facade portray the culture and art of the two peoples. The building is, therefore, a symbol of unity, mutual friendship, cultural amalgam and harmonious relations among the various peoples of my State prevailing since centuries and which made my people to live in peace and prosperity. I consider it a part of my duty as Ruler to preserve the same. Thus, Osmania University represents the best traditions of Hyderabad State and its noble culture should keep as its goal the broad-mindedness, fellow feeling and unity among students for, therein lies the welfare and prosperity of the country.
>
> On this occasion, I call upon the administrators and teachers of the University to strive to establish and maintain cordial relations between the teachers and the taught as well as friendly relations among the

students of various sects and creed because this is an important part of their job. Finally, I wish to say that since this is a residential University, teachers and students should live together on the Campus and lead a corporate life and create an academic, moral and social environment which is the best characteristic of any University. I hope that accommodation will be provided for all teachers and students on the Campus itself.

I now turn my attention to the students of this University and say a few words in response to their address. I feel please and gratified by listening your address and I appreciate the sentiments of loyalty expressed therein. I readily grant you permission by accepting your request to install my portrait in the Students Union building. My advice to you is that you must take full advantage of your career as a student. The facilities available to you now - learned teachers, fine and comfortable hostels, well-stocked libraries, well-equipped laboratories and vast play ground should be utilized to their maximum, for, all these are meant for you and your progress.

This is the time to acquire knowledge, expertise and moral character to equip yourself intellectually and morally for the battle of life which lies ahead of you. You must remember that service to your country and the Ruler is not an easy task; it requires ability and determination. You must prepare yourself for it now. The main benefit of a residential University is its Corporate life. So, it must inculcate the virtues of broad-mindedness, fellow-friendship, generosity and tolerance. These noble qualities make human character valuable and without them mere reading of books is of no good. Acquisition of these virtues is far more important than formal education or degree. No sane person can deny that this is the highest aim of the University's corporate life and its educational activities.

Finally, while expressing my joy at the inauguration of this building, I appreciate the work done by all those who are connected with it specially Zain Yar Jung, Ali Raza and Monsieur Jasper. I also appreciate the valuable services rendered by the present President of the Executive Council, Sir Akbar Hdei for the establishment and administration of this University.

Lastly, I Pray God, the Creator of all knowledge and learning that the Benefactor of the Worlds may grant this University, a rapid progress so that my country may enjoy its benefits for ages to come.

Amen

None of the above, sounds of a mean ungenerous man. Nizam VII's memory is deserving of much deeper, and gracious perception - from everyone.

Not so removed from the wonderful spirit of Osmania University (and the very many other learning and research institutions peppered in many areas of Hyderabad-Secunderabad) is the wonderful exhibition of the State's colourful past, housed, assembled, and displayed so well, in the Salar Jung Museum, by the Musi River.

Prime Minister to several Nizams, Afzal-ud-Daula (1857) and Mir Mahbub Ali Khan (1869), Sir Salar Jung amassed a wonderful collection of art and artefacts, from local and world sources.

In every respect, my wonderful new-found friends from Habsiguda, brought an added dimension to my many and varied experiences in India, and of India. The next chapter promises ever greater understanding and enjoyment of the many wonderful facets of Hyderabad-Secunderabad, yet to be discovered.

24. Lal Dighi's Spirit Rises To The Challenge

- recharging Calcutta's engine

As I write, an Australian cricket team is at present in Madras (*Chennai*), contesting sub-continental supremacy, with Azharuddin's and India's best exponents. Azar's team performs mightily, on hot spicy Indian food- Madrassi curries, *chaapathis,* and delicious *parathas,* the occasional *tandoor morghi* (chicken) with scrumptious accompanying *naans,* of so many varieties- Indian bread really (*roti*)- and for in-betweeners, fine *dosas, idlis* and *vadas,* as only south Indian cooks can turn out these appetising morsels.

But how might the Australian cricketers be settling in to their new and strange, and largely (personally) unknown situation? Their preparation for the Indian tour (most likely) would have been substantially related to physical fitness, and direction in- 'what pills to take' (or condition support remedies to quaff) to prevent or to reduce, the effects of dreaded eastern diseases- dysentery, cholera, typhoid, malaria, and other viruses and tummy wogs? Sensibly, precautions are necessary, and as well, a clear consciousness of heat dehydration from extreme physical exertion.

However, laden down with these little understood factors, the visitors' ability to concentrate upon cricket will have been significantly impaired, at least during the early stages of the tour itinerary, and would not subside (or at all) until many of these generally over-exaggerated fears, have been consigned to their proper and sensible place. This from one who has spent many decades in all parts of India in all manner of different situations, and for long periods, and in other Asian lands as well. Trust me, this is how things go.

Initially, the Australian cricketers (and nearly every visitor and certainly everything ex- the 5 star hotels), will treat with microscopic suspicion, everything they touch, drink or eat- and, breathe in. For the Aussies clearly it is NOT the recommended preparation for winning serious cricket matches. The author recalls one Antipodean cricket side touring India in the fifties with just eight 'reasonably' fit players- out of seventeen- half-way through a Test Match! Yes, they lost, to India.

Psychological problems can affect nearly every newcomer to the sub-continent, arising from difficult to shake off fears of serious illness being contracted, because of (mostly believed) less than strict hygienic measures, particularly in the handling of food. Even the universally indulged in regular brushing of teeth, sets visitors 'teeth on edge'. Most fears have no foundation, for popularised perpetuated theories (and myths) rarely pay any regard to civic improvements and the passage of time. In many respects, the very real health problems of 1950, are NOT the problems of today. For most visitors to India, it is a subject given obtuse confused attention, and even more poorly, or in any way, properly explained or delivered. Care yes- but ludicrous labelling, and *ad infinitum*- no.

Confirmation of the shortcomings in the Australian camp (on what to expect; on minimum precautions; on getting to learn and understanding something of Indian culture), have been quickly highlighted in the food department.

Indiscreetly ignoring respectful behaviour (to the host country), and putting commercial considerations foremost, Heinz (of the 57 varieties) made a great thing, of sending in twenty cases of baked beans. Hardly an effective saviour for any bowler expected to trundle twenty five overs of fast stuff in the March heat of *Chennai*! But Heinz suffered few rebukes and the foreign media had their fun. In the good relations stakes, a lot of learning is still obviously needed.

All this *tamasha* (show) might have overlooked that the Aussie cricketers were quartered at the resplendent 5-star TAJ COROMANDEL, a world-class establishment able to come up with the best palatable food, and in great variety, and qualitatively and hygienically able to satisfy the most fastidious guests (local and foreign)?

One must put serious questions to Australia's cricketing hierarchy- who only saw the humour (?) of the 'baked beans' bit- or are they no better than (most) foreigners, of properly understanding the state of current affairs, in present-day India? Ambassadorial 'duties' might have required better preparation, assessment and resolution, of (perceived) 'player- comfort' problems.

If Americans played cricket (and, except for nostalgic expatriates, in Williamsburgh and elsewhere, suitably togged out in the best gear and re-living past joys- they DON'T!), they would probably do what they (regularly) do when a U.S. team participates abroad- and it is not just confined to tours of 'uncertain' countries- they send in, food and drink, enough to cover the whole exercise (more a military operation, their 'systems' are so well-developed, and so expansive) from start to finish. Such delightful guests!! Oh dear, but then who is brave enough to contest with Americans?

Why does this fallacy still affect India's major cities (all well equipped with 5-star hotel accommodation- even for spoilt sportsmen, barely knowledgeable or ordinarily 'comfortable', with cuisine beyond McDonalds or K.F.C., or the Red Rooster, in their home environment)?

What prevents/gets in the way, of sensible intelligent advice? Travel brochures ordinarily skip/omit, or conveniently slide over getting deeply (and perhaps 'dangerously') involved in such intimate things as, diet- and the hardy perennial-constipation, which affects most travellers out of normal routine and subjected to rapidly changing environmental conditions- and as well climatic factors, which are in constant flux, pleasant and unpleasant, depending on the time of the year, and this- wherever in the world. Getting sensible accurate advice is no easy thing, although where the Aussie cricketers are concerned, one might expect them to be properly acquainted with expected conditions and forearmed. It is not their first tour, made to India.

Off the beaten track in India, perhaps it could reasonably happen that an unprepared visitor could encounter problems but *not*, if he or she is lodging in one of India's truly superb 5-star hotels and in a major metropolis! It is 1998, not 1898! Hasn't anyone spread the message? And if not, why not?

The author is well qualified to comment. As a new young greenhorn executive recruit (of a MNC) he was despatched to India, on a passenger liner first class, with the only forewarning (advice?)- given by a senior executive who had spent 22 years in Calcutta— —- "You'll put up at first at McDonnell's Boarding House" — —and— - "You must not address anybody by their christian name, but you must wait until you are properly invited and/or requested, to do this" —.

Nothing about the vastly different Indian culture, or changed living environment, or hints of 'time and tried' precautions, or most of all, of the Indian people themselves. Surprisingly (but as I was to discover for myself, not so surprisingly), the correct social 'form', and doubtlessly so 'in expatriate circles', overrode everything else. It was paramount. You were expected to 'pick up the rest', as you went along. Again- and somewhat oddly- very little advice of a helpful nature was ever offered by expatriates. The sink or swim philosophy prevailed. Stupid, really.

All very amusing now (even ludicrous) years later, and skillions of kilometres spent around India, to every imaginable place, and a lifetime residing in and visiting Asia/Pacific countries, all largely survived unscathed, and probably fitter for it all, than my erstwhile school chums, who never left 'healthy/comfortable' Australia. Perhaps their closest contact with India *etcetera,* was being at the cinema, seeing *GUNGA DIN!*

In a short while, the Aussie cricketers will be in Calcutta for the Second Test and will again grace the city's most magnificent cricket ground, Eden Gardens (Ranji Stadium). Alan Border's Australians were victorious at the same venue in 1987. The 1998 Aussies will undoubtedly stay at either The Oberoi Grand (nearby on Chowringhee), or at the Taj Bengal, by the Zoo at Alipore. Will they have the same 'comfort' problems there or, after several weeks in India, will they have asked enough questions, and got enough sensible answers (advice), to be able to sensibly get on with things? But not just that, but as well, realize that there are tens of millions of Calcuttans (many of them present at the cricket, cheering all good exploits, and performed by either side) and nearly a billion Indians, who also require to be recognized and to share equitably with whatever there is. Most Indians don't gripe and lament their situation. They are much more durable than that.

Some will know that Australia's women cricketers (but did *they* notice? Did *they* comment? Did *they* express their amazed feelings, with family and friends when they returned home?) played earlier this year at Eden Gardens before a cheering crowd of 60,000 spectators, of school children mostly, recruited by the State's Sports Minister as a special gesture to the visitors. Taylor's men will play in front of crowds, twice that number. An unforgettable experience, and one of awe, surpassing anything experienced even in Melbourne, where 90,000 once turned out for Worrell's West Indians, and where even larger single day's audiences descend upon the superlative M.C.G., for Aussie Rules Grand Finals.

53. Calcutta- Modern Apartment, at Dum Dum

54. The wonderful oasis, shared by all, the 'Victoria Memorial' and grounds.

55. Majestic Hooghly crossing - Vidyasagar Setu (Second Hooghly Bridge)

56. "Well-read" at Kalighat.

57. Hooghly transit-from Chandpal Ghat.

58. Russell Street refreshment.

59. Busy Dharamtollah Street intersection.

60. "Poor- but smilingly honest".

Yes, Eden Gardens ground in Calcutta, will surpass them all, and the enthusiasm of sports loving (sports crazy) Indians, will also surprise. To play on Eden Gardens before a 'full house' (120,000 fans), caps everything else any cricketer may experience.

Let us all hope that the Australians take away with them 'real feelings' and more honest impressions of Calcutta's greatness. The redoubtable 'world respected' Ed Hillary, first up Everest with Tenzing, and great lover and respecter of India, encapsulated his profound feelings, for the people and atmosphere of Calcutta, in his book *From The Ocean To The Sky.* Others, able to 'look beyond themselves' and who extend respect to everyone they meet, including Indians, never fail to experience and articulate similar enjoyment.

All this talk about cricket?- but no apology is due, as cricket is very dear to the heart of Calcutta's youth, and to older generations who have played the game, starting as kids on the bumpy uneven and uncordoned off 'temporary pitches' set up all through the seasons, on the Maidan. These 'pitches' criss-cross each other (no matter, getting a game is the thing), wherever there is some uncovered/unoccupied, space.

Except for the very privileged (boys who attend the top Public/ Private schools- Xavier College, La Martinere and others) most kids serve their 'apprenticeships' on the rough Maidan wickets, before graduating to the all-enclosed Maidan clubs- Mohun Bagan, East Bengal, Mohammedan Sporting, Rajasthan, or join other top Clubs- Kalighat and Bhowanipore etcetera, including the former bastions of expatriate cricket, the Eden Gardens (Ranji Stadium) and at Ballygunge (my former club, the C.C.C.), the latter now a composite cricket/rugby club.

The British are rarely thanked for it, but amongst their many, and enduring 'gifts'/contributions, to the leisure time of countless millions everywhere in the world, is or are, the 'no real cost involved pastimes' of football (of every kind), cricket, hockey; well in fact- all ball games, all multiple participation games. In continents like Africa and South America, and Australia, and in the sub-continent (India, Pakistan, Bangladesh and Sri Lanka), the benefits, enjoyment and opportunities created for everyone, are unsurpassable. In many respects, the pupils have learnt well, and frequently now out-gun the masters.

To represent his country at cricket is the ambition of every Bengali youngster. The enthusiasm (and seriousness) in which the game is played, takes the author back to his own boyhood, when cricket/ hockey/football was the bane of every mother's life. While there was a skerrick of light left, the game on the local sward continued until blackness shut things down. Calcutta's youngsters are imbued with the same spirit and have taken up the gauntlet, with great gusto. Saurav Ganguly is the local's cricketing idol.

If much has been made of 'activity' across the Maidan, know that it is merited. The Maidan is Calcutta's 'display window' and quite easily the foremost source of relief for most Calcuttans, and a panacea from the otherwise unrelenting burden- of making do in life; of incessant unrelieved toil; and of increasingly harsh and congested living conditions. But don't ever think that the people can't smile, can't look people in the eye and pass the time of day to each other. They do it better than most- than most people in foreign lands who believe themselves to be, materially better off. India puts more value on spiritual gain.

Before leaving cricket, as played internationally, and in 1998, the facts are that until not so many years ago, cricket everywhere in the world, was only played (and sensibly so), during each country's own normal season, and turn about with the more physical contact sports, rugby, hockey etcetera, which enjoyed prime place in the colder months. Nowadays, National cricket sides (and just about every other sporting code) are called upon to play 'filler tournaments' the whole year round. In cricket, promotional one day tournaments are staged in every imaginable and unlikely place around the world- as entertainment for the locals, who otherwise, have no local associations with 'playing the particular sport'. It is the era, of the marketing specialist, the 'turnstile mover'. Playing lengthier 5-day Test Matches in India's oppressively hot and humid summer months, in 45 degree Celsius temperatures, is no joke, but it is accepted in the name of 'funding the game', and of course paying the players, and meeting the handsome expenses of the ever expanding band of officials (carpetbaggers).

India wholly resides in the northern hemisphere, but because of 'the weather, uniformly affecting plains country in the sub-continent', the British very long ago, as progenitors of modern sport in India, reversed the seasons- playing hockey first, followed by soccer, and then rugby from April onwards, but not commencing cricket until the beginning of November round to the end of February, and, into early March, to wrap up the season. A wonderful compromise, although playing rugger on the C.F.C. in the sticky hot middle-of-the-year months, resembled a 'Turkish, or mud-bath!' Little wonder, Taylor's Aussies are finding very little to laugh about, *and* with Calcutta and Bangalore, yet to come! Begorra.

The 'silly season' has certainly arrived for international cricket, (but *not* local cricket competition), and the highly paid professionals must decide—"is it all worth it?" But money shrinks brains, and so the present torture will continue, and get worse. Playing 'out of regular season' on the sub-continent, i.e. India, Pakistan, Sri Lanka and Bangladesh, may not worry the local National sides, quite as much as foreign visiting teams. But that is the price the present gluttony exacts.

Because Calcutta, and perhaps every place, throughout the length and breadth of today's India, 'lives' on its past (and when tomorrow comes, today will be 'lived' as yesterday, joining the thousands of years that have gone before), only a small bit of serious attention is given to the future, beyond what is necessary to keep body and soul together, and to deal with just one more day 'tomorrow' which will be crucially important for most, anyway.

Of course, the infrastructure providers- of water, of electricity, of sanitation- necessarily look and plan further ahead. But momentous planning allied to grand vision is almost totally absent in the minds and hearts of the general population. How else would they have the grit, the courage, to patiently tolerate the mostly not improving conditions, and accept as inevitable, the unrelieved high levels of inconvenience most of them encounter, in their daily lives.

But in fact, no one is exempted, not even the most powerful (the privileged handful, relatively speaking, comprised primarily of politicians - the Chief Minister Jyoti Basu and his senior Ministers - the Police, and less conspicuous but sometimes there - the Army top brass) who, though they may sound their wailers, and 'cut' their way through the (often) dense traffic (which is frequently much more than Fire Engines and Ambulances, can accomplish), they too, like everyone else, must endure the frequent *bandhs* [daylight hours 6 to 6 union inspired shutdown affecting the whole city], electricity load-shedding and water problems (and frequent flash-floodings, which occur during each year's Monsoon-season, June to September).

(Author's Note: my apologies for what must be my most Dostoyevsky-like sentence.)

Change from the 'norm', is slow. Apart from lengthy (and often 'fiery') debate, 'meat and drink' for West Bengal's politicians and bureaucrats, there is always the vexed question of (1) how can matters be planned to avoid major disruption- while the work is being executed, which will be a long time rather than a short time, because of (2), finding the heaps of less than plentiful public funds, necessary to carry through the particular improvement/essential need. Despite the huge pool of manual labour which can be readily recruited to accomplish any project, nothing seems to be expedited- in Calcutta, in India. The days when Britain was Paramount Ruler in India, and could sweep everyone and everything else aside, often only for their own self-aggrandisement, are past!

In whatever way considered, the demeanour of Calcuttans is astonishingly refreshing to any discerning person from the western world, where dissatisfaction (amongst a world of plenty, of heaps more than any normal person needs) and selfishness and gross intolerance is rife, and where capacious commercialism is fast reaching abhorrent proportions. Consumerism is being allowed to ride rough shod over common decency, in most places, in the western world.

If the 'all devouring' western MNC's have their way, (three cheers for India putting a brake on their un-needed merchandise), the same 'breakdown of ideals and time and tested values' could wreak a trail of destruction, in India. It should not be allowed to happen. India's great traditions and compassionate respectful ways, are too valuable- for the world, and not just for India, to lose!

The 'general' western attitude to India, is that it is archaic, behind the times, drowning in the past. This position is not helped when India's own governments (all thirty or so of them) and its people, lack the will to widely and effectively ***broadcast far and wide around the world to everyone who will listen*** the wonderful cultural and 'people-wares' they are so richly endowed with, now topped off by some of the ablest technological and scientific skills to be found anywhere in the world.

Some good marketing is being done, but not enough of it and in a properly cohesive and collective organised way. An *Indian think tank* displaying flair, ingenuity and sound thinking, *and aided by sensible worldly-wise foreigners who 'know' India well,* could dramatically change India's poor, though nearly totally mistaken and erroneous, image- as peddled by the foreign camera and media bugs short on real flair and initiative.

Instead of T.V. incessantly and almost totally being 'held to close-ups', primarily in order to magnify and emphasise sensational (and usually as well, completely valueless) tosh, already worked to death, foreigners and India's own publicists should close down the lens, open the wide-angle and shoot into the distance and depict India's more valuable virtues of many descriptions, and comparable (with the best, most absorbing and interesting anywhere) subject matter of whatever kind, people, culture, scenery *et al.*

Ridiculous, that the trillions of yards of film taken at Mother Teresa's memorial service, did not produce, for showing to the world, a single wide-angle shot, of Calcutta's wonderful Hooghly River and its superb bridges, or of the multifarious activity going on, on the city's vast Maidan, or even some distance shots of the Red Road, or of inexhaustibly exciting Chowringhee, or Park Street, or of Dalhousie Square. Such negativity! So difficult to fathom. Such a lack of creativity, of respect and of common decency. Why have all these wonderful attributes/mannerisms/great urges to 'give something more, something of oneself'- done the bunk! Certainly is this so, where it comes to seriously depicting today's total India to the world at large.

The very best of Calcutta, is missed by so many- its own people, too! The French and the Italians may put on their vaudeville acts for their teeming millions of annual visitors, but 'the show of life', presented daily- in Calcutta and throughout nearly everywhere in hugely cosmopolitan (their colourful ones were imported long ago from many different regions of the world) India, beats most places.

But it is not its tawdriness, or its beggars (and in reality, there are not really so many, especially regarded amongst a huge population approaching a billion people), or the chance it offers to ridicule, that is paramount. Contrarily, it is the sheer volatility and versatility of the people and of the great diversity of styles and of 'things being done', which holds people, in thrall. It is not an act put on for an audience, it is the real thing.

The average 'contented, but not so well-off ' Calcuttan has to manufacture his own interests/his own fun/his own recreation. He plays cards; many of them are talented chess players; he loves to chat to his family and with friends, neighbours and workmates; he loves to watch cricket and soccer (a great favourite of Calcuttans); he sometimes takes his family to the cinema, and when his children are small, he takes them to the zoo, or to the Maidan. Prayer and obeisance to his Gods (and with Hindus, there are millions of Gods) constitute a very important and daily part of his life, either at home, or by visiting a nearby temple.

It is only the 'better-off' who frequent the sporting and recreation clubs (many of them occupying the myriad 'tents', scattered over the Maidan), while the 'well-heeled' have commandeered the vacated British Clubs, now not so strongly related, and predominantly visited, as in the expatriate era- for vigorous exercise- but to socialise and to idly chat. Ducking in to the Swimming Club, on Strand Road, on several previous visits in the last year, *there was no water*. Big extensions have been made to the buildings. Perhaps they should change the name of the Club?

But what of *Lal Dighi's* spirit? rising to the challenge? For all their amazing and special capacity to harmonize so many different cultures and religions, all living as it were 'under the one roof' and peacefully, collaboration in the civic affairs department, is not one of the Calcuttans', or any Indians', strong suit. Why so disparate when it comes to general 'people matters' is hard to reconcile with their other very prominent strengths in blending their basic lives, leaving room for everybody and everything and largely devoid of all or any serious conflict, except that created for personal ends and politicking purposes, when tempers are unnecessarily fanned.

Lal Dighi (literally Red Square- nothing to do with Moscow or Communists, and predating Marx and Lenin by hundreds of years), or Tank Square, or Dalhousie Square (as it was named when I looked out every day upon it, for many years, from 5 & 7 Netaji Subhas Road, on its western perimeter) or B.B.D. (Benoy Badal Dinesh) Bagh, as it is now officially named, but which will continue to be affectionately referred to as Dalhousie Square for a long time to come- defines the heart and the centre, of Calcutta's C.B.D., Central Business District.

Not a paved open space, but a large 'tank' of water, covering 43 *bighas* of land (approximately 25 acres), it was originally dug out in the early days of British settlement, circa 1700, to 'provide the inhabitants of Calcutta with (drinking) water, which is sweet and pleasant. No one may wash in it?'

The early British settlement of Fort William grew up around its perimeter, on all four sides, Lal Bazar Street to the north (the last block at its western end is wholly taken up with Writers' Building, which houses the Chief Minister, Ministers, and many of the bureaucrats heading up the Secretariat of the West Bengal Government); Old Court House Street on the eastern side; on the southern side Hare Street; and to the west Netaji Subhas Road, which links up at the north-western corner of Dalhousie Square (B.B.D.Bagh), to form Clive Street, still the leading 'business end' of Calcutta, hosting many major banks and mercantile houses, including the Stock Exchange and the Jute Exchange, the latter once the principal source of export revenue for India.

'Commercial Power' in British India, and up to the 1960's, was centred in the radius arcing in all directions from Lal Dighi, or as it was better known, Dalhousie Square. While West Bengal has surrendered much of its 'crown', to other States (Maharashtra and Gujarat in particular), it remains the largest and most important town in the north-east region of India, and a major port on the east coast of India.

Dominant in India's 'march to freedom' after the Mutiny (1857), and perhaps still the leading culture centre (the 23rd Calcutta Book Fair recently staged on the north-eastern corner of the Maidan attracted over 2.5 million (25 *lakhs*) book-worms/book browsers, during its twelve days, with an estimated 600,000 (6 *lakhs*) people attending on the last day. Nowhere else in India produces, or reads more books- mostly non-fiction ones- than Calcuttans). The disastrous fire which sent the author and thousands of others fleeing from the same venue, twelve months before, was thankfully averted, in 1998.

Calcuttans number people of all ethnic races, and religions from all regions of India. Many put down their roots there during the British days, intelligently aware that the British were not interested in smaller ventures, and in the myriad of ancillary trades that have to be present to service, victual, feed and clothe all (large) populations.

The Mahwaris (from Rajasthan) did their job well- the Birlas, the Bajorias, and Khaitans, and the Kanorias *et al-* and today, represent the richest and most prosperous and powerful of the immigrants, who stayed on to control India's major industries and export trades after the bulk of foreign firms de-camped India's shores in the late 1960's.

While not much reform, or not nearly enough, (land reform in particular) has taken place in many parts of India, keeping most *mofussil* labour on India's agricultural estate- seventy per cent of India's population- hostage to big landlords able to 'buy' political patronage, West Bengal's decline in the eyes of New Delhi (Central Government chose to quarantine West Bengal from any new large Public Sector enterprises for many decades) was particularly due to the Marxist State Government's sweeping changes introduced since 1967 (with just one gap of five years) not least in land reform in its State, which ushered in other concomitant problems.

But, while life for the people in the rural districts was markedly improved, some of this was at the expense of Calcutta- politically non-Marxist.

The 'buffeting' Calcutta took in the sixties and seventies, in its 'most violent anti-social era', turned investors away from the State and towards other 'more peaceful' States in India. The Calcuttan, quite naturally and all very inevitably, has been influenced by hundreds of years of being the major British centre of commerce, where most British activity in India took place, or was controlled from, up to the 1960's. Desirable or not, the Bengali took on some of the British 'show of superiority', over other Indians.

The major ethnic dweller in West Bengal, is the Bengali. Except in cultural circles (literature, dance, art, theatre and education) he has not dominated the business scene, but has for a long time, and even today, bowed to the itinerants from elsewhere in India, given more to trading and dealing. The huge clerical and manual labour forces in Calcutta and in the hinterland, have been there at the behest of the rich and powerful, whose domination has been now blunted by a Socialist Government leaning towards some 'pegging back of past discriminatory treatment'. Some, yes, was absolutely warranted, but a lot became 'too much'.

The 'great wheel' was allowed to turn, to go too far, and for too long. The resultant chaos put a brake on new investment of a substantial nature (from many quarters), and allowed a too long period of deterioration, to set in. The C.P.I. (Marxist) led by Jyoti Basu, realised things had gone too far, and during the past 3 or 4 years it has introduced new measures designed to attract investors back. But politically fired disruption still continues and still precludes any real or quick reversal of fortunes. New tricks well learned (and encouraged), take a lot of changing.

Such is Calcutta's problem. A great city, with so much wonderful talent, so much wonderful experience, and so much of just about everything to offer, but which is being thwarted, held back, by actions which itself manufactured and put into play. Just as India's own progress was unintentionally and unwittingly retarded by the voluntarily 'closing off of normal activity with the outside world', from 1947 up to 1991, a leeway not easily made up, as the rest of the world had made significant strides, West Bengal's own internal upheaval has played into the hands of the other twenty four Indian States, also avid for investment capital.

If one unprejudically compared Calcutta's attributes (across the whole spectrum), with the other major Indian cities, Delhi, Bombay (Mumbai) and Madras (Chennai), and the newer burgeoning centres, Bangalore and Hyderabad (Andhra Pradesh), it easily has most going for it. But it will need a peaceful, but positive 'people' revolution, and great resolution from everybody, to discuss and re-vamp the feelings and attitudes, and memories, of others- of other Indians equally desirous of winning most business/most laurels, for their own States, and as well, the favours of foreign investors- towards Calcutta/towards West Bengal. Such investors have the choice of many locations where their businesses will not be unscheduledly interrupted and disrupted detrimentally in the manner which has occurred and which regrettably still happens in West Bengal.

Memories are not rapidly extinguished and certainly not, in the harsh reality of the business world. Repairing lost faith requires tremendous effort- from everyone.

Possibly the stumbling block to 'real restoration' will not be removed until there is change of government (but it is hard to see that this is in any way imminent), or conversely by political and business consensus there is a huge, concerted and sincere programme put in place, and projected from every quarter. Business disruption is a key factor. It must be properly regulated, and serious stoppages only happen, when the most genuine and justifiable reasons are present. Wildcat strikes must be strictly prohibited and observed by all. Any exceptions will merely put everyone's hopes back to square one.

I lived for years in Calcutta. I watched its progress from the fifties up to 1965, and have witnessed its subsequent decline (although principally only in economic supremacy terms). While not many new industries may have started up, and many old long established ones been shut down, it would be ridiculous to discount the obvious many other changes which have occurred in keeping with normal living and rampant population increases. Calcutta serves the entire north-east region, supplying 'the staff of life' to millions of people and their multiple small businesses.

Yes, many positive things have also happened. The wonderful new Vidyasagar Setu (Second Hooghly Bridge) has been constructed, although not yet able to be properly utilized. The superb Metro has been completed, providing marvellously cheap and swift mostly 'below the ground' transportation. A number of splendid buildings have taken shape- on Chowringhee Road; on Strand Road (the extensive new Bank of India complex), and along the (new) Eastern Freeway. The City has a wonderful new football stadium, Yuba Bharati Krirangan, and the domestic terminal at Dum Dum Airport, excellently upgraded.

The 'second port' down the Hooghly at Haldia is working well, and fast developing. It is heartening as well to see commenced, the long overdue complete renovation and restoration of the City's famous City Hall, up the street from the still splendid High Court building, another of Calcutta's proud treasures.

But what has not happened, and what urgently needs to happen? My priority list for the 'turn of the century/of the millennium', Calcutta, would be:-

1) New technical training schools- many of them, for all trades.

In the past, 'tradesmen' have either learnt their skills 'on the job' at engineering works etc, or as 'handed down' by other casual tradesmen. While adept at 'temporarily' dealing with needs, it has meant a perpetuation of *kachha* work, *kachha* (or temporary, adequate to get the job done, or to perform the particular function- until it next breaks down) attitudes, of contentment with shoddy, cheap work.

'Kachha-ness' - has been allowed to infiltrate the standards, for doing EVERYTHING. The 'we can't afford the real thing, but this will get us by' syndrome, has anteaten proper standards of permanence, of decent proud workmanship. The 'put it up today, pull it down tomorrow' mentality, might provide continual casual work (for some remuneration), but it corrodes real progress. Replacement of ancient/ blunt tools, with modern sharp efficient ones, can be allowed to happen. But 'kachha'- let it be confined to unripe fruit (*phal*). Its present virulence is seriously hampering India's real progress.

2) A 'fair go' for pedestrians

At present pedestrians (who easily account for the greatest number of Calcuttans) are 'fair game', for motorists, whether public and or private buses, heavy trucks, jostling taxis and 'chauffeur driven' private vehicles. Unlike New Delhi, Calcutta has no underpaths across busy intersections, although Metro Stations now allow this to happen- if you've the time and are prepared to take the 'long way'.

Traffic lights are disregarded in many places (and at less busy times) if a motorist 'sees' a clear space i.e. clear of other cars, not people.

At the very least, Zebra crossings should be painted in on just about every major carriageway- and policed! More pedestrians are killed or injured in Calcutta, than other casualties involving motor transport.

There is a crying need for underpaths (or overpaths) in Park Street, at the junction of Chowringhee and further up the same street, in several places.

3) A tidy-up of The Maidan, and everything on it, from Dharamtallah/ Esplanade East in the north, right through to A.J.C. Bose Road, in the south.

All unwanted /non-registered premises to be removed. All rubbish cleared away. Tanks to be thoroughly drained, cleaned and refilled.

No more *'kachha'* exhibitions to be constructed but 'permanent' homes to be found for all these events, away from The Maidan.

The Maidan is for *all* the people to use at all times and is free.

A tidying up programme of the entire Maidan to be begun involving thousands of volunteers and civic minded citizens, plus horticultural technical experts, and as well, engineers co-opted from the Water and Drainage Sections, of the Calcutta Municipal Corporation, who might advise on and supervise essential irrigation works.

Gravel paths/tree plantings/in-ground irrigation equipment and permanent seating, to be installed in various places and properly maintained.

4) Greatly improved use of the Hooghly- for both commercial and private recreational purposes

During my third long trip (1997) in just over a year, to India, I crossed over the Hooghly to Howrah and then up river under Rabindra Setu (Howrah Bridge) to Belur, then returned to Chandpal Ghat, when I sought a ticket downriver to Garden Reach and, back. I was shocked to be told that all 'downriver' ferries had ceased to run, either because of poor results, or a wearing out of their small (private) boats.

Whereas in British times, the Hooghly swarmed with ocean-going cargo vessels, inland shallow draught paddle steamers, and barges and small motorized craft of many descriptions, the Hooghly is now nearly bereft of all traffic, apart from Government run passenger ferries (introduced only in 1985) following a fairly restrictive number of routes and destinations. Practically none, or no, private craft, of any kind, operate on the Hooghly, or make use of this expansive waterway. Sacred to all Hindus yes, but still difficult to understand why the people of Calcutta make no use of it, for recreational purposes. There may be reasons (above, lack of interest in water sports; or considered sacrilegious to use other than for bathing or religious ceremony); I have not heard of any.

If there are no 'serious' barriers precluding use of the Hooghly for recreational pursuits, where are the entrepreneurs? Leaving the 'on-shore congestion' behind, should have great and instant appeal to tens of thousands. It would 'open up the river, above and below Calcutta' precipitating the modern re-constitution of all the old foreign settlements, Chandernagore, Hooghly, Chinsurah, Serampore and Barrackpore and the creation of new resorts. Who will be brave and enterprising enough to begin this marvellous new and rewarding venture, which all can enjoy and benefit from?

5) Hugely overdue and very urgently necessary- the complete re-vamp, especially of the downstairs ARRIVAL SECTION of the International Air Terminal. The existing set-up is inadequate, frustratingly slow and a disgrace.

Until the arrival facilities are totally recast/re-designed, and extended, international airlines will not set down at Calcutta.

Accessing through Immigration and baggage collection is archaic and quite unable to properly service, a planeload (from Singapore, from Bangkok) of up to 200 passengers, especially late night arrivals. Two hours can be spent before reaching and clearing customs.

While every passenger is entitled to be treated the same, this situation is aggravated by the fact of many Indian Nationals bringing in with them many declarable (and bulky) items. There could be a case for permitting foreign passengers, in-transit through India with only limited luggage, to be separately processed. It is surprising that such an arrangement has not been sought after by India's own Government Tourist organisation, and by the International Airlines themselves, in deference to their passengers.

6) Excluding all foreign news media (reporters and photographers) who refuse to move away from only short focused shots - of Calcutta's worst features. Except that they apply a broader fairer brush, including the good and the interesting, with the bad (of which every large city in the world has its share), further entry banned.

Readers may think I am joking to promote such drastic embargo. Just a little, perhaps. Nevertheless, it is my belief that not many (people) could deny that much of the reportings today, particularly on Asian countries (and other African, Central and South American, Mid-Eastern countries – struggling to reconcile all manner of internal – and often very complex – problems), and put out as 'fact' – in their own countries – is frequently 'way off-beam', inaccurate and shallowly researched or understood, thereby missing the real meaning or substance – as a local sees it, or is affected.

True 'feel for' (*i.e.* honest feeling for) and genuinely compassionate understanding, can only happen by serious study and genuinely interested enquiry. There was a time, not so many years ago, when foreign correspondents were 'long term accepted (and thus – more acquainted and knowledgeable) residents. What they had to report contained dimension and balance – ingredients invariably missing these days, in a (western) world looking for sensation, as the networks compete with each other, for the advertising dollar.

Let us all hope that the media sees the 'error of its reporting', the injustices and injury it causes, where only better consciousness and understanding can bring proper rewards. Roll on the (great) day. Until the great day comes, more 'telling it' often and more emphatically and, as it is, by the Homesters, could be the remedy. As 'seen' from without, so often given the accolade (and believed as gospel), is not the same, as 'known' within.

Besides the above six (6) top priority items, there are many more urgent corrections needed, but once a concerted start is made on a number of them, excitement will mount, carrying everyone- Government, Municipal Corporations (all three of them, Calcutta, Howrah and Chandernagore) and all the people, along together- strongly united and with everyone coming forward with sound suggestions.

All of it is possible. Cohesion will achieve it. A brave new world will do wonders for everybody- and Calcutta will enhance its standing, most importantly- firstly amongst its own people, and secondly with other parts of India, and finally with the rest of the world. Everyone now- under Starter's Orders. Right- all begin! and don't stop until you have completed your mission.

25. Recalling My 'Chokra Days' And The Drama Of My First Advent To India

- In so many ways, nothing has changed

Very recently - in December - January/February 1998, I made a long visit to India for the tenth time in the last ten years. I had previously lived and worked in India, over twenty years before, for nearly ten years.

In the last ten years I have frequently walked along Chota Russelly Street (in Calcutta) and past what was formerly 'Kenilworth', Madath's Boarding House on the corner of Theatre Road (now Shakespeare Sarani). Since extended, refurbished and renamed 'New Kenilworth Hotel', Madath's was my home for the first twenty-one months of my initial stay in India. My original 'digs', it was also home, for scores of other 'first tourers' to India, many of them high spirited bachelors. It was a 'league of all nations', and a great place to forge new friendships, some of which endure to the present day. The laughter and *bonhomie* which used to regularly issue forth from the common dining hall, provided a wonderful unforgettable atmosphere. Who amongst us who were there, could ever forget the raucous 'from the bottom of the belly' laughter, of Ralph and Derek? Tracing the subsequent life journeying of 'my co-boarders' would fill an intriguing, even startling, book.

Over the past ten years I have talked to very many local Calcuttans, some of whom I knew in my *chokra* days, others new acquaintances. These chats have starkly highlighted the clear gulf which still existed in India's post-Independence days, between the expatriate commercial community and the local Indian population of Calcutta.

Even more surprising and revealing is how little each half knew in regard to how the other half lived their lives, or in particular, how 'separated' were the expatriates from their hosts. Indeed, apart from working contact and a smattering of sporting contacts, it is staggering to realise how remote the foreign contingent was, in everyday terms, from everyone else. Indians were privy to so little of foreign goings-on, particularly the social patterns and behaviour indulged in by the otherwise tightly controlled (by its own people) expatriate business community.

Intrigued by anecdotal references quoted by me in our conversations, my present-day Indian friends succeeded in persuading me that there could be some value and interest for others in this myriad (past) activity if some of it was recorded for posterity, if only to confirm that it took all kinds, and much that was different, to make that world go around, especially in the dramatic atmosphere of post-Independence India.

It was my good fortune to be born and raised in Australia, one of the cosiest, and at that time - the most innocent of social environments, anywhere in the world. Somewhat surprisingly and contrary to normal expectations, the culture shock I experienced upon finding myself in totally different India was not my main problem. It was not the strangeness of Indians and their ways (to me), which troubled me, so much, as my concerns in regard to the 'rip-roaring' frenetic lifestyle, pace and attitudes, of the expatriate community.

While pretty strictly monitored by firmly in place, foreign community 'un-written rules', the concomitant full-pelt social activities were dismaying, if not a tad overwhelming, to me, a practising Methodist, and a member of the Band of Hope, to boot! I recall writing to my mum in my early days expressing doubts that I wanted to 'stick around'; to serve out my four years contractual period. However, my strong unshakeably scrupulous mother had no doubts. She said, I must! I had given my word. As subsequent events have proved, her advice (as nearly always) was 'spot on'.

But I am racing ahead of myself (doubtless conditioned by maturer thoughts). Better that I start at the beginning of this 'fantastically different and transitional change in my life' and give a brief outline and a few random anecdotes of the new phase of my life - the passage to India; the short interval in Bombay which followed, and the long train journey across India up to arrival in Calcutta, and of the succeeding years, spent in India, before moving on to Indonesia and other parts.

A smile wreathes my face when I recall my initial welcome at Howrah Station. I had just completed my longest non-stop train journey. As well, I had landed in India only five days before; I had a raging cold, and I had barely eaten anything since I had landed at Bombay. Celebrations were definitely out, although a brave showing was called for, important first impressions, and all that! Ugh!

I had caught a dreadful head cold (worst of my life, before or since) on the run up from Australia on P&O's "Strathaird". Unused to the searing humid tropical heat, encountered when passing through the equatorial zone, I had trained the blower in my cabin on my face, when I slept. Disaster!

By the time I got to Calcutta I felt quite rotten. I rather jolted my welcoming party with my first enquiry *"did they know a good doctor?"* Imagine their shock. Heavens, the new recruit's first day of a four year 'tour' had not begun, and here he was, calling for a doctor! The prognostications for a long sojourn were not seen, as good!

How humorous for me to now relate that I've seen all of them off so far as revisiting India goes, (with just one exception), and here I am, in 1998, over forty years later, still charging around India and loving it. Such is the wonderful uncertainty of life.

In my era - the fifties and sixties, (foreign) service in India (and around the East) still carried considerable prestige and was surrounded by much privilege. As well, in proper behavioural terms, very much was expected from every expatriate. High standards were set in all things, and required to be met, at all times, by every one of us. It was true, that we were constantly 'on parade' and our conduct noticed, if we 'stepped out of line'.

We were led to believe we had been highly favoured and been set on the track of prospectively successful, interesting and lucrative careers. While it is a fact that many who reached to be *bara sahibs* (*numero uno*) in trading firms collected pretty handsomely, for most expats, any riches were confined to 'rich' experiences, and these were plentiful.

Yes, we were truly admitted to a very colourful life, one full of opportunities and marvellous experiences, particularly if you had initiative and was able to impose a measure of 'control' over one's varied life. Most managed to do this and scandals 'a la Somerset Maugham' were rare, despite the overwhelming numbers of foot-loose eager bachelors and - the shrewd 'stayers and players' amongst the married contingent!

Fitness was a fetish with most Britishers who served in India. Indeed, Noel Coward had the *sahibs* in mind when he wrote *Mad Dogs and Englishmen Go Out in the Midday Sun*. By my time, the *topi* or pith helmet had become *infra dig*. Most expatriates rarely sported any hats at all, even while we went hammer and tongs madly exercising and playing games, during the hottest weather.

Strangely too, most of us convinced ourselves that we felt 'less than well', if we missed out on early morning and evening (violent) physical exercise, seven days a week, all year round. While most Indians as a rule don't wear any head protection, a common accessory for many of them during the hot weather and in the Monsoon, is a black umbrella (faded by the sun). They otherwise seek the shade. Smart people.

Hard exercise (and a good sweat) was seen by most expats as a good antidote to illness, in a country widely regarded as 'the unhealthiest in the world'. Maybe it was once, but today (and in my *chokra* days too), it would be stretching a point to be so condemning. Apart from jaundice and the occasional 'crook tummy', most people I knew, kept pretty well, although most avoided leaving their 'effectively organized' home environment during their 'term of service'. Travel internally in India, rarely happened with many commercial expatriates, but those in Calcutta kept to a constant track - home to office, and to club, and to home, and to office ...... day in, day out, for the duration of their 'tour' (of duty).

My eastern learning experience had begun from the moment I'd settled aboard P&O's "Strathaird" at Station Pier, in Melbourne. I travelled POSH (port out/starboard home - the latter on my voyage to India). It was 'posh' to the extent that the traditional colonial Britisher's afternoon siesta, avoided the burning tropical 'afternoon sun', as we travelled westwards.

From the moment I passed up the gangway of "Strathaird" I entered into a whole new world of international adventure and experience.

Beginning at once, a whole lot of new learning was called for, not least, in respect of the 'correct form' expected from first-class seaborne travellers, and coming to terms, with, the significant 'colonial infected *bat*' (lingo/speech), a feature of P&O/Orient Line ship travel all along the way of the Suez Canal route - Cairo/Port Said (Egypt), Aden, Karachi, Bombay and Colombo - thence to the Far East, or down to Australia.

Many 'Indian hands' (expatriates serving in India) and other colonial territories spent their 'leaves' in Australia and New Zealand, ensuring that passage on the Australia/England run and vice versa, was never dull, and even full of intrigue. All of my sea voyages lived up to this reputation.

Imagine my confusion when (for the first time) I was asked ... *"will you have a chota peg?"* .... and even more so, when subsequently invited to... *"have the other, half"* .... It was a language of another world. As well, whisky was a new experience for me.

The shipboard crossing of the Indian Ocean was full of fun and interesting things to do (me being an early volunteer for Entertainment Committee duties). Our first overseas landfall was Colombo - my first taste of the exotic East, and what a very hot and very spicey introduction it was! Unlike anything I'd experienced before.

Moored in Colombo harbour, ferries transferred a very excited complement of passengers ashore straight into the waiting arms of eager hordes of trinket-sellers and the odd 'gulley gulley man' weaving his magic 'sleight of hand'. A beautiful green and luscious Colombo greeted us, marred only by the 'furnace-like' clammy heat. It was July and the monsoon had already arrived.

Australia's geographical remoteness was pointed up by the before then unseen (by me, anyway) wide array of 'foreign' goods on display and the remarkably lengthy list of foreign liquor which graced the shelves - Japanese, German, Dutch, Danish, and British lagers, all of them years preceding their appearance in my home country. Colombo had many delights to show off to us - of every description.

Despite dragging a fiery sore throat around all day (only relieved by my very first - and last - Jamaica rum), the enthralling scene of the Galleface Hotel, and adjacent green sward (shades of *ELEPHANT WALK* and Appuphamy) and the swirling palms and tropical waters of Mount Lavinia, captivated every one of us first-timers. Ceylon, (Sri Lanka) indeed, was and is, the epitome of a tropical island.

Back aboard 'our temporary floating home' at midnight, exhausted but happy, the sweltering heat kept most of us back from taking off to our 'hot-box' cabins, until "Strathaird" was well underway and turned northwards, heading for our next stop and my farewell point, Bombay.

A smooth passage, interrupted only by unscheduled drama when, early in the morning of the next day, the ship was put in 'neutral' while Doc. Moss applied his surgical skills to our most 'celebrated' passenger, Anoushka - a wonderfully interesting person and cuisine instructor to Aub and I.

A highly educated and sophisticated Egyptian from Heliopolis, the twenty-four year old world citizen Anoushka, had run foul of the Australian authorities because of her Communist Party membership. Anoushka was the cynosure of pretty well everyone aboard's attention and not just because of her politics. Highly voluptuous in appearance and extremely athletic, she was an intellectual stunner and a skilful exponent of table tennis to boot, ensuring always a full audience at her sports deck 'displays'. An exciting lady, in all respects, she was my table companion up to Bombay.

Our arrival in Bombay Harbour was greeted by a tremendous monsoonal downpour - and a sight of Ballard Pier covered from length to length, by a sea of black umbrellas (some a touch faded, but at one time black), hundreds and hundreds of them.

As I was to discover, everyone and his brother, amongst the Indian population, carries a black umbrella - for its (summer) shade, and in the monsoon season, against rain. The West-Ender left off his black rolled brolly when he came to India and took up his brightly coloured parasol (golf umbrella).

Battling against the driving rain and fierce windy squalls, tieing the ship up alongside was delayed, as our several struggling heaving puffing tugboats pushed and shoved us closer to shore. No Hollywood director could have scripted our arrival more dramatically.

Guest for several nights at Bombay's (and India's) grandest dame, 'the Taj Mahal Hotel', provided a welcome opportunity for assimilation of my new 'host' country. Concern for hygiene affects every newcomer. Food, in particular, is treated with grave suspicion. In the better establishments quite needlessly so, but it is something that has to wear off slowly. Mine took a week or so, whereafter feeling pretty famished, not unlike Paddy's pigs denied food by their own fussiness, I was ready to 'eat the trough'. Well, not quite perhaps, but I was by then mentally relaxed enough to begin eating and ready to tuck into my boarding house scran.

After shaking off their initial shock, my colleagues deposited me at my 'home' for the next twentyone months - Madath's "Kenilworth" in *Chota Russelly Street.* And what a tremendous twentyone months it was, a regular League of Nations, its scores of boarders hailing from many countries around the world, although predominantly people from the four Home Nations, England, Scotland, Ireland and Wales.

Starting out in the most 'junior in the house' accommodation, Madath's most modest suite at street level alongside C.R.S. (only a blank concrete wall separated me from the passing motley), after many internal moves,' step-ups', I ultimately found myself occupying the prime boarder's suite, 'in the main building', alongside the Proprietors' own quarters.

I might have believed I had 'been anointed'. Success! But any illusions I had, were very soon pricked. Putting a request to Mum that I had her 'permish' to squire her ravishingly beautiful teen-age daughter Vilma (a daughter of an Armenian/French mother and father) to Maxims, (a favourite haunt and night spot, at the Great Eastern, long since gone from the social map), soon had British 'apartheid' working in reverse. *"So sorry my boy - NO!"* Mum - a pox on her house - said *"she was broadminded - but"*. Way ahead of me that Mum, she had no illusions about what she planned, for *her* daughter!

White South Africa might have followed a universally condemned, pernicious and cruelly violent form of racial discrimination, but the British way of 'public discrimination' in India took a far more subtle and subdued form. In many respects it probably was akin to the old style class-conscious Britain, where every person slotted in to a particular place in society, mostly assigned by accident of birth!

The added factor in the equation in India (perhaps in all the countries around the globe 'colonized' by the British between the seventeenth and nineteenth centuries) were the native people, ordinarily deemed illiterate (uneducated) and accordingly generally regarded as inferior (to the white man).

The 'stigma' applied by the colonialists to mixed-bloods, (Eurasians, later labelled Anglo-Indians) lingered long after 1947. As well, it would appear that few Indians were ever formally accorded 'equal status', even though many of them, would have clearly exceeded in erudition, many of those in authority over them.

In British times, every person was graded socially, from Viceroy down to the newest *chokra* (newest junior expatriate), a kind of Whitaker's Almanac, applicable to India. While Indians might have been regarded as part of a separate social grouping, it should not be overlooked that Hindus (and they formed the majority of the Indian population) had their own caste (class) system, which was arguably more rigid by far, than anything the British colonizers introduced and applied.

While no apologies would be adequate for any inexcusably rude and arrogant behaviour displayed by some colonizers (there are louts and ego-trippers in every situation), and for the social degradation forced upon mixed-bloods (Hastings called them 'Eurasians' to differentiate between them and British expatriates ordinarily domiciled in India, at that time in history referred to as Anglo-Indians), in what at least it seemed to me, at no time in British India was it a cut and dried case of white complexions on one side of the line and black complexions on the other. It was much more complex than that.

India, was for everyone - rules, rules, rules. Not even foreigners were exempted. Proper overt public behaviour from all expatriates, was the 'unwritten rule', right through to the nineteen sixties. Step out of line and one paid the consequences, especially when fraternization dividing lines were exceeded. One young English insurance executive on his 'first tour', who was a close friend, 'bucked the system' and went ahead and married an Anglo-Indian stenographer, a Christian, and during Lent! He paid the penalty, by being summarily 'sent home', *sans* new bride, the same night! I know, for I drove him to Dum Dum Airport! He married at noon, celebrated the event at two (at the salubrious 300 Club, in 1998 now totally demolished and replaced by a large office building which covers every square inch of the ground), and was winging his way home - alone - to London at five. The 'gung-ho nature' of eastern (unrich) desserts, in full display! Wham! Wham!

61. Farewelling 'R.H.' from 5 & 7 and welcoming I.E.G. - Calcutta, 1954
(the author seventh from left, second row).

However, these kinds of happenings need to be seen in proper perspective. Ordinarily, young first-tourers were contracted not to marry during their initial four or three year term of overseas service. For starters, most couldn't afford to marry, anyway. Then, there was the sensitive ethnic problem and the probable sensible and genuine concern (of our elders) that a promising career could be jeopardised. This situation, or 'threatened dismissal' was never wholly satisfactory to everyone, but few suffered as a result of its existence. Liaisons carried on during subsequent 'tours' of duty, received nowhere near the same attention. By then, you were apparently seen as author of your own future?

Personnel of foreign business-houses (Birds, Andrew Yule, I.T.C., I.C.I., Balmer Lawrie, etc. etc.) conformed to quite rigid traditional norms, particularly in observing the strict 'pecking order', seniority ordinarily followed 'time served', in the Indian Branch (of the Company's world-wide operations). The person who arrived one week before you, was literally your senior, for observing protocols, back or front seat positions in office cars and suchlike. A bit of British military order and precision, practised on the civil lines!

The newest arrival was 'Junior Bloggs', and it was his place to 'bring up the rear of the procession'. But it all worked amicably. Everyone knew 'the form', knew where they fitted into the scheme of things. In fact, such procedure is still largely followed in the Indian bureaucracy, and in commercial firms, especially amongst subordinate staff, everywhere in India, even today. British systems still prevail very much but, and quite rationally, clearly delineated and defined 'order' (not tyrannical), can dispose of all doubts and can never be a totally bad thing.

Until one 'moved up the list' and was allocated Company accommodation, Madath's, and McDonnell's (in Bishop Lefroy Road), were the first-up favourite boarding establishments for single foreigners and for some married couples with no children, or whose children were 'at home' at school. No International schools existed at that time in Calcutta, nor were they considered, as the British at that time held to the view that the development of foreign children 'suffered', if they were kept back in India.

Different attitudes prevail in our more enlightened (democratic) times, with International schools flourishing all over the world and throughout the tropics, catering for the primary, and sometimes secondary education of expatriate children, whose parents have been seconded to foreign countries.

In former times, children of expatriates serving in India were 'sent home' at age five or six to not inexpensive Prep schools. They periodically joined their parents at vacation times. Such family separation severely tested relationships - many children becoming strangers to their parents. I have no doubt that this price was paid by many expatriate families serving in colonial territories. The lives of my own Scot's cousins were affected this way, largely separated at an early age, from their parents, long time servers in Burma (Myanmar).

Clothing is one commodity which is ordinarily inexpensive in India, where the common ingredient cotton has been extensively grown for centuries, and is accordingly, relatively inexpensive. Tailors (and dressmakers?) abound everywhere taking orders to be made up by cheap but proficient labour. Fashion labels are only just now beginning to appear. But for most people, the *derzi* (tailor) attends to their clothing needs, usually calling at the customer's home.

We expatriates received an initial 'tropical clothing allowance', with which we had ourselves measured up for shirts (always custom-made and nearly always double-cuffed, white cotton) and white duck trousers - a dozen of each. Durable quality and strong enough to endure scores of 'slappings on stones' by our humble *dhobis*. First 'tour' (four years) always white, although office jackets could be fawn or some other pastel shade.

Having passed the test and now regarded from second tour as 'seniors', coloured linen or panama suitings were permitted to be worn. Statutory dress for 'formal' occasions was *khana kapra* (black evening dress, or white shark-skin jackets, cummerbund - 'Red Sea' kit - black bow ties, NOT pre-tied! *Most infra dignitatem*!).

Every dinner or cocktail invitation - and most formal gatherings were held in Calcutta in the 'cool' season November/February - clearly stated the dress, time and place. No room was left for slip-ups, for any embarrassment. However, many men opted for 'black bow tie' for going to dinner evening wear, knowing it to be acceptable gear whatever the occasion. This contrasted to 'off-season' procedure, when impromptu invitations (no food at home but 'no matter, the *memsahib* next door has a good *bawarchi* - [cook], who'll provide') were common place. Food eaten was replaced the next day.

With no Austin Reed or Marks and Spencer in India, most clothing was 'made to measure'. Except for really good stuff, when you might go to Rankens, Samuel Fitze or Barkat Ali, (and today - to Raymonds) *derzis* fitted us out with most of our regular needs, down to boxer shorts (hilariously, very identifiable all around the world as 'made in India').

Mochis - shoemakers, made our shoes patterned on styles advertised in foreign magazines. You chose your style and material and the *mochis* did the rest, from cricket boots right through to evening shoes. One rowing colleague of mine, a down-to-earth Kiwi, owned just one pair of shoes, brown leather with rubber soles, in which he rowed, worked and partied - I don't think he slept in them? Or perhaps, only sometimes!

One intriguing 'British Indian' custom which continued to be generally followed by most expatriates (particularly those persons who had begun their service in India pre-World War II) was strict observance of annual dates for defining the changing climatic seasons. Whether the rains actually arrived weeks early, or weeks late, the fifteenth of June was 'officially' Monsoon- season arrival day.

The fifteenth of November formally signalled the start of 'the cold weather', in Hindi, India's *thanda mausem.* Religiously on that date, older (*pukka*) expats changed from hot weather *kapra* (light weight clothing) to cold weather (heavier) clothing, regardless of whether it was still boiling hot or not, and *vice versa* on the fifteenth of February, when the 'old orders' (and doubtless, military factors spawned the original dress rules) decreed that winter was past and it was time to change back into 'hot weather' *kapra.* Again, winter could be staging a late surge, but no matter 'form was form'.

Mohandas Karamchand Gandhi (the Mahatma), had some chastening remarks for the expatriate British (even though he referred to 'the English', a common mistake many people make, when what they really intend is 'British', much to the chagrin of Scots, Welsh and Irish) regarding sensible wearing apparel, for Indian conditions. Writing in 1922, Gandhi observed...."*only their insularity and unimaginativeness have made the (English) retain the (English) style of dress in India, even though they admit that it is most uncomfortable for the Indian climate"*

Accounts of the early days of British colonization leave little doubt that aggravated body temperatures contributed to many early deaths. A read of William Hickey's intriguingly revealing *Memoirs* (British India *circa* 1800) or a visit to the Park Street and Lower Circular Road cemeteries provides ample confirmation of the consequences of slow (or unwilling) adaptation.

In such antithetical setting (something many expatriates never came to terms with, or wished to?) the ritualistic practice was never wholly left off, right up to the closing days of the British staffed commercial presence, in India. At a time when air conditioning was still the preserve of the very senior, more than one young office jacketed knotted tie British *chhota sahib* sweltered manfully, under the whirring overhead *punkahs* (ceiling fans) hell bent on maintaining the superior attitude.

Much has been written about the habits of the old world adapting to the requirements of the new (please see on *-Australia's Rich Natural Heritage,* for what happened there), but adopting sensible attitudes to the differing environment and climate was a slow and sometimes painful process. Examples are numerous. Many more could be given.

But, beyond all dispute, life in India for expatriates was definitely not all play. Work was our first priority. Everything else was required to fit around it and for most expatriates it was just that. Despite the vagaries of Indian weather, for centuries the British had strongly believed that frequent hard outdoors physical exercise was beneficial to sustaining good health, regardless of the climatic conditions.

Strong adherents of this notion, the degree of participation amongst expatriates in Calcutta, was fantastic (fanatical might be a truer description). Every, yes *every* morning well before breakfast, (except Sunday, when most of the day would be given up to cricket, golf, rowing, tennis, and for others of us, woven around morning or evening church attendance), before breakfast, it was customary for a goodly number of us (Indians too), to swim, row (at Dhakuria lake), run or ride - around Calcutta's magnificent racecourse, or get in up to twelve holes of golf (at the R.C.G.C. or at Tolly), then get back home, ablute, have breakfast and be in the office by 8.15 a.m. On Saturdays, most worked to 1.30 p.m. after which it was hockey, rowing, football, tennis, squash, or a half-day cricket match. A ritual followed by most expatriate (men) in India, throughout the year.

Most week day evenings after work, it was football (rugby or soccer), squash, tennis (at the 'Slap') or rowing training, then home, dinner at 8.30 p.m., followed by an hour or so's work then lights out at eleven. Saturday night we 'played up', either at Princes or Firpo's going on to the 'Golden Slipper', and around dawn, finally to Spence's Hotel, for bacon and eggs, then home for kip.

Those of us who were 'captives to our highly programmed body clocks' would be up and about as usual (after just a few hours sleep) and as often as not over the cold weather, bowling the first over at Ballygunge at 10 o'clock! The pace was hectic and it never changed in all my years in India, for indeed most 'believed' they 'felt' better with constant exercise. There wasn't much sickness, but the 'change-down' at retirement was known to bring about some abrupt endings - for some. Also, for all the criticism that it cops, and for all of its congested living, it must be said of Calcutta that it is a marvellously convenient place in which to get around.

The central Business District attached (as of course it still does, in 1998) to Chowringhee, the Maidan, the River, Park Street, the Clubs (the social ones, The Light Horse, Bengal, United Services and to an extent Calcutta and Outram Clubs plus the really composite ones - the Saturday Club ('the Slap'), Swimming, Cricket, Football, and Squash), to the wonderful spacious Calcutta Racecourse (and its Turf Club and 'Pat Kingsley' Polo Ground), and as well to the most favoured living areas - those adjacent to Chowringhee, and a little distance off, at Alipore (over Tolly's Nullah), and at Ballygunge.

Most expatriates who resided in Calcutta, after WWII and up to the mid-sixties, ordinarily lived and moved in a very tight radius of just a few kilometres. All so marvellously convenient (and no differently today, it all still is, for the better-off Indian).

Only the up-market Tollygunge Club (with its golf course, tennis and swimming), the superb Royal Calcutta Golf Club nearby, and the Rowing Clubs at Dhakuria Lake (C.R.C./Lake/Bengal and

University Clubs), were more distant, and even then, only a few more kilometres away.

The close proximity of every facility, then and now, maximised our usage of time and resulted in nearly every one of us taking on a 'fairly massive' workload (i.e. work, plus sporting, plus social - activities) far in excess of anything we could have got anywhere near accomplishing in our home countries. At our 'digs' we had servants to do most domestic tasks.

Yes indeed (and in 1998 much the same happens, but for many more Indians) for the privileged, Calcutta planned and assembled by the British after 1800, is a wonderfully convenient place to live and work.

For its (huge) size, Calcutta's unique situation and possibilities for a full energetic life, eclipse any other large metropolis, on earth. A fact of life completely unknown or ignored, by every harsh uninformed inexperienced critic of Calcutta since Kipling's fleeting Calcutta experience was grabbed, distorted and made legendary, a hundred years ago.

Not so surprising, Hong Kong and Singapore (both erstwhile British colonial territories) provide comparable living/working/ clubbing and sporting convenience, to that provided in Calcutta. All examples of British precision and good planning. Surprising, how the real facts of anything, can get mutilated by either innocent or deliberately false, telling.

Living life at a high pitch (and most not leaving town) it wasn't surprising that the expat. community (and the Calcutta one, including people on tea estates etc, up-country, numbered approximately 5000 - out of a local Indian population of many millions) displayed much flair and initiative and constantly looked for innovation to 'ginger-up' its social activities, enjoyed mostly at either the Swimming Club (on Strand Road) or at the 'Slap' (the Saturday Club).

Amateur floor shows and musicals were regularly staged, with members making up the casts. There was plenty of talent amongst the expat. community and the opportunity to 'create fun' was never missed. When the Calcutta Symphony Orchestra folded at the New Empire, there was always Liesl Stary, Brian St. John Conway, Edgar Cleaver

62. The author joined by P.C.Duggal's excellent performers, Jullundur, Punjab.

and Gordon Simpson, to provide a feast of piano and organ music. There were also the fraternities - the Vingt-et-un set, and the Twelve Apostles, to enliven proceedings and to entertain their guests at Tolly or at Burdwan's Palace, often aided and abetted by the great Calcutta identities, Burdwan and Cooch Behar, and the redoubtables, Hutch, Pearson Surita and Boris Lissanovitch.

Keeping healthy was important not only for the individual but as well, in the Company's interest. At that time, whisking up replacements from elsewhere in the world was costly, and as well, not readily convenient. Maintaining good health had every merit.

No country or organization anywhere in the world, took tropical ailments more seriously, than did - and doubtless it still does - the British Institute for Tropical Diseases, in England. Precautionary jabs or tablets for typhoid, cholera, smallpox and malaria were seriously and religiously maintained, by all expatriates, although most expat. commercial types in India rarely got geographically much beyond their urban precincts as for many, the *mofussil* (up-country rural India) spelt problems, uncertain food and water, and running the risk of contracting the expat. medicos' favourite staple - amoebic dysentery.

Not funny of course, if one copped a 'wobbly tummy'. Better just a mild dose, which thereafterwards provided sufficient truthful excuse for respectfully declining any too rich or too spicy 'small eats', at public functions. While some 'old hands' might have cracked hardy and considered a daily intake of Johnny Walker the best preventative, most people preferred to give cirrhosis the go by, and stick with the conventional remedies. Common sense generally won the day.

While we are on about 'crook tummies', a word or two about diet would be appropriate. One of my wiser *bara sahibs* (bosses), a solidly grounded person who never let Eastern Service 'go to his head', strongly believed that 'plenty of regular and good basic food' was a vital component for staying well, in the tropics – he unequivocally believed quantity should make up, for diminished quality. The trouble-free history of his family, and as seen today many years on, provides positive testimony for his theory.

Although a lot of beef, lamb (mutton) and pork was, and is, grown in India, it is only variously eaten. As well, it was deficient in nutrition. A fair assessment of all such meat that was grown, would be, that it lagged far behind the rigorously controlled produce grown in Western countries. But given the poorer ingredients they had to work with, it was nonetheless amazing what our *bawarchis* (cooks) could rustle up, from basically inferior quality meat and vegetables. Many of them would have even put our much vaunted 'magicians' (army cooks) to shame.

Chicken (*morghi*) was plentifully available and though fowls rather than chickens, the filleted chicken produced by these fellows (paid no more than Rupees eighty a month – then £6 approx, plus lodging)would have no peer, anywhere. Their puddings (schooled, many of them, by English *memsahibs*) were superb. I've never tasted (and enjoyed) better steam puddings, caramel custards (*krammel* custard), or *souffles*, anywhere.

Fresh fruit of many kinds was available all the year round, with *pomelos, papaya* (paw paw), *amrud* (mangoes), or grapefruit, standard breakfast starters, for most expatriates, followed by the old English traditional, bacon and eggs, toast and marmalade. Kellogg's has since arrived, but few Indians eat porridge or cereals. Great standard for nearly all Indian dishes is rice, which fills bellies, but is not reckoned to result in the acquiring of strength and/or stamina, sufficient to win either the Olympic hundred metres, or marathon. It is nonetheless remarkable the hard normal work many of India's large labour force do manage on such basic fare.

Until India's foreign exchange reserves dried up in the late fifties (they dipped to their lowest point in 1990, being the catalyst for abruptly 'opening up the economy', since when reserves have moved up over $30 billion), one could buy lots of foreign goodies – Chivers Jams and foreign liquors, etcetera. Local industries stepped in to fill the gap.

Except for late Sunday lunch (*tiffin*) when non-sports engaged expats devoured copious helpings of Indian curry, (for many also, washed down with copious quantities of Beck's beer), few Europeans ever emulated the 'better-off' Indians penchant, for late sitting (around 9 p.m. or later) curry meals. Except that one could 'sleep late' (ten a.m.), such cuisine was not encouraged, nor ordinarily compatible with normal expat working routines.

In the post-colonial period, fewer foreigners 'took to the *mofussil*', unless their work demanded it, preferring to spend most of their tour with the 'devil they believed they knew'. In Calcutta, this meant the controlled, supervised position, within a five mile radius of their town residences. A pity, because the real India is in the country and the opportunity to explore and meet more of the ordinary Indians was not availed of, and lost. The British form of social apartheid in India was never completely left-off.

Sport provided the best opportunity for mixing with our host country, particularly amongst horse-racing enthusiasts and golfers, where many close friendships were formed. Not much in the way of close ties came of encounters on team sporting fields - i.e., cricket, football and hockey, where fraternization began, and usually ended, with the particular fixture itself.

Generally the foreigner spent his leisure time at his 'foreigners only' clubs, most of which combined sporting, recreational and dining facilities, all of them quite top class, anywhere in the world. For the most part, contact with Indians was confined to business, apart of course from the retinue of house servants, all of whom gave marvellously loyal service.

Sport and leisure were fine while this activity kept expats. mentally and physically tuned up. But above everything else, business responsibilities held first priority and there was very little absenteeism amongst foreigners. An unwritten code prevailed of 'not letting down your colleagues'. Every member of foreign staff was expected to pull his weight and any 'poodlefaking' soon got its just desserts.

Additionally, it was usual to value one's Company's public face, and its reputation. In all overseas countries, the priority of place was accorded the Company and less importantly, the individual's place in it. 'Who you worked for' was paramount. It was 'that man from Bird & Co.' or 'that man from the Howrah Flour Mills', who 'made a spectacle of himself', in public. The expatriate's own identity wasn't seen as important as the Company's reputation. But it was not challenged, for it made good sense.

As already mentioned, 'step out of line socially' and your term in India could summarily end. Harsh stuff perhaps, but the 'right' public appearance was strictly defended and maintained. Exceed the 'unwritten expatriate rules' or rigid code of behaviour, for us people, guests in another's country (this may sound a tad hypocritical and of course in a way it was) and you stood a pretty good chance of being on the first plane home. Most expats. understood (and recognized), the implied threat.

In what many bachelors justifiably called 'sexless gulch' (because of racial taboos, although there was plenty of romancing behind the scenes), socially acceptable romantic endeavours in Calcutta for single expats were limited throughout most of the year, and only fleetingly improved with the arrival in the 'cold weather' - December/ January - of the 'fishing fleet' from Britain.

Anglo-Saxon daughters visiting their mums and dads had themselves a ball enjoying virtual unlimited attention and choice of social partners. Typical of such, the experience of one lass from Perthshire who exclaimed..."*this is the fourth time I've been to Maxims this week*" ... each time with a different escort! Lucky Ellen. Hard cheese, Richard, and John, and Bob, and Bill.

I wonder how many of you are familiar with John Master's "*Bhowani Junction*", made into a film starring Stewart Granger and Ava Gardner? Many a Victoria Jones, the Anglo-Indian beauty played by Ava Gardner propped up the foreign business sector's secretarial services, and very competent Indian women played their part as well. All displayed skills and capabilities of a very high order, but any public liaison 'out of office' was frowned upon, certainly discouraged, if not totally embargoed. Here, the 'foreign' *memsahib* (though I'm sure, not all of them), her domain (as seen by her) challenged, sometimes would presumptuously demand (of hubby), that she be spared 'embarrassment at the club, amongst her bridge-playing lady-friends, from social tittle-tattle', arising from the romantic adventures of her husband's young assistants.

Many a humorous story can be related, but with due respect, the racial discrimination unfairly directed at Anglo-Indians (one parent Indian) was as shameful as it was permanently injurious to so many innocent persons. With Independence, it might have faded or should have been dropped, but regrettably it persisted. It was not the fault of the Anglo-Indians as for a very long time, not accorded a respected place in normal society by foreigners, as well as by orthodox Indians, their chance of improving their status and with it their living conditions, had been always severely restricted. They remained in most respects, in Indian society, 'the odd-ones out'.

A 'social stigma' wilfully and wrongfully (however conveniently) applied, the system represented a throwback to colonial times, initially and not so unnaturally created, by dint of distance (Britain was a long way off from India) and the humiliating deprived social status endured for so long by the hundreds of thousands of Tommy Atkins who served long tours of duty - many never returned home - in India, in the 18th, 19th and 20th centuries. Could they be blamed for 'looking around them' for female company?

The offspring of such liaisons (although in fact, all levels of society in India participated at some time or other) - many lovely people - were branded, and became involuntary victims of history. After Indian Independence, many Anglo-Indian families took up British passports (one happy consolation and long overdue), becoming responsible citizens in many British Commonwealth countries, particularly Canada and Australia.

For the British, it was not so much the question of colour, but it had more to do with social status and degree of individual acceptability. The more senior the expatriate, the more power one could (and did) exercise to overcome any difficulties associated with Indian and/or Anglo-Indian couplings. Junior expats never enjoyed the same licence. In real terms it was hypocrisy at its worst, but so far as the Anglo-Indian is concerned, an era that should, for most of them, be now largely behind them.

First tours of duty for expatriates post-war were usually of three or four years and more often than not, with no intervening holidays. Strangely, but not wholly explanatory, many expatriates (and I met them all the time) never 'wanted it to appear' that they got any 'personal' enjoyment from being in India, (an attitude of India is not good enough for me, I'm here under sufferance), but they lived for the day when they went on their three months or six months furlough. Definitely, a most quirky attitude, and smacking of ungraciousness – to their host country.

The not uncustomary opening gambit of many conversations in India went... "*when are you going on leave?*"... "*Oh, in two years, four months and three day's time*". Many expatriates willed their lives away.

And these were no isolated cases. Hope springs eternal to be sure, or at least many must have believed so, or believed a successful aftermath would be theirs, after India?

For many of us, India would be a 'temporary stopping place', and we would go on to the Company's other Branches dotted all around the world, before finally returning home to take up responsible positions in Head Office or joining other firms in senior positions.

One stop, thirty and forty year service, in just one single foreign field, died out soon after the second world war. Better communications, enabled more frequent and less costly - in time and money - 'home-leaves', and inter-territory transfers. The era of the '*koi hais*' (all knowing foreigners in India) was ended. As well, the pace of Indianization was stepped up, finally giving India control over herself and over her own destiny.

With reputedly over two million Britishers buried in India, it would be entirely reasonable to believe that great shafts of very fond memories of time spent in India remain among many British families. The India Library in London contains the single greatest collection of books and artefacts on India, ensuring that echoes of India go on and on, and on.

Some final affectionate thoughts. For most expatriates there can be no argument that service in India opened up for them a stupendous 'new' world. While the odd grumble was understandable, in their heart of hearts, most would afterwards admit to having experienced and enjoyed some great times and learnt much, from their time in the sub-continent. For me, returning years later and being reunited with many of my old staff, and on equal terms, has been one of the joys, and confirmation of perhaps the greatest advancement wrought by Independence - proper recognition, and however belatedly, properly due - to all Indians.

26. Repaying Enjoyed Experiences

- the story of how, The Changing Face of Calcutta, came to be written

One very famous conductor gained a reputation for never responding to an enthusiastic concert audience's clamour, for an encore. He steadfastly maintained that the publicized programme which the orchestra had just performed represented a receipt (and not a bill), and nothing more was due. Throughout his renowned career he never wavered from this position, no matter how much his 'popular appeal' could have suffered.

For me, the boot was on the other foot. I owed a big debt to India and to her people (reasonably never fully repayable) which I'd so far not done a thing about tangibly reciprocating. Service in India had come at the outset of my career and unquestionably had contributed significantly to the moulding of my lifelong standards, and to the shaping of my thinking about a lot of things, not least, my attitudes to others, taking in their ethnic origins, colour or social status. I could not have been favoured with a better tutor, India, through which to observe, learn and be instructed. The India dating from 2500 B.C. and my particular post-Independence India, had it all; had seen it all and been through it all.

What had taken me almost a lifetime to properly observe and absorb, hear and heed, came early in his life to the great man, Albert Schweitzer. Born into a loving home and comfortable circumstances, he was unceasingly challenged by inner voices asking *"What have I done to deserve such blessings?"* To which ultimately came the answer... *"To whom much is given, of him shall much be required."* The same answer is there for all of us, whether, in material terms, rich or poor. Weightier virtues are not denied to any one of us.

For several years I had been taping text books and essential course reading for sight-handicapped tertiary students in Melbourne, while the whole time being disturbed by constant inner thoughts... *"If this happens here, what occurs in India, where there are many millions of similarly afflicted people. Who assists them to go forward to beneficial productive lives, when perfectly normal people aided by the best that can be provided, often achieve little more than the basics? How much harder, more difficult, for the handicapped to go forward (climb up)".*

Although I had lived in India for nearly ten years, and had witnessed many things, I knew practically nothing of the nitty gritty of these matters, in that country. A whole lot of change was clearly ahead of me, but for now, one step at a time, each properly attended and efficiently completed.

Initially however, my first goals lay with visually handicapped people in my own country, and what I might do to assist them more, and bring 'light into their lives'. Sharing with them some of my past overseas experiences seemed to have merit, particularly those I myself had thrilled to, while serving in Asia. I would be their eyes. I set to to map out a programme for revisiting a lot of fascinating, though to many-unknown places, where I had enjoyed out-of-the-ordinary events, with the difference that this time, I would tape 'word pictures' on my Walkman. The bonus for me would be making new friends and developing my personal respect and understanding of the region's diverse and colourful people.

After several months systematically sifting through mountains of material which I had accumulated during the eastern part of my career, and putting in place an outline of my proposed journey - one of enlightenment for me, and for those others not blessed with every faculty, August 1987 saw me ready to set out for Asia, a journey that is still ongoing ten years later, even as I write these lines.

Almost half of the stories in this volume were gathered during my first twelve week sojourn in India, in 1987. Subsequent events, nine long visits since, have seen some updating and refinement, for as any writer knows, this process can go on for ever. There is very little of anyone's previous writings that can not be improved upon.

Coming after an absence of twenty-five years, and vast population increases in India, my initial foray would be most important. Repeating my earlier experiences would either re-activate my fascination or I would turn away, mission already accomplished.

Let us then return to my initial 1987 re-discovery venture which began at what is probably the most fascinating and 'internationally populated' hotel in the whole world, Bombay's glittering Taj Mahal. Not simply an hotel, but an important player in Indian history, and a bastion of indigenous fightback - for in its time its creation had restored Indian native pride, dignity and integrity, and had provided positive encouragement for the future.

I followed no pre-arranged fixed schedule, and had no forward bookings, but I knew India well enough to find accommodation and fix up travel needs as such need arose. I had set points to re-visit, but travelling alone, I could deviate when and wherever the mood took me.

After my brief stop in Bombay at the celebrated Taj Mahal hotel (to be sure, you need to be a real Prince, at least a merchant prince, to put up in this opulent palace for very long) my next stop was Pune, where I had a date with Apa Pant, retired Indian diplomat, philosopher and writer (*A MOMENT IN TIME, et al*) whom I had met several times many years earlier when he was Political Officer at Gangtok, in Sikkim. Until his permission had been obtained (authorized by New Delhi) no foreigner could go farther into the mountains in Sikkim, which country shared a border with Chinese-dominated Tibet.

The vista from Apa Pant's official residence in Gangtok would evoke the envy of every person, anywhere in the world. If there is a *Shangri-la,* then this is surely it. The view across the bungalow's terraced rose gardens falling away in front of you, looks out into the distance on the snow-capped Himalayas to the west of Kanchenjunga, a truly breathtaking and superlative sight. It requires a great effort to withdraw one's gaze, it is so magnificent.

Leaving Pune and going on to north India, Delhi and the Garhwal and then down to Agra, I soon realized that more than myriad taped descriptions of individual points of interest were needed - the message of India was too big, too vast and too extensive. More than a series of short stories, a longer book (or books) was needed, if proper justice was to be done. India, the whole of India, is a compelling scenario.

So the die was cast. I would transfer my research to a book, one that followed my own format and which set down the impressions

India had made upon me, and would continue to make on me, not for a second or third time, but for the umpteenth time, for the canvas constantly changes. There is always more, much more, never less.

Three months carefully detailed travel and research in India up to this point of my return, had barely scratched the surface. I returned home to evaluate my material and to map out my future programme.

But before the task could be begun in real earnest, an important part of my daughter Alexandra's, character growth (and seventeenth birthday celebration) had to be attended by introducing her to life in, and the customs of, the United States, United Kingdom and Europe. That mission behind me, I was ready to begin serious work on my book - by intensive research at home, and abroad, complemented by more visits to principal sources in India.

What subject would I choose to write about? There were so many. Who did I wish *to inspire, to delight, to elevate and to instruct?* A formidable enough task (for me) for any writer. No matter what subject on India one selected, the canvas of that country is so broad and so vast, and so profound, that one would still be doing little more than leaving a barely perceptible mark on the surface.

It would not be enough to tread the same well-worn ground, already prejudicially and/or superficially described *ad infinitum* by sincere but (in more recent times) itinerant foreign scribblers. Something which could make some positive contribution - to India, to Indians today, was called for.

It is no surprise that no one person, Indian or foreign, has succeeded in writing a modern epic, which embraces the whole of India. The nearest anyone has come to achieving this goal, would be Pandit Nehru. His *DISCOVERY OF INDIA*, which stops forty years short of today, is still the finest 'commentary of the evolution of free India, and its first substantiated history 2500 B.C. up to Independence, 1947, and by supplements, ten years further on'. Every person interested in today's India, might use Nehru's wonderful book as their 'first primer'. It provides an excellent basis for understanding India's past heritage and for comprehending why so much in modern India is, as it is today.

Ultimately, it came down to writing about strongly held feelings which might reasonably translate into positive benefits, most of all, for Indians themselves. While familiar with much of India, dearest to me was the welfare and plight of Calcuttans, in whose city I had worked and resided for nearly ten years. Neither personally known or properly understood by very many, but still unkindly and unthinkingly denigrated, by Indians and foreigners alike, (regrettably, and *ad nauseam,* and to the point of anachronistic absurdity by foreign journalists, *eg*. The Black Hole, and the grime and poverty that even today abounds everywhere in India, without explaining the genuine reasons for such, or paying any respect to the amazing and wonderful qualities of the Indian people, able to endure such conditions and still 'get on with living' without weeping and complaining ceaselessly) my decision was not long delayed.

The greatest, but least used or understood growth-producing factor for people, 'honest-praise' and sympathetically critical and constructive comment - would be my most sincere and best service which all foreign observers might thereafterwards consider to learn from, and use.

There is not a city or a place in the whole of India that holds more significance in the life of modern independent India, than Calcutta. Of the whole of the erstwhile British Empire, outside of London itself, no other city in the whole Empire up to 1947, had more importance than Calcutta. Although Bombay (Mumbai) has made up a lot of ground in the years since, the future of India is still significantly bound up with whatever befalls Calcutta. It is that important. It simply can not, and must not, be ignored.

My first task was to make up lists of topics that I wished to thoroughly research. My initial folio one consisted of eighteen subjects, from 'Calcutta's modern beginnings', down to 'choice of title' (for the book). Folios two to six, added nearly 150 more subjects, and more still were added as my work proceeded,

Every important facet of the City's life would be investigated - even the complement of jails, to analyse the social and psychological factors which contributed to the committing of crime. Some different light would thereby be shed on the moral make-up of Calcutta's people, allowing better understanding.

For myself, I set an extensive programme, one which would considerably enhance my knowledge of India, although in reality, it would still amount even then to no more than a fleabite of the prodigious treasury of knowledge pertaining to the country, and of Indians. That there would be many unheralded and unscheduled pleasant surprises for me along the way, went without saying.

My collection of information, (and for this exercise, one necessarily and essentially needed to go back to the earliest data on India, its pre-history from 2500 B.C., and work right through up to the present day by extensive reading, mostly at Melbourne and Latrobe Universities, plus scouring my own and others 'libraries'), was already quite voluminous by the time I set out on my second research trip to India, in June 1988.

I had put in hand correspondence to many specific points around the world, seeking explicit and authentic details on many particular topics, *viz.* to Stockholm and Oslo, to obtain Nobel Prize details; to the Carnegie Institute in Washington to obtain details of the Czar's Peace Conferences of 1899 and 1907, which dealt with the 'dum dum' bullet, and there were many more specific topics I wished to thoroughly check through multifarious enquiries to libraries and institutions, in Britain and America.

But external research, reading and correspondence can achieve only so much. Active 'on the spot' investigations might be tedious and frustrating and - hugely time-consuming, but it is the most factual and valuable method of all. There can be absolutely no dispute that this is so, and such of course was essentially needed, in respect of my Calcutta story. You can write for information until you are blue in the face, but prompt detailed replies (or any replies!) are not the strong suit of Indians. However, in today's terms it is the same story everywhere.

I already knew the public, business and people structure of Calcutta (of India) reasonably well from years living there. But even for me, enquiries were painstakingly difficult, and nothing was easily won, or 'handed to me on a plate'. The population of Calcutta had doubled, while the metropolis 'living space' had scarcely expanded. Tracing and unearthing records, particularly Government records, called for much sleuthing and perseverance. While much was achieved, delving into certain procedures (like Government's classified archives and civil prisons) met a brick wall, even if you knew someone, who knew someone, or else became too protracted to proceed with them any further. A pity.

For the most part, in India (or anywhere else, for that matter), for enquiry to reap effective results, you must start at the top. This is the traditional way and very much so in India. Where however in the western world you could be - curtly or otherwise - fobbed off and get nowhere, or referred to No.27, thankfully this does not happen in India (in over forty years, I've never personally encountered or seen displayed - any bumptiousness or discourtesy, by *Indian* executives). Graciousness is part of Indian culture and sincerely practised.

One is always courteously received, even briefly, and then introduced to a responsible person capable of supplying the answer, or the particular thing you are seeking. Being helpful is a refreshing Indian trait. Basic respect is common, whether to a foreigner, or by the mightiest chief to the lowliest office peon (messenger). Very little, or no arrogance, is ever in evidence. Something the world could poach and adopt.

Having retained a reasonable grasp of Hindustani (a mixture of Hindi and Urdu), also gave me an advantage, and perhaps a little added respect. Taught to me in my initial working days by Indian *Munshis,* using Saigal's faithful (Hindi ed) Grammar, it substantially meant that my pronunciation would, most times, be understood, a failing oft times obvious in spoken foreign languages taught by non-Nationals, and other than in the land of origin. Meeting people half-way increases respect and admiration, a very helpful factor in a foreign country.

But for all these plus points in my favour, most of my information had to be ground out. Nothing came easily or quickly. India is a huge country and many people have to be served besides yourself. Perseverance, courteous persistence, knocking on the right doors, is required in great chunks.

If you aren't possessed of patience, either you'll learn it or quickly retire, defeated. Frustration is an over-used expression relating to India. More often than not it is a case of the foreigner not doing his or her preparatory homework and thinking every Indian must jump, if you bark a command (but no more can yours be a command, but it must be a request). Meticulous preparation, correct enquiry procedure and right source of enquiry will 'get things moving'.

I was to undertake more research trips to India - in 1988, 1990, 1992, 1993/1994, 1995 before I could begin, and before I could complete the initial draft manuscript of my book, which afterwards underwent a score or more edits, until I could be satisfied with its accuracy and look around for an Indian Publisher in India in February/April 1996.

Other full-time work commitments had delayed the writing of the Manuscript. Having read Nicholas Monsarrat's *THE MASTER MARINER*, especially the second volume *DARKEN SHIP*, I was conscious of the method Monsarrat adopted in developing the framework of his novels. It served him very well. It was a great model for me.

Despite considerable career participation, over many years and in many countries and cultures, framing and delivering copious numbers of Memorandums, Manuals and Instructions, and as well indulging in voluminous correspondence, both business and personal, when it came to writing books 'that people will find interesting enough, to read' - that was another situation entirely. New skills were called for.

A lifetime of constant reading, of others' works of all description, is a big leg-up but over and above everything else, come inherent writing capabilities that come from the head/the heart/life's experiences - they can not be taught. Try emulating Tolstoy, Hardy, Thomas Mann or Galsworthy, or Graham Greene, and you'll get your answer at once - it just isn't possible. These great writers defy the efforts of all others to replicate their originality, their unique story-telling capabilities, in short, a quality, a genius, which alone is theirs.

In the final analysis I suppose, it comes down to yourself and the degree to which you are inspired. It can be a formidable challenge, as it was for me, all along the way. Acquiring knowledge, digesting it, compartmentalizing it, sorting it, and regurgitating it, readably and interestingly, can also be exhilarating. It represents a considerable challenge. There never can be any 'sure-fire' result.

A writer's life is a lonely life, for the gathering of one's thoughts in coherent form calls for intensive uninterrupted concentration. Constant reference is made to dictionaries, grammar books, atlases and one's copious notes, besides the pile of material one has available for never-ending cross-referencing. Accuracy and authenticity is

63. Cover picture *The Changing Face of Calcutta*

imperative. Poorly researched work condemns otherwise good work to mediocrity because of its credibility lapses.

In my case, choosing a subject and a foreign land, five thousand miles off from my own, added a further dimension or in fact, many dimensions. But I was no stranger to India for I'd served a long apprenticeship and held much conviction that this was what I wanted to do. I'd read and heard too much that was false and misleading - about India - there was always an urgency for accurate description. For too long contemporary India has been mis-represented, innocently and otherwise.

Dismissing the romantic fantasy of 'old' India that many (foreign writers) exclusively latch on to (to the exclusion of the other ninetynine percent that is independent India, present day) as representing India's only worthwhile contribution to the world at large, and according to Indians their rightful and important position in any discussion of yesterday's and tomorrow's world, vested in me a great responsibility, a factor which has always remained at the centre of my consciousness.

Laying out the whole format of the book at the outset, eliminated most uncertainty and hesitation in direction. The course was clearly marked out ahead. The great value of knowing where one is headed, recalls the frightening experience of the famous Polar explorer, Admiral Byrd. Alone in the deep winter for six months at the North Pole accumulating scientific data, Byrd used to walk each day outside his submerged hut. He would set markers every fifty feet. In a 'white out' one day, he looked back but nowhere in any direction could he see a marker! Put yourself in his place!! He kept his head and the rest is history.

Except for the opening 'lead in' chapters in my book, the order of sequence was not a crucial factor. Every chapter could stand on its own. Also, every known or applicable piece of information on a particular topic or subject had not got to be crammed in, in the one segment. Properly, and for maximum suitability and rememberability (and reader enjoyment) points can go in where they do the best job and where they would be best understood and enjoyed by the reader. Flexibility had to be the keynote, and is, essentially, particularly in non-fiction (who hasn't struggled to 'get through' dry-as-bones unadorned facts!).

Many know of Flaubert's agony in searching out the right word for his fiction - he would spend days, even weeks, before deciding on the complete suitableness (suitability) of a single word or phrase, to convey his exact meaning. Every (serious) writer goes through similar distress, although fortunately for nearly all, for a lesser period than Flaubert. Every 're-reading' of text results in some change. It happens to everyone, and is all very normal, for there are umpteen ways of expressing something which will pass muster, but only one which is the proper fit.

The success (or otherwise) of every new chapter depends very much on the opening gambit. It should 'impact' upon the reader and go on from there. For me, my most rigorous mental gymnastic sessions were 'getting the opening sentence right'. For some chapters I might 'put down my pen' for days, a week, while tossing around, and weighing up, various suitable constructions. Once decided, then the rest of the text rapidly fell into place.

Interspersed with research trips to India (to Calcutta, particularly), and enormous correspondence, in order to clarify detail, by mid-June 1995 the first full draft of my manuscript was completed, but little did I realize then that my real work had only just begun.

To gauge probable reader acceptance I put copies of my manuscript to several divergent quarters, in Calcutta. All but one expressed satisfaction and delight with the way I had approached and treated my subject - quite differently to how any others (writing on Calcutta and Calcuttans) had done it before me.

But then the stereotypical way others had depicted Calcutta was my bone of contention and constituted the prime spur for my wanting to 'set the record straighter'. Criticism based on inadequate research or spiteful comment, has no place, anywhere. Disappointing however for me, the only dissenting critic was a long-time friend and encourager. His inexplicable *volte face* has never been explained. I can only hope that he found the equanimity to read the final rendition and re-cast his earlier judgement, acknowledging such as precipitate, also possibly subjective, and perhaps too - a tad ungracious.

Many people only want to hear (or see) what they wish to hear (or see). In our less than ideal or perfect world, there will always be three opinions - yours and mine, and the right one. It has ever been thus, and is not about to change. What a dull world it would be, if we all thought similarly; held the same opinion!

Being the central player in my book, I naturally hoped that Calcutta would do 'the whole job' and its professionals also be entrusted with its publishing. However, and because of what is often said (possibly with little factual foundation), that Indian businessmen are over-cautious and not high up in the league of entrepreneurs and 'risk-takers', my quest for a Publisher, would be an arduous one.

Thousands of new books are published every year in India, more perhaps than anywhere else in the world, although nearly all of them are serious non-fiction, and generally attracting limited audiences. Books that appeal to a wide readership are uncommonly rare. Indian Publishers with international connections are copying present world marketing hype and pushing 'pulp fiction', but to achieve any real success with Indian readers, contented with their huge store of religious mythology, there will need to be a whole lot more 'reader-conditioning' processes resorted to. Acquired habits going back over centuries will not be easily changed, and 'fact' or long-held legend, will remain kingpin for discerning Indian readers, for a long time yet.

New Delhi is the 'pivotal' centre of India and has the ability to arc out in all directions, around India, and internationally, through the disparate local population and the diplomatic community which functions there. New Delhi (the old, and the newer bit from 1913-1931) is perhaps the most 'neutral' of all the large Indian cities, but even today after fifty years independence, the heart and soul and doings of millions of normal 'Delhi-ites' unconnected with diplomatic or governmental functions, are almost wholly unknown and unseen alongside the backdrop of Edward Lutyens' and Herbert Baker's square mile or two of 'voluptuous New Delhi'. So much apathy exists, but no one objects; no one complains! Strange.

I was fortunate in finding a publisher for my book, (although not a West Bengali), with the perception to see 'the real thrust and meaning' contained in my book, and quick to see the potential for wide readership appeal, particularly in West Bengal, but also amongst Indians elsewhere in India, and Indian emigrants living successful lives in overseas countries. British interest in India will continue for a very long time, and Americans, the most democratic of all the world's people, display a sincere warmth and affection for India and are the world's most cosmopolitan readers.

Entrusting nine years of highly emotive and intensive work on Calcutta, to Indians (and north Indians), to publish, and market world-wide, with vigour and genuine enthusiasm, was not decided without a good deal of consideration, and some apprehension. We might love one another and trust one another, but truth and common sense requires that our different cultures (all of the parameters that that word includes) and the different way we often do things, as well as how each of us view things, are recognized and properly understood.

The hustle and bustle demanded in the western world, would be hugely tempered by the slower more patient approach, which is the norm in India. Ordinarily - frustration, exasperation, impatience - are quite foreign to the demeanour of Indians. Whether good or bad for us, we foreigners monopolize such feelings, such emotions, instead of pausing, taking a deep breath, and emulating the Indian's *sang froid.*

After years of toil (and intense concentration) every Author hopes no more serious snags will arise. My final 'problem/anxiety' came in final choice of published title. My original title (and easily the best and most appropriate one) had been arrived at after much deliberation. *Rekindling the Flame - a celebration of Calcutta,* was a perfect description. With an eye to sales, and Calcutta's mis-read notoriety, Publishers wanted something more literate, more readily seen/ discernible. In succession we agreed on - *Enigmatic Calcutta: the Eternal City / Enigmatic Calcutta / Calcutta meets the Challenge,* before compromising on *The Changing Face of Calcutta.* I still prefer my first firm choice.

From 'go' to 'whoa' - producing a book, especially something that you feel so strongly about, and which relates to a foreign country and a foreign people, requires great commitment. (Indeed, many people queried the value of my spending so much time and effort on what 'they' believed - but never me - was a hopeless and probably unappreciated task.) Yes, it can often be (and it was) a long journey, and one can but hope that one has been scrupulously fair and honest in everything and will be seen to have been, and that the message conveyed is noticed and accepted with equally good grace by the principal protagonists, India and Great Britain. History can never be erased, but also it can never be changed (ask Omar Khayam). Accordingly, to admit that mistakes of judgement and action occurred, is to take on some of those wonderful but highly elusive qualities - modesty, fairmindedness, and maturity. By such actions we all grow just a little bit, and become better world citizens.

27. Putting Pep Into Life!

- an invitation to be adventurous

In today's world human resourcefulness is regarded as a highly prized quality and clear evidence of such quality, prospective to a successful career. What we do with our leisure time is believed to indicate how we approach life in general.

Adventure can mean taking risks or putting our bodies to tougher feats of endurance. So being adventurous, and exhibiting a preparedness to take on tough challenges, can be rewarding in multiple ways.

Adventure can be many (different) things to many people. For most of us 'being adventurous' means participating in an exciting new undertaking or enterprise - something that is wholly outside our normal routine and quite removed from anything we've ever previously experienced or believed we had the 'guts' or capacity to successfully undertake, unassisted, or in equal collaboration with other like adventurers.

For as long as man has roamed the earth urges of this sort have affected people. The pages of history and of adventure books relate many stirring tales of courage and enterprise. The present times are no different. Men and women everywhere, dream of escaping from the enslavement of everyday routine and of experiencing something that will lift them out of their present ritualistic lives.

Yes indeed, many of us yearn to 'get the adrenalin flowing' and be taken out of ourselves. Whether this chemical change helps or not, we generally believe that it does do something which is uplifting and beneficial, and which causes us to believe that 'we've grown a bit', or even 'a whole lot' through our endeavours.

Well you know - such pursuits are factually within the reach of nearly every one of us. All that is needed (over and above financial considerations) is the resolve and enthusiasm to 'give it a go'! The requisite formula is really quite simple, a mixture of - *'WILLING, WANTING AND DOING'*, plus of course - *PLANNING.*

So, next time you've got a holiday period coming up, surprise yourself and resolve to experience something wholly new, something which might open up a new exciting phase in your life.

Travel/adventure magazines of every imaginable kind abound, opening doors and minds to leisure activity. They spread their net and favours to every nook and cranny of our fascinating world. Never before have facilities and opportunities been so alluringly dangled before prospective adventurers.

All you have to do is reach out to savour totally new, invigorating and scintillating experiences. Exciting fresh objectives can be rewarding in many different ways.

In thinking of what real purposeful adventure constitutes, we are reminded of the exhortation and good advice of one of the greatest adventurers of the 20th century, the Himalayan climber Frank Smythe. He said that... *"no man (or woman) has ever really lived until he (or she) has looked into the heart of Nature and has learned to appreciate the magnificent earth on which he (or she) has been created."* Such fine and challenging words are for every one of us.

Nowadays, as never before, it is possible to fly, sail, motor to, or tramp into countless places and destinations. Where you finally reach to or what you do when you get there, is entirely up to yourself, and will depend upon how well you've researched and planned; and equipped yourself beforehand to take on the venture.

The economies contained in such 'planned' forays into Nature may also pleasantly surprise you. Surprisingly, you can find that the principal expenditure involved comes down to your own input. Enduring memories of a unique happy experience set the seal on everything and become lifelong memories of having accomplished and enjoyed something quite out of the ordinary.

Taking time out to thoroughly plan 'your' adventure holiday can pay wonderful and rewarding dividends. A wealth of travel literature is available for you to consult. As well, in nearly everyone's

64. Selection of Pictures (Adventure in India).

home there is already a repository of conveniently on hand planning material, in the form of atlases of all vintages, history and geography books, also encyclopaedias if you want to get really technical.

Perhaps going to the same old destinations year after year, and sunning yourself while relaxing with a Daiquiri or 'cold one', is refreshing from the viewpoint of physical relaxation. But, just think, you have spent a lot to change very little and in reality another opportunity to break out, and be adventurous, has been lost!

The call of adventure once heard and responded positively to, introduces fresh elements into otherwise fairly orthodox lives. So, next time you plan your holidays resolve to take the plunge and do something DIFFERENT - from what you did the last time and the time before that, AND, before that again! You'll enter a whole new phase of living. Zest for the new, the different, the revitalising, will transform your life. All dullness will evaporate. Positiveness will take over, relegating negative thinking to the dustbin.

Now comes decision time. What should I do? Where should I go? Raft across the Pacific? Scale Kanchenjanga? Swim the Panama Canal? While you need not go to these lengths, in reality the sky really is the limit. You could of course trek out of Darjeeling, and experience the sheer majesty and immensity of the Himalayan mass or put your pack on your back and enjoy the wonders of Ladakh. The destinations which beckon the world over, are infinite.

Perhaps if you are of a mind, you could journey to South America and make it overland to Punta Arenas and thrill to the dramatic landscape of Tierra del Fuego. Or in season, you could launch yourself out of Aberdeen and 'explore' the folklore of the Orkneys and the Shetlands and even reach up and out to the Faeroes, and to Iceland, with its geological wonders.

All of these 'adventure' holidays are singular experiences and there are oodles more, equally enthralling and fascinating, yet realistically all of them are quite within the reach of all of us. All that is needed is the resolve and the desire (and it will surprise you - not a great deal of money).

Wherever you visit, the moods of the seasons introduce vastly different conditions and accordingly provide endless interest, diversion and entertainment. And wherever you go, 'be an explorer' by taking time out to consciously observe the land, its inhabitants (particularly if you are venturing in a foreign country), and its plants and animals. Such attention can bring considerable added enjoyment and pleasure. You will come away a changed enlightened person, aptly fitting Pierre Pfeffer's belief that - 'one talks well, only of what one knows well'.

Yes, the people of other lands, their lifestyles and (different) customs, can intrigue, enthral and fascinate, all pluses of travel. While your camera may record some great shots for you, by far the really unforgettable features (memories) of any trip are your own mental pictures. These endure forever and can provide many wonderful rememberable instant playbacks, all of them bringing infinite pleasure. Constant 'camera eyes' can (and regrettably do) miss a lot. Next time, try giving equal play to your own eyes and senses. You may find the difference very pleasing!

It also goes without saying that conscious effort to meet and enjoy the local people adds a wonderful extra dimension to one's travels. Indeed, it is the stuff that leaves fonder memories! Rightly, growls and scowls get the reception they properly deserve. Smiles, on the other hand, smooth the way to general harmony and as an extra bonus wherever you venture, - 'open doors', if not to homes, almost certainly to hearts!

Maintaining a sunny disposition particularly in another man's land makes every traveller an ambassador for universal togetherness. This is a quality we could all do with a whole lot more of. Respect for local customs and a tolerance of the way things are sometimes done can be the big 'pay-off' and the difference between wholesome happy memories of a super holiday or 'haunting' ones! The choice is yours. It is incontestable that 'nice attitudes' ordinarily beget 'nice attitudes'.

Go to it! Best of luck with your planning and a great trip.

28. Australia's Rich Natural Heritage Of Sun, Sand And Sea

- a blessing not always appreciated

The phenomenon of Australia's vast storehouse of natural geographical riches isn't so much that it is there, (and something which all we Australians so bountifully blessed should marvel at!), but that this 'fortuitous bounty' plays such a commanding role in the lives of Australians.

It is easy to take such great and good fortune for granted and not think much about how this state of affairs evolved, or the extent to which all Australians are affected by it, as everyone assuredly is. Very few, escape its influence.

For a nation of predominantly pale skinned people of mainly Anglo-Celtic and/or of European extraction, (even while Asian migration and totally different cultural interests and habits are affecting the past balance), with ancestors given more, in earlier times, to beach strolling fully garbed in their Sunday best than cavorting in a bathing costume, the extent of the pull towards sea-side recreational activities is probably unique among peoples anywhere in the world.

In the northern hemisphere only a small percentage of the populations of cold-water countries gravitate to the shoreline. Even in modern times of increased affluence and opportunity for leisure, little change is evident from age-old pastimes. Similarly, not big numbers of indigenous people inhabiting tropical countries spend much time at, or on, or in - the water, beyond that part of the population whose livelihoods depend upon occupations worked at or from the shoreline.

Certainly, there is a uniqueness about 'home-grown' Australians' fondness for outdoor activity, especially leisure indulged in and upon our great stretches of golden coastline and on the adjacent inland waterways.

By a stroke of unintended good fortune (it must be reasonably doubted that Captain Cook, our modern founder and by reputation, one of Britain's ablest navigators of any era, gave much thought to these prospective pleasures when he recommended Botany Bay as an alternative penal colony?!), Australia and its people are inheritors of a climate and a sea-scape that is the envy of other people all around the world.

But the gusto which attends present day Australian sea-side activity was not always so. Inherited lifestyles and habits die hard and many generations of Australians were to come and go, before 'old world' traits and traditions were discarded. Today, the Australian ethos is less influenced by the heroics of our 'bush' pioneers and more, by the love and pull of the sea. With increased prosperity the tough resilient image derived from our earlier colourful pioneering beginnings has been supplanted by the sunnier image of the sparkling, more relaxed, livelier, and much happier sea picture.

The Great Dividing Range runs down the entire east coast of Australia for over 2,000 miles, in places hardly more than 100 miles distant from the Pacific Ocean. The highest point of this mountain chain barely exceeds 7,000 feet, but this geographical barrier does much to dominate and influence Australian weather patterns.

Keep to the east of the Divide and life can be pleasant. Away to the west the harsher dry climate of the great inland 'plains' country (oppressively hot in summer and, surprisingly, bitterly cold in winter when the westerlies blow) automatically favours living along the coastal belt, something Australians have enjoyed doing since white migration began over two hundred years ago.

Unlike the United States of America where substantial river systems exist to support large populations, far from either the eastern or western seaboards, Australia is not so well placed. Nevertheless, inland Australia does play host to quite extensive pastoral and agricultural communities situated quite distant from the coast where inland streams or artesian bores provide life-supporting water, ordinarily enough to allow habitation. Farming (mainly sheep grazing) is adapted to meet the drier, more limiting conditions encountered as one moves further west and north. Instead of sheep to the acre, in the far outback of Australia, it becomes acres to the (one) sheep.

65. Sydney Harbour Bridge and Opera House.

66. Known around the world - Bondi Beach, Sydney.

67. THE TWELVE APOSTLES - Port Campbell.

68. Magnificient Caloundra (King's Beach).

69. Tranquil Pearl Beach and entrance to Hawkesbury.

70. Portsea (ocean beach) at low tide.

71. London Bridge-Port Campbell, Victoria.

72. Purity in all its glory. Yonder, Bass Strait.

Considering the harsher climatic conditions encountered the farther one moves inland from the vast coastline which encircles Australia, it is eminently very sensible and very natural, that Australians favour their temperate coastline, and the considerable benefits that can go with living and playing, by it. In a population which now exceeds 18 millions, it is confidently reckoned that upwards of one million families own a water craft, for sailing, paddling or, powerboating.

Beach and rock fishing have many enthusiastic adherents, all eager to 'make a catch'! Fish of many kinds inhabit Australian coastal waters - tailor, whiting, snapper, bream, flathead, John Dory, trevally and many others - all in plentiful supply, depending upon the seasons, the weather and the tides - aspects which test the experience and skills of the amateur fisherman, big numbers of whom take their pastime very seriously.

Queensland offers abundant facilities along the whole of its two thousand kilometre stretch of coastline. The Great Barrier Reef provides an enormous bonus with its superb island resorts, especially in winter. In tropical north Queensland, summers can be awfully hot, and oppressive - more like conditions felt in South Asia, during summer.

Sydney, with its magnificent Harbour and excellent surfing beaches around it, north and south, is probably unrivalled (in the whole world) for the number of people living, working or 'playing' close to the sea, and 'due to the universality of Bondi' (perhaps with Waikiki the best known surfing beach in the world), it gets most publicity of anywhere in Australia.

The fact of course is, that there are hundreds of superlative surfing beaches and boating inlets to be found everywhere along Australia's extensive coastline, particularly east, west and south - the possibility of meeting a crocodile on the northern coastline is not encouraged!

While southern Queensland (all the year round) especially the exceptional Sunshine and Gold Coasts, adjacent north and south of Brisbane, and New South Wales, and to a lesser extent Western Australia, are said to 'have the climate' (and it is a fact their coasts are the most developed *and* that they have many superlative beach resorts), some of the greatest and most testing of Australia's natural adventure parks are to be experienced in Victoria and along the east coastal areas of South Australia.

The wonderful beaches below Sydney and down to Victoria highlight how wonderfully catered for Australians are, for these quite marvellous places are not patronised so much. Maybe it is because the water is colder, yet for the more adventurous types the exhilaration that is possible to get from experiencing marvellous Mallacoota in Croajingolong National Park, Lake Tyers and the Ninety Mile Beach from Lakes Entrance and from boating out of glorious Metung in the Lakes National Park is tremendous.

Moving further south into Wilson's Promontory National Park a treasure trove awaits the fit tourist who is prepared to hike into what are some of the most fabulous solitary beaches in the whole of Australia, besides reaching to the lowest point of the mainland.

Passing on to Philip Island, if you are English, twin pleasures can be enjoyed - one of Australia's largest Fairy Penguin colonies, and the nostalgia of lunching at Cowes. Across Westernport Bay, one can see the beautiful Flinders Peninsula reaching down to majestic Cape Schanck. The descent to 'The Pulpit' down the wooden staircase is a must, and is especially exhilarating on a wet blustery day when the 'white horses' are 'galloping' across Bass Strait at high tide. It is an experience forever remembered and a sight not readily forgotten! Very dramatic! Also great value tramping into Bushranger's Bay before or from Cape Schanck, can bring great delight. Rugged and spectacular, it never ceases to thrill its patrons, at whatever time of the year.

The pride of Melbourne is 'the Peninsula' and the turbulent but tremendously exciting 'back-beaches' at Sorrento and Portsea. Being the best surfing beaches closest to Melbourne, surprisingly these places boast only a handful of patrons on their wonderful beaches, for most of the year. For the past one hundred years the coveted playground of the establishment and the rich, temporary dwellers are not encouraged. As a result of this exclusivity only very limited resort facilities are available. More's the pity, for this peninsula is quite lovely and hardly more than an hour's easy drive from Melbourne and - although quite treacherous rips and huge surf, greet the surfer, a day's fun at these wonderful beaches has no peer - at least, in Victoria. Surfboarders relish the conditions.

Going south-west from Melbourne and reaching Victoria's second city, Geelong, one can profitably spend a little time savouring the delights of the Bellarine Peninsula, Portarlington and Queenscliff, before proceeding along to join the Great Ocean Road at Torquay. A wonderfully scenic drive on a narrow (exciting) road with superb scenery one comes to Lorne and Apollo Bay, before crossing through the pretty Otway forest to the even more rugged southern coast adjacent to Port Campbell and Peterborough. Here you find Australia's 'ninth wonder of the world' (if as is claimed - the Empire State Building is the eighth?) - the tremendous sea-scape known as 'The Twelve Apostles'.

Over the centuries, the pounding seas of the turbulent Bass Strait have 'eaten into' the coastline, leaving segments of harder rock left standing offshore after the softer limestone has been eroded by wave action. Strung along miles of coastline they provide a dazzling array of tall stacks, pinnacles and arches like warships in battle line ahead. It is spell-binding stuff and a photographer's dream. There can be few minutes/hours of complete exhilaration, more enjoyable than the wonderful isolation spent at the mouth of the Sherbrooke River, where it spills into the turbulent sea. Cheek by jowl with dramatic nature, it is hard to leave. It is simply magnificent.

West of Warrnambool and reaching along the coast beyond Portland to Cape Bridgewater, a vast volcanic lava flow plain sweeps from the north and the east to meet the sea. Petrified forests give way to rugged boulder-strewn steep cliffs plunging down to boisterous seas pounding the shores from the restless Bass Strait.

Entering South Australia, one encounters an amazing change of character in the area reaching up to Lake Alexandrina. Extensive stretches of parallel lines of dunes separate windswept sandy beaches from swamps and lagoons, just inland. This fascinating corner of Australia, is very thinly populated and is visited by only a few, yet it teems with interest for those adventurous souls sufficiently intrepid to venture into it.

Passing across the turbulent Great Australian Bight where the seemingly endless flat topped plateau of the Nullabor spills over with dramatic abruptness to the shores of the Great Australian Bight, we are surprised by over a hundred miles of spectacular vertical limestone cliffs - the Bunda Cliffs. These plunge over 75 metres vertically down to the sea, but because of the remoteness of this sparsely populated area of southern Australian few persons know of them, and in consequence, they are seen and marvelled at, by only a handful of road travellers prepared to leave the Nullabor Highway - and EXPLORE! Nowhere else in the world will you find anything like it - Ireland's more accessible and consequently better known Cliffs of Moher pale by comparison.

Nature's playground abounds all around (and through) Australia. Its possibilities are unlimited and would occupy several lifetimes for anyone to properly experience them. It is little wonder that modern Australians partaking of innumerable outdoor pastimes, whether at work or at play, bear the tremendous imprint of Nature. This lifestyle shapes the Australian's moods and attitudes. It would be surprising thing if this were not so.

The next time doubts are expressed or criticism is levelled by either Australians or foreign visitors about Australian's supposed mixed up priorities and preference for leisure, it behoves all of them, to spare a thought for environmental factors and interpose the question: *"Assailed by so much of Nature's gifts, is it really so unnatural?"* Perhaps the further question follows: *"Is it really such a bad thing to be shaped by one's environment?"* The answer to this must surely be an emphatic - NO! After all, most peoples of the world have just that happen to them too!

29. A Treasury Of Wisdom And Wit

- a good tonic for us all

from many good and well-intentioned contributors.

As this Volume of Essays is devoted to India and to expanding the world's (and Indians themselves) knowledge, understanding and appreciation of India, it is fitting that a great twentieth century Indian should lead the way

ALL OF US - TALK OF INDIA,
- AND ALL OF US
DEMAND MANY THINGS, FROM INDIA.
WHAT DO WE GIVE HER, IN RETURN?

WE CAN TAKE NOTHING FROM HER
BEYOND WHAT WE GIVE HER

INDIA WILL ULTIMATELY
- GIVE US
WHAT WE GIVE HER,
IN LOVE AND SERVICE
AND PRODUCTIVE AND CREATIVE WORK.

- Jawaharlal Nehru
First Prime Minister of India
1947 - 1964

APA PANT - Indian Diplomat and Political Officer, Gangtok, Sikkim 1953-1959

1) WHEN there is friendship and understanding

- peace and stability can never be built on foundations of hate, fear, pride and anger.

2) WHEN there is friendship in the heart, protests are put aside.

- it is an affectionate interest in the other person, his or her country, the history, geography and cultures - factions which build up and sustain one's identity - that creates the right conditions for a friendship to prosper.

Pride, egocentricity and a feeling of superiority can never allow friendships to grow, however much money etcetera, one may have.

It is only a genuine interest in, and a candid appreciation of, the very differences, in language, culture, food, clothes, habits, music, dance and literature between oneself and the other person or country, which can lead to friendship and understanding.

With an affectionate interest in the other person and his country, all doors are unlocked and you get invited to partake and participate, in his or her, identity.

Then you function with a different and joyful ease and become effective in bringing about a real transformation.

Share yourself - you will be exhilarated and be re-born.

3) GREATNESS resides in the control of desires and the minimisation of wants.

Only a mind that is without fear, anger, hate, violence or anxiety, has the energy to be intelligent and compassionate.

4) JOY, ENERGY, LOVE all the time there, timeless, silent, beautiful.

You must always be aware of it and you will never miss your way. These silent moments of joy and love, are this energy. Being under the illusion that you are separate from it, is ignorance.

To fulfil oneself, an individual must be awakened to a more profound and subtler intelligence.

VANDANA BAKHSHI - Advocate, Magistrate and Judge (Calcutta)
— — a heartwarming welcome

YOU ARE WELCOME HERE,
BE AT YOUR EASE

GET UP WHEN YOU ARE READY,
GO TO BED WHEN YOU PLEASE

HAPPY TO SHARE WITH YOU
SUCH AS WE HAVE GOT

THE LEEKS IN THE ROOF
THE SOUP IN THE POT

YOU DON'T HAVE TO THANK US
OR, LAUGH AT OUR JOKES

SIT DEEP, AND COME OFTEN
YOU ARE ONE OF THE FOLKS

THE MOTHER - Aurobindo Ashram, Pondicherry
.... she stirred the hearts and minds of many.

WHEN YOU HAVE NOTHING TO DO,
YOU BECOME RESTLESS, YOU RUN ABOUT,
YOU MEET FRIENDS, YOU TAKE A WALK,
TO SPEAK ONLY OF THE BEST; I AM
REFERRING TO THINGS THAT ARE
OBVIOUSLY NOT TO BE DONE.

INSTEAD, SIT DOWN QUIETLY
BEFORE THE SKY, BEFORE THE SEA,
OR UNDER TREES, WHATEVER IS POSSIBLE
(In Pondicherry you have all of them)
AND TRY TO REALIZE OF THESE THINGS

to understand, why you live
to learn you must live
to ponder over what you want to do, and what should be done
to consider the best way of escaping from the ignorance,
falsehood and pain, in which we live.

More from - THE MOTHER

EVERYDAY UNDERTAKE - something which is difficult,
something that will do you good. Unless you
try something beyond what you have already mastered, you will
never grow.

The people of the Punjab have a song which goes as follows -

The bulbul does not always sing in the garden;
And the garden is not always in bloom;
Happiness does not always reign,
And friends are not always together.

The conclusion to be drawn from this song is that we cannot expect to be always happy, and that, to know how to be patient, is useful.

ON HINDUISM - idealism in a life, one lived to 100 years.

The first 25 years - is devoted to study

The second 25 years - is devoted to work

The third 25 years - is devoted to travel
(and visitation to Shrines)

The final 25 years - is given over to solitude and peace

P. R. BAKHSHI

THE UNITED STATES POST OFFICE

- inscription on building, corner Eighth and 34th, opposite Madison Square Garden, New York.

NEITHER SNOW - NOR RAIN
NOR HEAT - NOR GLOOM OF NIGHT
STAYS THESE COURIERS
FROM THE SWIFT COMPLETION
OF THEIR APPOINTED ROUNDS.

Wonderful words (qualities) 'to live by'

SELF-CONTROL COURAGE CHEERFULNESS PATIENCE

PERSEVERANCE PRUDENCE SINCERITY RIGHT JUDGEMENT

MODESTY THE SIMPLE LIFE/ORDER/DISCIPLINE

SELF-RELIANCE GIVING SYMPATHY UNDERSTANDING

INTEGRITY STEADFASTNESS LOVING FAMILY.

Anon

ACTUAL REQUEST for compassionate (casual) leave by office clerk, in Calcutta (circa 1958)

"As my wife has suddenly got cough and cold, and headaches all over her body, and as I am the only husband in the house to look after her, I humbly request you for a day's leave, for which act of kindness, I shall never be grateful".

- two things stand like stone

KINDNESS IN ANOTHER'S TROUBLE, COURAGE IN YOUR OWN.

Adam Lindsay Gordon
-Australian Poet (1833 - 1870)

- good advice

COMMITTEES OF TWENTY
DELIBERATE APLENTY.

COMMITTEES OF TEN
ACT, NOW AND THEN.

BUT - THE MOST JOBS
ARE DONE
BY COMMITTEES OF ONE!

Anon

NO ONE CAN EXPRESS WELL,
WHAT HE DOES NOT UNDERSTAND

Anon

MONEY - IS A SINGULAR THING

- it ranks with love as man's greatest source of joy.

- and it ranks with death as his greatest source of anxiety.

Over history it has oppressed nearly all people, in one or two ways

1) either it has been abundant and very unreliable

or

2) reliable and very scarce

However for many, a third affliction - Money has been (is) unreliable *and* scarce

J. K. Galbraith
Famous American Economist
(1908 -)

WHAT WAS ONCE - OR, IS STILL?

IN ENGLAND - everything is allowed, except what is forbidden

IN GERMANY - everything is forbidden, except what is allowed

IN RUSSIA - everything is forbidden, even what is allowed

IN FRANCE - everything is allowed, even what is forbidden

- with thanks to TIME/LIFE and Rudolph Chelmionski

SOME WERE REVERED

- one of them, Lord Canning (1812-1862)
Governor General, (and first) Viceroy, of India 1856 - 1862.

Inscription on plinth of his statue in Victoria Memorial Gardens, Calcutta.

In that high office,
During the perilous crisis
of the Sepoy Mutiny (1857)
He displayed with entire success,
such fortitude, judgement
and wise clemency
As proved him worthy of his
illustrious father
and justly entitled him
To the lasting gratitude of his country

(Buried with his father in Westminster Abbey)

Footnote: Lady Canning's distinguished casket occupies the north veranda of St. John's Church, Council House Street, Calcutta.

---

and another –

WILLIAM CAVENDISH BENTINCK
(Governor-General of the Presidency of Fort William in Bengal - From 1828, and first Governor-General, of India, from November 1834, until 1835).

WHO, During seven years, ruled India with
eminent prudence,
integrity and benevolence;

WHO, placed at the head of a great empire,
never laid aside
the simplicity and moderation,
of a private citizen:

WHO, never forgot that the end of government
is the welfare of the governed;

WHO, abolished cruel rites;

WHO, effaced humiliating distinctions;

WHO, allowed liberty to the expression of
public opinion;

WHOSE constant study was to elevate
the moral and intellectual character
of the nation, committed to his charge.

This monument was erected
by men,
Who, differing from each other
in race, in manners, in language and
in religion.

Cherish with equal veneration
and gratitude
The memory of his wise, upright
and paternal administration.

Calcutta, 4 Feb 1835
Richard Westmacott
London

Footnote: The Movement started by Ram Mohan Roy to end the practice of suttee (widow burning) was endorsed by Bentinck, who abolished it - in 1829.

IF YOU AIM AT NOTHING, YOU ARE BOUND TO MISS THE TARGET

Anon. Woodburn Cottage
Dr. Graham's Homes, Kalimpong

OH, WAD SOME POWER THE GIFTE GIE US
TO SEE OURSELVES AS OTHERS SEE US?
IT WOULD FRAE MONY A BLUNDER FREE US,
AND FOOLISH NOTION.

Robert Burns, "To a Mouse"
(1759 - 1796)

OUR GREATEST GLORY IS NOT
IN NEVER FALLING
BUT, IN RISING
EVERY TIME WE FALL

Confucius
(551 - 479 B.C.)

OBSTACLES -

PROBLEMS AND OBSTACLES,
ARE THOSE TERRIFYING THINGS WE SEE
WHEN WE TAKE OUR EYES
OFF OUR GOALS

Anon

JOB APPLICANT (Bombay, 1960)

- factual, to illustrate the skills present, and the dearth of jobs available in India. A country which has a huge number of multiple skilled graduates, competing for many fewer positions. Many go overseas. The applicant listed his (extensive) qualifications, thus,

D.Sc, Ph.D., A.M. Inst. B.E. (LONDON)
M.Mech. E.A. (Ind), A.M.I.S.E., A.M. Inst.E. Tech. (LONDON)
"MECH., ELE, & INDUST, ENGINEER"
M.Comm., P.S.A.A., B.Comm. F.I.C.A., F.B.S. Com. (LANGS)
"INCORPORATED ACCOUNTANT AND AUDITOR"

RE: POST OF CARGO SUPERVISOR

Dear Sirs,

I have pleasure in submitting my application for the above mentioned post and tender for your information the following proforma: -

My technical, commercial and accountancy qualifications have been amply supplemented & opulently crystallized by holding multifarious responsible EXECUTIVE & ADMINISTRATIVE position in highly reputed EUROPEAN & INDIAN largest Commercial/Industrial Concerns for the last many years, being completely conversant with modern methods of Business-administration & Managerial-Practice, Industrial-Works-Organisation & Production control, Personnel-management & Wage-administration technique, Plant Engineering & Waste-elimination, handling Trade-negotiations and Business correspondence, Import-Export procedures & formalities, Customs-clearing & Shipment forwarding, Systematic storage & Distribution, Job-analysis & Evaluation, modern Stores-Practice & Inventory-control, exercising sound judgment for Material-utilisation & mechanised handling, submitting Quota-applications & Procuring inviting, Scrutinising & analysis Quotations, Estimating & Costing etc, of heterogeneous description with modern Scientific out-look, combined with a flair for systematic execution of work in running the Departments most efficiently and expeditiously.

More-over, I have been intimately acquainted with all the ramifications and rudiments of Mercantile-laws, Economics, Company-laws, Factory-act & Labour-legislation, Banking,

Accountancy & auditing, Income-tax & Sales-tax handling; having thorough knowledge of cost-conscious approach & critical analysis of all technical problems with the latest innovations in the field of business technique & accomplishment, geared with innate aptitude for appreciating the practical & economic significance of Industrial development & research, and ability to incorporate the same in works routine with a clairvoyance sense of responsibility and rational approach.

I am capable of assuming independent and entire charge of modern, Commercial/Industrial Concern, synchronising inter-alia the introduction & development of business, finding the prospective buyers, studying their psychology, conducting high-level salestalk, making field investigations of Market-potentialities and solicitations of Consumer preferences, explore new Markets, formulating sales-promotion schemes, Advertising & Publicity etc, with the implementation of greatest business acumen, integrity, efficiency and all in good-faith to warrant the evolution of pre-determined production & business schedules and other incidental synthetic data to suit Employer's requirements on potentially economical basis.

I am fully energetic, young with robust physique and commanding personally gifted with unimpeachable business integrity and conspicuous creative organising ability, together with the supreme control over large labour-force & supervisory staff, I shall prove to be an asset to your organization.

I remain,
Yours faithfully

S Madiali

Postscript: The (monthly) salary the job attracted was Rupees three hundred and seventy five per month (equivalent at that time to thirty pounds English money)

- in a lighter mood.

More good advice to men

"THEY ARE THE FOOLS WHO KISS AND TELL"
WISELY HAS THE POET SUNG
MAN MAY HOLD ALL SORTS OF POSTS
IF ONLY - HE'D HOLD HIS TONGUE!

Anon

ALI'S RECIPE FOR LOVE AND PATIENCE

TAKE A FEW CUPS OF LOVE
ONE TEASPOON OF PATIENCE
ONE TABLESPOON OF GENEROSITY
ONE PINT OF KINDNESS AND
- A QUART OF LAUGHTER
MIX IT ALL UP AND LET IT
STAND AWHILE
THEN SERVE IT TO EVERYONE
- WHO COMES TO YOUR DOOR

YOU MAY BE IN COMMAND
- BUT, ARE IN CONTROL?

Anon

BE BOLD, BE BOLD, AND
EVERYWHERE, BE BOLD,
- BE NOT TOO BOLD!

Spenser's "Faerie Queene"
(1552-1599)

An interesting observation - by James Martin (1998)

God so loved the world, that he gave his
Only begotten
Son, that whosever believeth in him should not
Perish, but have
Everlasting
Life

St John 3-16

Food for thought.....rushing to conclusions....

ONE MAN'S SOLEMNITY IS
ANOTHER MAN'S DEAD-PAN WINK!

Ambrose Bierce (1842 - 1914)

QUALITY - is never an accident

But it is the result of
High intention, sincere effort
Intelligent direction, and
Skilful execution
It represents the wise choice
Of many alternatives

Anon

HISTORY - is not a science, nor

is it an art; though the
historian must, as writer -
be an artist, too.
He should write well,
lucidly and eloquently;
and is not harmed by
a lively imagination.

Anon

WOMEN - those adorable but unfathomable creatures (the best ones)

- women in love
- spurned women

HEAV'N HAS NO RAGE
LIKE LOVE TO HATRED TURN'D
NOR HELL A FURY
LIKE A WOMAN SCORNED

"The Old Bachelor"
William Congreve (1670-1729)

Seizing the chance (to give help) - when it presents

I ONLY PASS THIS WAY ONCE
ANY GOOD THAT I CAN DO,
ANY KINDNESS THAT I CAN SHOW,
LET ME NEITHER NEGLECT IT,
NOR DEFER IT
- FOR I SHALL NOT PASS
THIS WAY AGAIN

Anon

Mother Teresa's lasting legacy to the world -

The fruit of SILENCE is Prayer

The fruit of PRAYER is Faith

The fruit of FAITH is Love

The fruit of LOVE is Service

The fruit of SERVICE is Peace

(Mother Teresa's visiting card - 1997)

HAPPINESS

Is a perfume,
You cannot pour on others
Without getting a few drops on yourself

Anon

DON'T WORRY

There are three days in every week
About which we should not worry
One is YESTERDAY, with its mistakes
And cares, its aches and pains
Yesterday has passed forever beyond our control.

The other day is TOMORROW
With its possible adversities and blunders
Until its sun rises we have no stake in tomorrow
For it is yet unknown.

Which leaves only one day - TODAY
Anyone can fight the battle of just one day
It's only when we add the burden of
Those two awful eternities
YESTERDAY and TOMORROW
That contentment will escape you.

Anon (Queenscliff, Victoria 1986)

Some of the most profound and intriguing sentiments

Robert Browning ("Christina" c.1840)

...She should not have looked
at me, if she meant that I
should not love her!

Christopher Marlowe (1564 - 1593)

....Oh, thou art fairer than the
evening air
Clad in the beauty of a thousand stars...

Robert Herrick (1868 - 1938)

...There is a lady sweet and kind,
was never face, so pleased my mind.
I did but see her 'passing by'
yet will I love her 'til I die'....

Reinhold Niebuhr (American Theologian 1892 - 1971)

God grant me the SERENITY
- to accept the things I cannot change,
The COURAGE - to change the things I can
and the WISDOM to know the difference.

(Saint) Ignatius Loyola - Founder of the Society of Jesus (1491 - 1556)

The will to live, to live life
out to perfection, in action and in passion.

To give and not to count the cost;
To fight, and not to seek for rest;
To labour, and not to look for any reward
- save that of knowing, I do thy will.

SAINT FRANCIS OF ASSISI (1182 - 1226)

- lover of Christ and of men, and birds, and animals, and flowers, who washed the feet of lepers, and was a friend of the oppressed and abandoned.

(Recited too, at Mother Teresa's request at the 1979 Nobel Peace Prize Ceremony, in Oslo)

A SIMPLE PRAYER

Lord, make me the instrument of Thy Peace
Where there is hatred, let me sow love;
Where there is doubt, faith; where
there is despair, hope; where there
is darkness, light; where there
is sadness, joy.

O Divine Master, grant that I
may not so much seek to be
consoled, as to console; to be
understood, as to understand,
to be loved, as to love. For it
is in giving that we receive;
it is in pardoning, that we are
pardoned; it is in dying that
we are born, to eternal life.

DEO GRATIAS

Footnote: Jesuit teacher, Christopher Willcocks, (Blessed Sacrement Church, Melbourne) has set the piece to music *The Prayer of St. Francis* which was sung at the upper Basilica in Assisi, in January 1986, during the Choir's tour of Europe. It was pure magic.

Albert Schweitzer (1875 - 1965)

- one of the twentieth century's greatest and noblest, of men. Also doctor four times over - of music, of theology, of philosophy and of medicine.

....profound words, spoken yesterday? No - at the turn of the century, 1900. What will be said in 2000, when another 100 years have passed?

inter alia ....*"when reviewing every field of human activity in order to determine and evaluate what had been achieved, this was done with an optimism that seemed incomprehensible.*

Everywhere it seemed to be assumed, that we had made such progress in inventions and in knowledge that the ethical and intellectual spheres in which we lived had soared and would never decline.

My own impression was that in our mental and spiritual life, we had not only descended below the level of previous generations, but were living on their achievements - and that some of this heritage was melting away, in our hands."

John Bunyan (1628 - 1688)

WHO SO BESET HIM ROUND
WITH DISMAL STORIES,
DO BUT THEMSELVES CONFOUND;
HIS STRENGH THE MORE IS.

NO LION CAN HIM FRIGHT,
HE'LL WITH A GIANT FIGHT,
BUT HE WILL HAVE A RIGHT
TO BE A PILGRIM

George Bernard Shaw (1856 -1950)

The more a man possesses over and above what he uses, what he (essentially) needs, the more careworn he becomes.

Benjamin Disraeli (1804 - 1881)

The secret of success is constancy to purpose.

And finally, and fittingly, profound words, from Bengal's most revered son, poet, philosopher *et al*

RABINDRANATH TAGORE (1861 - 1941)
from *Gitanjali*, NOBEL PRIZE for LITERATURE
(1913)

WHERE the mind is without fear
and the head is held high,
WHERE knowledge is free;
WHERE the world had not
been broken up into fragments
by narrow domestic walls;
WHERE words come out from the
depth of truth;
where timeless striving
stretches its arms towards
perfection;
WHERE the clear stream of reason
has not lost its way into the
dreamy desert sand
of dead habit;
WHERE the mind is led forward
by thee into ever-widening
thought and action
into that heaven of freedom,
my Father
let my country awake

Santiniketan
West Bengal

73. The great Bengali - Rabindranath Tagore.